Personal Catholicism

Martin X. Moleski, S.J.

Personal Catholicism

The Theological Epistemologies of
John Henry Newman and Michael Polanyi

The Catholic University of America Press
Washington, D.C.

The Catholic University of America Press

Washington, D.C.

Copyright © 2000

The Catholic University of America Press

All rights reserved

Printed in the United States of America

Library of Congress Cataloging-in-Publication Data

Moleski, Martin X., 1952–

    Personal Catholicism : the theological epistemologies of John Henry Newman and Michael Polanyi / Martin X. Moleski.

        p. cm.

    Includes bibliographical references and index.

    1. Knowledge, Theory of (Religion)   2. Catholic Church—Doctrines. 3. Newman, John Henry, 1801–1890. 4. Polanyi, Michael, 1891– . I. Title.

BX1753.M575 2000

230'.2'01—dc21

99–41885

ISBN 0–8132–0964–1 (alk. paper)

To my parents
Desmond and Ruth Moleski

Contents

Conclusion: Breaking into Dogma   180

Foreword

In the present book Professor Moleski deals with two of the thinkers who have most influenced me, especially in my thinking about faith and reason. Like many others, I found it difficult to understand how faith could go beyond the reach of probative reason and at the same time be utterly certain to the believer. That problem proved almost insoluable when approached within the categories of explicit knowledge. But Newman, in the course of writing his Oxford University Sermons, came to see that we know more than we can say, and that this unexpressed knowledge is what warrants us in making the unconditional assent of faith even though the truth of its content eludes logical proof. Our prior inarticulate presentiments often guide our investigation and enable us to discern more than could be produced as evidence in a court of law. By building tacit knowledge and the inspirations of grace into his analysis of faith Newman made a notable advance.

The implications of this advance for theological method are still not fully appreciated. I began to find some guidance in this matter when, quite by chance, I came across Michael Polanyi's *Personal Knowledge* on a library shelf. Polanyi, who was not a theologian, became acutely aware of the importance of tacit awareness in his reflections on the history of science. He noted that the great scientific discoveries are regularly made by reliance on antecedent intimations, and are transmitted to others by the personal trust that disciples place in the authority of their masters or that of the scientific community. These great insights, I realized, could be transferred to theological questions such as the nature of prophetic insight, the importance of discipleship, and the authority of tradition. Religious knowledge, I concluded, advances and perpetuates itself by methods akin to those that Polanyi attributes to the scientific enterprise.

It would be impossible to understand my own theological contributions, such as they are, without being aware of my indebtedness to Newman and Polanyi. They have greatly helped me to work out the theory of symbolic communication that underlies my doctrine of revelation. In addition, the theory of models I have proposed in my treatment of various themes (such as Church, revelation, faith, and theology itself) was constructed with a view to the tacit presuppositions of theologians who perhaps never reflected critically on the perspective from which they were approaching the data. In my ecumenical labors I have found that doctrinal disputes between churches could often be alleviated and even transcended by the realization that theological traditions have to be understood in terms of the orientations and concerns of their authors. Once these are recognized, it often becomes possible to harmonize positions that previously seemed contradictory.

Both Newman and Polanyi rank high among the pioneers in the history of the post-critical movement in epistemology. They pointed out the limitations of the methods that had become current since the time of Descartes and Spinoza. Newman was fiercely critical of the rationalism of John Locke and William Paley, which led to weak and desiccated styles of faith. He was equally critical of the emotionalism of Anglican Evangelicals, who treated religion as a matter of the heart rather than the head, of feeling rather than truth. Newman himself refused any such dichotomy. He maintained that the mind does not work reliably in the religious sphere without the concurrence of the heart and that the truths of the faith must be seen as good for the believer. Unlike geometric formulas, they must be life-giving and salutary.

Polanyi, a century later, mounted a massive critique of the "critical program" in science. In its place he sought to erect a "fiduciary program," which admitted the priority of belief over all other forms of knowledge. In particular, he criticized the method of doubt that had dominated the theory of science since the time of Descartes. He showed how this same attitude of suspicion, by creating a moral vacuum, lay at the root of grievous sociopolitical aberrations.

As Father Moleski illustrates at length in these pages, Newman and Polanyi exhibit many common traits. In their theory of knowledge both represent a shift from the formal to the informal, from the explicit to the implicit. Reflection on their experience convinced them that formal argument is more useful for verifying what is already known than for achieving new advances in knowledge, whether in science or in religion. They attached primary importance to the tacit ingredient in knowledge and to spontaneous or intuitive reasoning. They called attention to the roles of affectivity and creative imagination in leading the mind forward in its search for truth. They acknowledged the importance of trust, of tradition, and of authority for the transmission of personal knowledge and for paving the way to progress. In so doing they recovered certain insights that had been characteristic of the medieval Augustinian heritage.

The systems of these two authors are exceptionally useful for dealing with the major issues that trouble the theological climate today. In the realm of religious knowledge, we are plagued by a kind of "culture war" between objectivists and subjectivists. Defenders of orthodoxy rather commonly see religious truth as something that already exists in some impersonal way and has to be inserted into the mind of the believer. They act as though the truths of faith could be fully contained in propositions whose credibility can be demonstrated by rigorous arguments. But the arguments, on examination, seem to fall short of strict proof. And potential believers protest that they do not want to be converted by syllogisms. They hold, quite correctly, that religious truth should fulfill an inner need or desire and should make them better for possessing it.

By way of reaction, the failure of objectivism has given rise to an unhealthy subjectivism. Many of the intellectual leaders of our time hold that since the truth of faith defies demonstration, we are entitled to accept or reject it on grounds of feeling and personal preference. A subjectivist style of religiosity, often accompanied by philosophical relativism, is much in favor. Applied to religion, subjectivism engenders a rather tentative and individualistic adherence to Christianity or, alternatively, to some non-Christian religion or New Age religion. All religions tend to be evaluated subjectively, in terms of felt satisfaction.

In contrast to both objectivism and subjectivism, Newman and Polanyi proposed what may be called a triadic model of knowledge. They saw truth as an achievement of the intellect when it ponders the meaning of the data presented to the senses. The empirical world offers complexes of potentially significant data. The significance has to be unveiled by allowing the data, taken in context, to disclose their meaning to an intelligent subject, somewhat as letters on a page give rise to ideas in the mind of a literate reader. It is all-important not to impose one's preconceptions on the real, but to let reality evoke in us the meaning that it truly has.

The post-critical position, on the one hand, goes beyond objectivism because it recognizes that the inquiring mind brings personal presumptions and skills to bear on the process of discovery. On the other hand, this approach avoids subjectivism because it insists on the imperative to obey the precepts of conscience and to submit to the self-evidence of the real. The personal, as Polanyi said, transcends both the subjective and the objective. "In so far as the personal submits to requirements acknowledged by itself as independent of itself, it is not subjective; but in so far as it is an action guided by individual passions, it is not objective either" (*PK*, 300; Moleski, 93).

In systems that correspond to the insights of these two great writers we have an apt remedy for the sense of isolation and drift that afflicts the modern mind. Both Newman and Polanyi, in their respective fields, had a sense of membership in a community with a tradition and with stringent standards of truth and authority. They insisted upon discipline and discipleship, on integrity and commitment. Above all, they respected the personal character of belief and knowledge. In making judgments, we have to rely upon, and evaluate, our own powers of apprehension.

Quite apart from the particular beliefs that Newman and Polanyi espoused, their method seems to me well suited to sustain what Martin Moleski in his title calls "Personal Catholicism." Sociological Catholicism is, for a variety of reasons, in decline. Men and women of our day do not adhere to a faith simply because it is handed down to them by their parents or is the dominant faith of the community in which they were reared. Having profited, as they should, by exposure to the tradition of their elders, they must assimilate its elements into their own interpretative framework, thus arriving at personal conviction. They must find in the faith what Polanyi calls a happy dwelling place of the mind (*PK*, 280). The mind, with its native orientation to the real, cannot be satisfied with a subjectivism that disregards the truth-content of faith. For Catholics, it is axiomatic that the gospel, as transmitted through Scripture and Catholic tradition, is true for all times and all places and that it is to be confidently proclaimed as good news for people of every kind and condition. Believers can have this assurance if they adhere to the faith with the type of personal assent so luminously described by Newman and Polanyi.

As a former teacher of Father Moleski, I am delighted to see that his doctoral studies have borne fruit, among other places, in this volume. In reading it I am reminded of the dictum of Leonardo da Vinci: "It is a poor teacher who is not surpassed by his own students."

Avery Dulles, S.J.
Laurence J. McGinley Professor of Religion and Society
Fordham University
January 25, 2000
Feast of the Conversion of St. Paul

Acknowledgments

I am deeply indebted to Alan Weinblatt, who introduced me to
Michael Polanyi's writings and who labored mightily to make sense of
my honors thesis at Boston College; to John Ford, C.S.C., my dissertation director at The Catholic University of America, without whose gra-
cious and patient attention to detail I would have despaired; to
William Wallace, O.P., who served on my board and whose philosophy
of nature demonstrates the vitality of the Aristotelian and Thomistic
tradition in the modern age; and to Avery Dulles, S.J., who was my first
advisor at Catholic University and whose work shows how the epistemology of tacit knowledge illuminates and deepens our understanding
of the Catholic tradition.

I wish to thank Susan Needham, my editor, for her sharp eyes and
gentle suggestions which have greatly improved the clarity and correctness of the text. I also want to thank the many Jesuits with whom I
have lived during the development of this book, especially Tom Kret-
tek, Joe Rossi, Frank Herrmann, Pat Lynch, and Jim Higgins. Their understanding, compassion, and good humor have filled my days with
grace.

I dedicate this book to my parents. They give me life, sustained me
in countless crises, taught me to believe, to hope, and to pray, and sent
me to the Jesuit schools where I found my vocation.

Martin X. Moleski, S.J.
Canisius College
February 17, 2000

Abbreviations

Newman

Apo *Apologia pro Vita Sua: Being a History of His Religious Opinions.* Edited and with introduction by Martin J. Svaglic. Oxford: Clarendon Press, 1967.

AW *John Henry Newman: Autobiographical Writings.* Edited with introductions by Henry Tristram. New York: Sheed and Ward, 1957.

Dev *Essay on the Development of Christian Doctrine.* New York: Sheed and Ward, 1960.

GA *An Essay in Aid of a Grammar of Assent.* Edited and with introduction by Nicholas Lash. Notre Dame: University of Notre Dame Press, 1979.

Idea *The Idea of a University: Defined and Illustrated in Nine Discourses . . .* Edited, with introduction and notes by Martin J. Svaglic (1960). Notre Dame: University of Notre Dame Press, 1982.

LD *The Letters and Diaries of John Henry Newman.* Edited by Charles Stephen Dessain et alia. Oxford and London: 1961– .

DN *A Letter Addressed to His Grace the Duke of Norfolk on Occasion of Mr. Gladstone's Recent Expostulation.* In *Newman and Gladstone: The Vatican Decrees,* introduction by Alvin S. Ryan. Notre Dame: University of Notre Dame Press, 1962 (1875).

PN *The Philosophical Notebook of John Henry Newman.* Edited by Edward Sillem. Louvain: Nauwelaerts, 1969.

TP *The Theological Papers of John Henry Newman on Faith and Certainty: 1801–1890.* Edited by J. Derek Holmes, assisted by Hugo M. de Achaval; introduction by Charles Stephen Dessain. Oxford: Clarendon Press, 1976.

US *Newman's University Sermons: Fifteen Sermons Preached before the University of Oxford, 1826–43.* Introductory essays by D. M. MacKinnnon and J. D. Holmes. London: S.P.C.K., 1970 (3d ed., 1871).

VM *The Via Media of the Anglican Church Illustrated in Lectures, Letters and Tracts Written Between 1830 and 1841.* London: Longmans, Green and Company, 1901 (3d ed., 1877).

Polanyi

KB *Knowing and Being.* Edited by Marjorie Grene. Chicago: University of Chicago Press, 1969.

LL *The Logic of Liberty: Reflections and Rejoinders.* London: Routledge and Kegan Paul, 1951.

PK *Personal Knowledge: Towards a Post-Critical Philosophy.* Chicago: University of Chicago Press, 1962 (1958). "Torchbook Edition," with unique preface—New York: Harper and Row, 1974 (1962).

SFS *Science, Faith and Society.* Chicago: University of Chicago Press, 1946.

SM *The Study of Man.* Chicago: University of Chicago Press, 1959.

TD *The Tacit Dimension.* New York: Doubleday and Company, 1966.

Introduction

"The kingdom of God is as if a man should scatter seed upon the ground, and should sleep and rise night and day, and the seed should sprout and grow, he knows not how." (Mk 4:26–27)

The first purpose of this essay is to construct a dialogue between a man of faith from the nineteenth century and a man of science from the twentieth. Though widely separated by time, by their respective fields of specialization, and by their religious outlook, they seem remarkably akin to one another in their understanding of the operations of the human mind. The second purpose is to bring the results of this epistemic integration to bear upon disputed questions in Roman Catholic theology.

I first came across Michael Polanyi's writings in the spring of 1972. Professor Alan Weinblatt of the English Department at Boston College recommended reading *The Tacit Dimension* as part of a study of how we create and appreciate new beauty in poetry. Ten years later, at Catholic University, I took a course on Theological Epistemology from Avery Dulles that featured an extensive survey of Polanyi's works. In the next semester, the fall of 1983, John Ford presented a course on Newman's theological writings. With the reflections from Dulles' course still fresh in my mind, I was struck by how much ground Newman and Polanyi seemed to have in common. After beginning to work on this as a dissertation proposal, I discovered that Dulles has called attention to the similarities of the two positions several times over the last two decades,[1] but there seemed to be no dissertations, books, or

---

1. "Theologians in the past have generally paid far too little heed to the individual logic of discovery, as outlined by authors such as Newman and Polanyi" (*Survival of Dogma* [New York: Crossroad, 1982] 40). "Polanyi's heuristic theory, all too briefly outlined here, is admirably suited to account for discoveries which break out of the framework of what had antecedently been considered possible. His 'logic of discovery' has many points of similarity

articles devoted to the topic per se. I am grateful to each of these three men for the help they have given me in understanding Polanyi and Newman.

In the *Grammar of Assent*, John Henry Newman confronted the question of how a Christian can legitimately assent to what cannot be fully understood and cannot be strictly proven. At the climax of his argument that faith provides certitude, he appeals to "the personal action of the ratiocinative faculty, the perfection or virtue of which I have called the Illative Sense."[2] Rooted in human nature, this is the power by which we face facts, discover new interpretations of the facts, evaluate positions with a subtle, flexible, wordless logic, and use converging inferences to ground assent. Newman concluded that the illative sense is the ultimate criterion of truth for all "concrete reasonings," and therefore is the instrument, from the human point of view, of the kind of certitude proper to the Christian faith.

Michael Polanyi developed a strikingly comparable epistemology from an entirely different starting point: understanding the kind of certitude proper to discoveries in the physical and human sciences. If Newman aimed to show the rational structure of faith, Polanyi aimed to show the fiduciary structure of reason. Like Newman, but apparently without being directly influenced by him, Polanyi appealed to the power of the mind to gain knowledge informally, personally, and tacitly—the more deeply we examine what we know, the more profoundly we realize that "we know more than we can tell."[3] In *Personal Knowledge*, Polanyi assessed the importance of this 'tacit knowledge' for the whole range of human understanding.

Where Newman focused on the illative sense as an essential *means* of acquiring knowledge, Polanyi concentrated on the tacit and personal *quality* of what we know. The illative sense is that which enables the mind to gain, enrich, correct, and deploy tacit knowledge. The evidence for this claim will be drawn primarily from two books: Newman's *Grammar of Assent* and Polanyi's *Personal Knowledge*. The first two

to what Newman previously described under the rubric of the illative sense" (*A Church to Believe In* [New York: Crossroad, 1982] 43). There are several references to Newman in his "Faith, Church and God: Insights from Michael Polanyi" in *Theological Studies* 45 (1984) 537–50. Dulles also recommends his article in Johannes B. Bauer, *Entwürfe der Theologie* (Graz: Verlag Styria, 1985).

2. *GA* 271.
3. *TD* 4.

chapters will examine each author's epistemological masterpiece in it-self and then follow the key themes through the remainder of each man's works. The third chapter will explore the similarities and differences between the two positions; the fourth will provide some of examples of how post-critical consciousness benefits the conduct of theology; the Conclusion presents a post-critical view of particular concerns in Roman Catholicism.

A guiding metaphor for this project is "conceptual cartography." If we think of an epistemology as a map of the mind,[4] then our first task is to project one man's map on another's so as to determine to what extent their respective explorations of this intellectual territory may reinforce or correct the other's observations. It is the essence of map-making to neglect inessential features of the land in order to compress the important aspects into a manageable tool:[5] a map designed to show how to travel the interstate highways must show state boundaries, the location of cities, and the general contours of the highways themselves, but may discard topographical data, rainfall patterns, agricultural details, and small, local roads, whereas a map designed to show the pattern of fresh-water distribution in the land may ignore practically everything that is essential to the highway map.

When attempting to compare maps, one must take into account the fundamental methodologies of the map-makers; a Mercator projection generates quite a different image of the world from that of an "equal-area" representation, but both cover exactly the same ground. In order to compare Newman's map of the mind with Polanyi's, one must select a few salient features that reveal the lie of the land in each system, then "project" those features from a common viewpoint in order to de-

4. Polanyi observes that "all theory may be regarded as a kind of map extended over space and time" (*PK* 4). Newman also valued maps: "Who has not felt the irritation of mind and impatience created by a deep, rich country, visited for the first time, with winding lanes, and high hedges, and green steeps, and tangled woods, and every thing smiling indeed, but in a maze? The same feeling comes upon us in a strange city, when we have no map of its streets. Hence you hear of practiced travellers, when they first come into a place, mounting some high hill or church tower, by way of reconnoitering its neighborhood. In like manner, you must be above your knowledge, not under it, or it will oppress you; and the more you have of it, the greater will be the load" (*Idea* 105–6).

5. "A map is the more accurate the nearer its scale approaches unity, but if it were to reach unity and represent the features of a landscape in their natural size, it would become useless, since it would be about as difficult to find one's way on the map as in the region represented by it. We may conclude that linguistic symbols must be of reasonable size, or more generally that they must consist of easily manageable objects" (*PK* 81).

termine how closely the two maps correspond to each another. The process of selection and projection necessarily distorts the original images, but this is the price one pays when a third party attempts to answer the question, "Do these two thinkers view intellectual reality in the same way?"

Where Newman and Polanyi's visions of the mind correspond, they support each other's position, just as the maps of two explorers confirm each other, even though they may not have followed the same trail into the new territory. I cannot find any evidence that Newman's epistemology in any way influenced Polanyi's. One may well argue that both men were moved by a common culture, especially by an Augustinian current within it, and therefore that they are not to be considered "independent" thinkers; even so, many others born and raised in the same culture have neglected or repudiated this aspect of our heritage. Even if Newman and Polanyi were mining the same vein in the Western tradition, each found his way into it by his own personal exploration and should be given due credit for marking out paths that others may follow.

Personal Catholicism

I. Newman's Notion of the Illative Sense

This chapter gives a brief synopsis of Newman's major work in epistemology; the next chapter similarly summarizes Polanyi's position. The goal of this chapter is to link a series of concepts to each other: to define knowledge in terms of certitude, to define certitude in terms of assent, and show that the illative sense is that which determines when and how to assent. Newman introduces the term "illative sense" in the last three chapters of *An Essay in Aid of a Grammar of Assent*, as a "grand word for a common thing."[1] This "grand word" refers to the theme of informal reasoning, to which Newman returned repeatedly over three decades of reflection.[2]

For Newman, "illative sense" meant the power by which the mind generates and evaluates inferences.[3] It might also be called "the rea-

1. Zeno, *John Henry Newman: Our Way to Certitude: An Introduction to Newman's Psychological Discovery: The Illative Sense and His "Grammar of Assent"* (Leiden: E. J. Brill, 1957), 2, 263 (in a letter to Charles Meynell, November 17, 1869).

2. In the ninth chapter of *An Essay in Aid of a Grammar of Assent*, edited with an introduction by Nicholas Lash (Notre Dame: University of Notre Dame Press, 1979; hereafter cited in notes and text as *GA*), Newman quotes from his 1837 work *The Prophetical Office of the Church* and then uses the term "illative sense" to sum up his reflections on informal reasoning and to demonstrate the continuity of this thought (*GA* 296–97). Zeno notes that the "doctrine of the illative sense may be found in the University Sermons when [Newman] speaks about implicit and explicit reason" (Zeno, *Certitude*, 13; cf. 168). Newman makes a parallel distinction between informal and formal inference, and speaks of informal inference as one of the distinctive operations of the illative sense (*GA* 283).

3. In the nineteenth century, Newman's classically trained audience probably recognized the common Latin root of "illative" and "inference," but for most twentieth-century readers, "illative" is alien and uninformative. "Inference" is constructed on the present stem of "fero," to bear or carry, while "illative" derives from "latus," the past passive participle of the same verb. It is bad enough that there is no visual clue for the uninitiated that "fero" and "latus" are related, but it is even worse that when "in" was prefixed to "latus," the "n" from the prefix gave way to the "l" of the root. Newman's original audience may also have been familiar with "illative" as an adjective describing words or phrases which introduce a conclusion (e.g., therefore, hence, as a consequence, etc.). For such readers, the phrase would have been resonant with meanings; for many of us today it is an impediment to understanding what Newman is talking about.

soning sense," "conclusive awareness," "consciousness of consequences," or "the judging faculty." In some contexts, the best transla-
tion into contemporary English might be "the power of insight," "rational intuition," or "inferential instinct." Without setting aside such
resonances arising from the roots of the phrase, I also suggest that the
illative sense is the conscience of the intellect, i.e., that self-reflexive
aspect of the reasoning mind which questions, evaluates, and guards
the integrity of its own reasoning process.

Newman himself used "illative sense" in only one of his many writings, but as a brief survey of his life and works will show, this rather
awkward (even ugly) term embodies one of the most important and
fruitful themes of his life's work.

Biographical Context of the *Grammar*

Newman described his birth and early years in these words:

John Henry Newman was born on February 21st, 1801 in Old Broad Street in
the City of London. He was the eldest of six children. His father, whose family
came from Cambridgeshire, was partner in a Banking House in Lombard Street.
His mother was of one of the Huguenot families, who left France for England on
the revocation of the Edict of Nantes. Shortly after the peace of 1815, the Banking House wound up its accounts, and paid its creditors in full, but the effort involved his father personally in difficulties, which ended in his premature decay
and death.[4]

Although Newman was "brought up from a child to take great delight
in reading the Bible," he lacked "religious convictions."[5] Trevor notes
that "by the time he was fifteen he had reached a general skepticism
which required only a step to become conscious atheism."[6] In the fall
of 1816, Newman was converted to evangelical views by Walter May-
ers, "a clergyman of twenty-six, who had recently undergone conversion and became an Evangelical."[7] However, Newman's conversion ex-

4. John Henry Newman, *John Henry Newman: Autobiographical Writings*, edited with introductions by Henry Tristram (New York: Sheed and Ward, 1957; hereafter cited in notes
and text as *AW*), 10.

5. John Henry Newman, *Apologia pro Vita Sua: Being a History of His Religious Opinions*, edited with an introduction by Martin J. Svaglic (Oxford: Clarendon Press, 1967; hereafter cited in notes and text as *Apo*), 14.

6. Meriol Trevor, *Newman: The Pillar of the Cloud* (Garden City: Doubleday, 1962), 16.

7. Charles Dessain, *John Henry Newman* (Stanford: Stanford University Press, 1966,
1971), 3.

perience did not fit neatly with the evangelical paradigm; it did not take place in a single moment as did Saul's conversion on the road to Damascus, Luther's recognition of the supremacy of God's mercy, or Wesley's experience of being warmed and illuminated from within, but was a process lasting for five months, "from August to December 1816."[8] In that same December, Newman entered Trinity College, Oxford; he passed his exams for the Bachelor of Arts degree four years later (*Apo* xiii).

In April of 1822, Newman was elected a fellow of Oriel College and came under the influence of Richard Whately, the latitudinarian and anti-Erastian leader of the "Noetics."[9] For six years, Newman participated in this "group intent on restoring the philosophy of Aristotle to a position of honor and respect in the university curriculum."[10] Newman remained committed to Aristotle throughout his life. In the *Idea of a University*, he says, "While we are men, we cannot help, to a great extent, being Aristotelians, for the great Master does but analyze the thoughts, feelings, views, and opinions of human kind . . . In many subject-matters, to think correctly, is to think like Aristotle; and we are his disciples whether we will or no, though we may not know it."[11]

It is probably in this context that Newman developed his understanding of "phronesis," Aristotle's notion of judgment, which the *Grammar* uses as a model for the "illative sense." Phronesis is the "directing, controlling and determining principle" in "matters of conduct" that cannot be settled by the application of formal rules (*GA* 277). In such cases, the quality of one's own character is what decides the issue of what is to be done. Similarly, the illative sense is supreme, personal, and not bound by rules (though it may be aided by them); it is the "directing, controlling, and determining principle" in *intellectual* matters, especially "the affirmation of truth" (*GA* 277n).

Ordained an Anglican priest in 1825, Newman began moving away from his Evangelical roots—"it was his parishioners who first shook his confidence in the specifically evangelical doctrines; the coachmen,

---

8. Trevor, *Pillar,* 17.

9. Dessain, *Newman,* 7.

10. James W. Lyons, *Newman's Dialogues on Certitude* (Rome: Catholic Book Agency, 1978), 60.

11. John Henry Newman, *The Idea of a University: Defined and Illustrated in Nine Discourses,* edited with introduction and notes by Martin J. Svaglic (Notre Dame: University of Notre Dame Press, 1982; hereafter cited in notes and text as *Idea*), 83; cf. *GA* 354.

pub-keepers, young females and the rest just would not fit into the categories of Saved and Unsaved."[12] In 1826, Richard Hurrell Froude, soon to become one of Newman's great friends, was elected fellow of Oriel College. Froude was a disciple of John Keble, and the two together represented "the old High Church tradition at its noblest."[13] In that same year, Newman preached the first of the *University Sermons*. Although the sermons were presented over the next seventeen years, the unifying subject of the collection was the right use of reason in religion. D. M. MacKinnon considers these sermons a response to the empiricists, especially Hume, Locke, Mill, and Bentham, meeting them "on their own ground."[14] In his 1871 preface to the third edition of the *Sermons*, written the year after the publication of the *Grammar*, Newman highlighted the theme of implicit and informal reasoning, which operates "without a direct recognition . . . of the starting-point and path of thought from and through which it comes to its conclusion" (*US* xi–xii). As we shall see, it is the illative sense which governs the conduct of implicit reasoning, and it is implicit reason which stands at the foundation of faith: "Faith, viewed in contrast with Reason in these three senses, is implicit in its acts, adopts the method of verisimilitude, and starts from religious first principles" (*US* xvi–xvii). In the sermon "Implicit and Explicit Reason," Newman anticipated many of the points developed at greater length in the *Grammar*:

The mind ranges to and fro, and spreads out, and advances forward with a quickness which has become a proverb, and a subtlety and versatility which baffle investigation. It passes on from point to point, gaining one by some indication; another on a probability; then availing itself of an association; then falling back on some received law; next seizing on testimony; then committing itself to some popular impression, or some inward instinct, or some obscure memory; and thus it makes progress not unlike a clamberer on a steep cliff, who, by quick eye, prompt hand, and firm foot, ascends how he knows not himself, by personal endowments and by practice, rather than by rule, leaving no track behind him, and unable to teach another. It is not too much to say that the stepping by which great geniuses scale the mountains of truth is as unsafe and precarious to men in general, as the ascent of a skillful mountaineer up a literal crag. It is a way which they alone can take; and its justification lies in their suc-

12. Trevor, *Pillar*, 58.
13. Dessain, *Newman*, 9.
14. John Henry Newman, *Newman's University Sermons: Fifteen Sermons Preached before the University of Oxford, 1826–43*, with introductory essays by D. M. MacKinnon and J. D. Holmes (London: S.P.C.K., 1970; hereafter cited in notes and text as *US*), 10.

cess. And such mainly is the way in which all men, gifted or not gifted, common-ly reason,—not by rule, but by an inward faculty. (*US* 257)

The "inward faculty" which operates without rules and which is inca-pable of being fully formalized or articulated is, in the *Grammar*, called the illative sense.

   Personal difficulties in 1827 and the death of a sister in 1828 helped turn Newman away from "liberalism" (*Apo* xiii). Controversy over Catholic emancipation and consequent civil intervention into the af-fairs of the established church led Newman to break with Whately in 1829.[15] Four years later, another controversy over the relationship be-tween church and state sparked the Oxford Movement and helped to deepen Newman's commitment to the notion of revealed religion and "a visible Church which maintained an objective Truth with divine au-thority."[16] Over the course of the next twelve years, Newman's patristic studies confirmed "the idea of a visible Church" and ultimately led him to Rome. His *Essay on the Development of Christian Doctrine* was writ-ten at the end of his Anglican career and published shortly after his re-ception as a Roman Catholic in 1845. Newman claimed that his study of history led him from Protestantism to Catholicism—"If ever there were a safe truth, it is this. . . . To be deep in history is to cease to be a Protestant."[17]

   The perception of the identity between primitive Christianity and nineteenth-century Catholicism depends on seeing that "a living idea becomes many, yet remains one" (*Dev* 135). Gaining this insight is more an act of informal rather than formal reasoning, just as the devel-opment of the idea is an informal rather than a formal process. New-man uses the methaphor of growth to emphasize how "a body of thought is gradually formed" in the knower "without his recognizing what is going on within him"; only after the idea has taken root, formed many connections, and flourished in the garden of the mind can formal logic be "brought in to arrange and inculcate what no science was em-ployed in gaining" (*Dev* 138). In passages like this, Newman rejects a Cartesian model of clear and distinct ideas, capable of being expressed in unambiguous propositions; for him, an idea is not fixed and sharply

   15. Trevor, *Pillar*, 83.
   16. Trevor, *Pillar*, 154–55.
   17. John Henry Newman, *Essay on the Development of Christian Doctrine* (New York: Sheed and Ward, 1960; hereafter cited in notes and text as *Dev*), 5–6.

defined, but is a view that gives rise to many different propositions under different circumstances. Formal reasoning depends upon informal reasoning, and so "the spontaneous process which goes on within the mind itself is higher and choicer than that which is logical" (*Dev* 139). Newman's series of conversions from skepticism to evangelical Christianity, then to the patristic Anglicanism of the Oxford movement, and finally to the dogmatism of Rome illustrate the slow but powerful development of an idea within one man's mind. Just as the "living idea" of Christianity changed often in its growth in history, but retained its integrity, so the idea of a revealed religion, planted in Newman's heart at his first conversion, remained one through all suprising phases of its development within his personal history.

For "20 or 30 years," Newman attempted to write an "Essay on Assent."[18] The collected philosophical and theological papers of Newman show the "succession of commencements" from 1846 on.[19] During this same period, Newman carried on a correspondence with Hurrell Froude's brother, William, "the person above all others whom he wished most dearly to influence"—"one of the leading scientists of the day, Fellow of the Royal Society, freethinker, and lifelong friend."[20] The correspondence was collected and edited by Gordon Harper, who notes that "the potentiality of the illative sense" was one of the central issues in the dialogue: "Newman had for a long time been working toward this conclusion, that in the illative sense lay the means of establishing his case, but he had not so far developed it in words."[21]

Newman developed *The Idea of a University* between 1851 and 1858, while serving as the founding rector of the Catholic University of Ireland. The discourses and essays in this volume take up the question of knowledge as it is related to the purposes of a university. In his preface to the 1852 edition of the discourses, Newman described the development of "the instinctive just estimate of things as they pass before

18. Meriol Trevor, *Newman: Light in Winter* (Garden City: Doubleday, 1963), 384–85.

19. John Henry Newman's *The Philosophical Notebook of John Henry Newman*, edited by Edward Sillem (Louvain: Nauwelaerts, 1969; hereafter cited in notes and text as *PN*) has notes dated from 1859 to 1888. *The Theological Papers of John Henry Newman on Faith and Certainty*, edited by J. Derek Holmes, assisted by Hugo M. de Achaval, with an introduction by Charles S. Dessain (Oxford: Clarendon Press, 1976; hereafter cited in notes and text as *TP*), are dated from 1846 to 1886.

20. Gordon H. Harper, *Cardinal Newman and William Froude, F.R.S.: A Correspondence* (Baltimore: The John Hopkins Press, 1933), 1–2.

21. Harper, *Newman and Froude*, 25–26.

us, which sometimes indeed is a natural gift, but commonly is not gained without much effort and the exercise of years" (*Idea* xlii). In the language of the *Grammar,* it is by means of the illative sense that the intellect comes to such instinctively appropriate judgments. "Sound judgment"[22] depends on and nourishes "a connected view or grasp of things" (*Idea* xliii). The act of adopting a view precedes investigation, for it is the view that makes questioning possible. Without an integrating standpoint, "when we hear opinions put forth on any new subject, we have no principle to guide us in balancing them; we do not know what to make of them; we turn to and fro, and over, and back again, as if to pronounce upon them, if we could, but with no means of pronouncing" (*Idea* 375).

Because taking a view of things is so essential to the life of the mind, we will make efforts to force experience into a coherent framework: "though it is no easy matter to view things correctly, nevertheless the busy mind will ever be viewing. We cannot do without a view, and we put up with an illusion, when we cannot get a truth" (*Idea* 57). Newman was not overly concerned about the problem of false interpretations because "as far as effectiveness goes, even false views of things have more influence and inspire more respect than no views at all" (*Idea* xliv).

For Newman, there is no such thing as knowledge without a view to give it meaning: "When I speak of Knowledge, I mean something intellectual, something which grasps what it perceives through the senses; something which takes a view of things; which sees more than the senses convey; which reasons upon what it sees, and while it sees; which invests it with an idea" (*Idea* 85). Note how the description of knowledge as something "which sees more than the senses convey" sets Newman's position apart from the empirical tradition. The adoption of a view *gives* meaning to the data of the senses: "That only is true enlargement of mind which is the power of viewing many things at

---

22. "What we need at present for our Church's well-being, is not invention, nor originality, nor sagacity, nor even learning in our divines, at least in the first place, though all gifts of God are in a measure needed, and never can be unseasonable when used religiously, but we need peculiarly a *sound judgment,* patient thought, discrimination, a comprehensive mind, an abstinence from all private fancies and caprices and personal tastes,—in a word, Divine Wisdom" (*Apo* 64—a quotation by Newman from his *Prophetical Office;* emphasis added). When Newman defines "illative sense," he calls it "right judgment in ratiocination" (*GA* 269).

once as one whole, of referring them severally to their true place in the universal system, of understanding their respective values, and determining their mutual dependence" (*Idea* 103). There is also a hermeneutic circle here: the illative sense is conditioned by views already adopted, but it is also the means by which we take a view of complex realities (GA 287–88).

In 1864, Newman became embroiled in "an affair of honor, only one step removed from a duel,"[23] provoked by Kingsley's remarks about the integrity of priests in general and about Newman in particular. In the *Apologia pro Vita Sua*, Newman gave an account of the development of his own religious ideas. To some, his transformation from a defender of Anglican theology to a critic of it may have seemed "perverse or hypocritical."[24] In order to show that the progression of his religious commitments was reasonable, Newman explored his own notion of reason and provided a sketch of his theological epistemology (*Apo* 29). Seven propositions are embedded in a single extended sentence:

1. The "absolute certitude" about "the truths of natural theology, or as to the fact of a revelation" derives from "an *assemblage* of concurring and converging possibilities."

2. The peculiar character of this kind of knowledge is due both "to the constitution of the human mind and the will of its Maker."

3. Certitude is a "habit of mind."

4. Certainty is "a quality of propositions."

5. "Probabilities which did not lead to logical certainty, might suffice for a mental certitude."

6. Certitude based on the convergence of probabilities "might equal in measure and strength the certitude which was created by the strictest scientific demonstrations."

7. "To possess such certitude might in given cases and to given individuals be a plain duty, though not to others in other circumstances . . ."

That which declares that the mind possesses sufficient evidence and which enforces the duty of remaining certain is, in the *Grammar*, the

23. Trevor, *Light*, 320.
24. Trevor, *Light*, 344–45.

illative sense. In the *Apologia*, Newman called it Private Judgment—
"not formed arbitrarily and according to one's fancy or liking, but conscientiously, and under a sense of duty" (*Apo* 30). Even though Newman portrayed himself as striving to develop a kind of logic that would
rationalize the certitude appropriate to the Christian faith, he dissociat-
ed his approach from "paper logic" because "it was not logic that carried me on; as well might one say that the quicksilver in the barometer
changes the weather" (*Apo* 136). Newman's own illative sense was
clearly the root of his conversion. When Newman finally found the key
to writing the *Grammar*, he placed St. Ambrose's maxim on the title
page as a reminder of the difference between "paper logic" and the
force of insight gained informally by "the concrete being that reasons":
"Non in dialecticâ complacuit Deo salvum facere populum suum [Not
by dialectics did it please God to save His people]" (*Apo* 136).

The *Apologia* may have made the *Grammar* necessary. In order to
combat the rationalistic and anti-dogmatic models of his contempo-
raries, Newman needed to defend his view of "truth in religion." To one
observer, the mentality explained in the *Apologia* failed to rise above "a
sentiment and a taste":

In September, 1864, Fitzjames Stephen wrote for *Frazer's Magazine* [volume 70,
265–303] an article, "Dr. Newman's Apologia," in which he suggested some of
the scientific objections to Newman's argument, pointing out that the "considerations which finally decided him [Newman—to become Catholic] were of a sen-
timental rather than of a rational kind." He specifically attacked Newman's view
of accumulating probabilities as making for certainty, and showed how they
tended rather in the opposite direction, and concluded that "This misapprehen-
sion of the nature of probability vitiates the whole of Dr. Newman's theory." He
held, as did Froude, that "It is the first of intellectual duties always to reserve for
ourselves a liberty of doubting on every question whatever, however firm may be
our present belief, however sacred the matter to which it applies." Froude felt
that the article stated his own view, "with a rigor and clearness which is quite
beyond my power."[25]

Although Newman did not respond directly to this article, it seems fair
to speculate that such charges would have motivated him to clarify his
view that certitude depends on converging lines of thought brought to
conclusion by the illative sense. His reaction to this criticism does not

25. Harper, *Newman and Froude*, 176–77.

seem to have been strong enough to qualify as a "calling" to issue a response, as Kingsley's remarks had "called forth" the *Apologia*.[26] When
Froude urged Newman to answer this criticism of the *Apologia*, Newman indicated some doubt about whether he would be able do so: "On
the one hand I scarcely ever have written without an urgent or compul-
sive force applied to me—on the other hand it is of course a matter
which requires great and careful investigation."[27]

Newman spoke of the *Grammar* as his "hardest work."[28] When it
emerged as his "last full-scale treatise," it had been decades in the
making.[29] After the surprising success of his *Apologia*, published in
1864, Newman felt refreshed and renewed, and he began to seek
"some other means of doing good, whether Propaganda cares about
them or no."[30] In 1866, he suddenly realized that the key to understanding the kind of certitude proper to religious faith lay in distinguishing between inference and assent,[31] and he found himself able to
finish the project that he had begun so long ago:

> For twenty years I have begun and left off an inquiry again and again, which
> yesterday I finished. . . . I began it in my Oxford University Sermons; I tried it in
> 1850—and at several later dates, in 1859, in 1861 . . . but, though my funda-
> mental ideas were ever the same, I could not carry them out. Now at last I have
> done all that I can do according to my measure.[32]

If it is true that Newman's "fundamental ideas were ever the same,"
then the "illative sense," one of the key concepts of the *Grammar*, is
really new terminology rather than an entirely new notion. The
phrase crystallizes one aspect of what Newman had been driving at
through all these years of rumination on the informal foundations of
certitude.

Newman felt antipathy toward the methods employed by the Roman theologians of his day,[33] and therefore positioned his theological
reflections as an "essay" rather than a "treatise." In the *Grammar of As-*

26. Trevor, *Light*, 512.

27. Harper, *Newman and Froude*, 178; John Henry Newman, *The Letters and Diaries of John Henry Newman*, edited by Charles Stephen Dessain, et al (Oxford: Clarendon, 1961– ; hereafter cited as *LD*), XXI, 245.

28. Lyons, *Dialogues*, 12–13; Trevor, *Light*, 467.

29. Dessain, *Newman*, 147, 148.30. Trevor, *Light*, 364.

31. Lash, introduction to *GA*, 7.

32. Newman, February 13, 1870, in a letter to Richard Hutton; *GA*, 1.

33. Trevor, *Pillar*, 403.

sent, Newman engaged in controversy with several different kinds of opponents. The position he wished to advance is that "certitudes are attained in theology";[34] this stance is defined against a background of both philosophical and theological controversy. On the question of what certitude is in general and how it may be obtained, Newman took issue with various models of rationality suggested by skeptics (Hume and Montaigne),[35] empiricists (Locke and Froude),[36] utilitarians (Bentham and Brougham),[37] and idealists (Kant and Berkeley).[38] On the specific question of what religious certitude is and how one can obtain it, Newman opposed his view to fideism,[39] Evangelical sentimentalism,[40] evidentialism (Paley),[41] and liberalism (Whately).[42] In comparing his views to those of his opponents, Newman did not simply contradict them, but often granted qualified acceptance to part of their position, as when he expressed his deep respect for much of Locke's philosophy (GA 137–38).

In 1874, an argument with William E. Gladstone gave Newman an opportunity to clarify his view of papal infallibility. Prime Minister during the First Vatican Council, Gladstone was in close correspondence with Lord Acton about the events in Rome.[43] In "The Vatican Decrees in Their Bearing on Civil Allegiance: A Political Expostulation," Gladstone objected to the assertion of "Papal supremacy."[44] Ryan notes that

34. Lyons, *Dialogues*, 5. "Certitude . . . is essential to the Christian" (*GA* 74).

35. Zeno, *Certitude*, 59. Newman himself experienced the lure of skepticism in his youth (Trevor, *Pillar*, 16) and watched his brother, Frank, wander from Evangelical zeal to thoroughgoing skepticism (*Pillar*, 155, 518, 521).

36. Lyons says Newman chose Locke as the closest representative of William Froude's position (*Dialogues*, 6, 19).

37. GA 88–90.

38. Zeno, *Certitude*, 60; Newman refers to Kant once in *PN* and five times in *TP*.

39. Newman's concern was not with any particular fideist, but with protecting the uneducated faithful against the charge of accepting the faith without having sufficient reason to do so (Lyons, *Dialogues*, 16; Dessain, *Newman*, 152).40. It was especially clear in his account of his conversion to Catholicism that Newman intended to rule his religious life "by reason, not by feeling" (Zeno, *Certitude*, 114; Dessain, *Newman*, 73). In his youth, however, Newman had studied Evangelical theology and identified with it for a time (Trevor, *Pillar*, 32), until experience in parish work and contact with Whately gave him other perspectives (*Pillar*, 58, 80, 253).

41. GA 330.

42. Lyons, *Dialogues*, 9.

43. Alvin S. Ryan, introduction to John Henry Newman, *A Letter Addressed to His Grace the Duke of Norfolk on Occasion of Mr. Gladstone's Recent Expostulation*, in *Newman and Gladstone: The Vatican Decrees*, introduction by Alvin S. Ryan (Notre Dame: University of Notre Dame Press, 1962 [1875]; hereafter cited in text and notes as *DN*), x.

44. Ryan, *DN*, xiii.

"nearly half of the entire essay" deals with Gladstone's proposition "That Rome requires a convert, who now joins her, to forfeit his moral and mental freedom, and to place his loyalty and civil duty at the mercy of another."[45]

Newman felt that his response to Gladstone was "likely to be [his] last publication."[46] Gladstone's attack gave Newman the opportunity to distance himself from the English Ultramontanes, "who for years past have conducted themselves as if no responsibility attached to wild words and overbearing deeds; who have stated truths in the most paradoxical form, and stretched principles till they were close upon snapping; and who at length, having done their best to set the house on fire, leave to others the task of putting out the flame" (*DN* 76). Newman observed dryly that "there are partizans of Rome who have not the sanctity and wisdom of Rome herself" (*DN* 167). He aimed instead at a "moderation of doctrine, dictated by charity" (*DN* 184, 192). For Newman, the Church's "direct statements of truth" or "condemnation of error" weighed "as lightly as possible on the faith and conscience of her children."[47] In such declarations, the Church only asks what is necessary for the preservation of revelation and does not intrude on other areas of personal conscience.

Against Gladstone, Newman upheld the right of the papacy "to determine in the detail of faith and morals what is true and what is false" (*DN* 152); against the Ultramontanes, Newman upheld the primacy of conscience outside the narrow field of papal authority: "So little does the Pope come into this whole system of moral theology by which (as by our conscience) our lives are regulated, that the weight of his hand upon us, as private men, is absolutely unappreciable" (*DN* 115).

Although the *Letter to the Duke of Norfolk* was written just a few years after the *Grammar,* Newman uses none of the technical language developed in the earlier work. In particular, the phrase "illative sense" never appears. Instead, in this work, "the sense of right and wrong" seems to have many of the qualities ascribed to the illative sense in the

45. Ryan, *DN,* xv.

46. *DN,* 75; on page 199 he calls the essay his "last words."

47. *DN,* 192. "To be a true Catholic a man must have a generous loyalty towards ecclesiastical authority, and accept what is taught him with what is called the *pietas fidei,* and only such a tone of mind has a claim, and it certainly has a claim, to be met and to be handled with a wise and gentle *minimism.* Still the fact remains, that there has been of late years a fierce and intolerant temper abroad, which scorns and virtually tramples on the little ones of Christ" (*DN* 197).

Grammar. In one notable passage (*DN* 132–33). Newman says the moral sense is:

— the first element of religion;
— delicate;
— fitful;
— easily puzzled, obscured, perverted;
— subtle in its argumentative methods;
— impressible by education;
— biassed by pride and passion;
— unsteady in its flight;
— at once the highest of all teachers, yet the least luminous.

Apart from the first predicate, which asserts that conscience is the foundation of religion, all the others apply equally well to Newman's understanding of the illative sense, which he sees as fundamental to all knowledge. (The close correlation between Newman's notions of conscience and the illative sense will be explored further at the end of Chapter III.)

As part of a uniform edition of his works, in 1877 Newman issued a third edition of *The Via Media of the Anglican Church.* Since this defense of Anglicanism contained statements which he was now "sorry to have made," Newman provided a preface to this edition, along with some footnotes in the text, as a "refutation" of his earlier position.[48] Ironically, one of the last people he chose to engage in controversy was himself; consequently, he speaks of himself in the third person in the preface. In reviewing his work, he did not feel it necessary to recant everything in it: "Large portions of these Lectures are expositions, nay, recommendations of principles and doctrines, recognized in the Catholic Church, and in these portions, now that I take up the Volume afresh as a Catholic, I have nothing or little to alter" (*VM* xvi–xvii). As in the *Letter to the Duke of Norfolk,* Newman again refrains from using the philosophical terminology he developed in the *Grammar.* The closest reference to natural inference, informal reason and the illative sense is in a remark about "an instinctive course of reasoning which leads the mind to acknowledge the Supreme God" (*VM* lxx).

---

48. John Henry Newman, *The Via Media of the Anglican Church Illustrated in Lectures, Letters and Tracts Written Between 1830 and 1841* (London: Longmans, Green and Company, 1901; hereafter cited in notes and text as *VM*), ix.

In 1879, Newman was made a Cardinal. On this occasion, Newman characterized his life's work as a conflict with religious liberalism:[49]

Liberalism in religion is the doctrine that there is no positive truth in religion. . . . It is inconsistent with any recognition of religion as *true*. [Liberalism holds that] Revealed Religion is not a truth, but a sentiment and a taste. . . . Devotion is not necessarily founded on faith.[50]

Fifteen years earlier, in his *Apologia*, Newman had portrayed himself as a defender of dogma:

My battle was with liberalism; by liberalism I mean the anti-dogmatic principle and its developments. This was the first point on which I was certain. . . . From the age of fifteen, dogma has been the fundamental principle of my religion: I know no other religion; I cannot enter into the idea of any other sort of religion; religion, as a mere sentiment, is to me a dream and a mockery. (*Apo* 50–51)

Although Newman continued to wrestle privately with questions of philosophy and theology,[51] to publish new essays,[52] and to edit and republish former works in the 1880s,[53] there were no major shifts in his conduct of the battle against "the anti-dogmatic principle." Trevor observes that "The Development of Religious Error," published in 1885, recapitulates the great theme of his career:

He took up the central question of Reason, using illustrations from his University Sermons, written fifty years since. Thus, incidentally, he demonstrated the continuity of his ideas. He emphasized once more that the reasoning faculty was an instrument which could be used correctly and yet come to false conclusions if the argument proceeded from faulty initial assumptions.[54]

49. "Newman was not opposed to all forms of liberalism. For instance, he had no quarrel with scientific progress professed by the liberals. Nor was he opposed to liberalism as a political movement, since in this context liberalism generally means the concession to popular demands chiefly in politics" (Lyons, *Dialogues*, 2).

50. This is a speech Newman made in Rome in 1879 when he was raised to the rank of Cardinal (Dessain, *Newman*, 165).

51. The last entry in the *Theological Notebook* was made in 1886, while the last in the *Philosophical Notebook* was made in 1888.

52. Most notably, "Inspiration in its Relation to Revelation" and a subsequent comment on that article in 1884. This article is republished with an extensive introduction by J. Derek Holmes and Robert Murray in the book *On the Inspiration of Scripture* (London: Geoffrey Chapman, 1967; 101–31).

53. The *Apologia*, for example, did not reach its "definitive edition" until 1886, twenty-one years after its first appearance as a series of pamphlets ("A Note on the Text," *Apo* xi).

54. Trevor, *Light*, 624. Trevor notes immediately that this is not the main theme: "But the core of the essay was the exposition of Newman's views on the World."

Newman died on August 11, 1890, at Edgbaston. "Although the unseen world was so vivid to him, he yet knew the limitations of Revelation, and asked to have inscribed on his memorial tablet the words, 'Ex umbris et imaginibus in veritatem,' 'Out of shadows and images into the truth.'"[55]

Purpose and Structure of the *Grammar*

It may be helpful to reflect for a moment on the metaphor employed in the title of Newman's essay. Newman advocates teaching grammar in his preface to *The Idea of a University* because it inculcates "the idea of science, method, order, principle, and system; of rule and exception, of richness and harmony" and provides the groundwork for the development of "the largest and truest philosophical views" (*Idea* xliv–xlv). A grammar defines fundamental linguistic terms, declares principles of correct speech, and licenses exceptions to its own rules. "Grammar, in this sense, is the scientific analysis of language, and to be conversant with it, as regards a particular language, is to be able to understand the meaning and force of that language when thrown into sentences and paragraphs."[56] If grammars in general describe the formal conditions of correct speech, without regard to the contents of what is said,[57] a grammar of assent would describe the conditions of correct assent, without concern for the contents of the assent. Newman's title, then, raises the question whether there are, in fact, "principles or rules" that govern assent.

The central weakness of approaching assent as a grammatical construct is that a "grammatically correct" assent might still be false, just as a grammatically correct sentence might be false. In mathematics, Kurt Gödel showed that any formal system powerful enough to express the questions of consistency and coherence cannot settle those same

55. Dessain, *Newman*, 169.

56. *Idea* 250. Newman was commenting on Johnson's definition of grammar as "the art of using *words* properly."

57. "'Grammar' is precisely the total of linguistic rules which can be observed by using a language *without* attending to the things referred to. The purpose of the philosophic pretence of being merely concerned with grammar is to contemplate and analyze reality, while denying the act of doing so" (Michael Polanyi, *Personal Knowledge: Towards a Post-Critical Philosophy* [Chicago: University of Chicago Press, 1962; hereafter cited in notes and text as *PK*], 114). Polanyi's criticism of the grammatical dodge is directed at Wittgenstein, not Newman.

questions.[58] Similarly, it seems impossible to create a formal linguistic system that is flexible enough to speak of all the things which we value but that is strict enough to rule out nonsense and falsehoods automatically. Even in the highly restricted field of number theory, such a system of complete identity between grammatical correctness and truth is impossible to obtain. One might also note that effective communication may purchase impact at the expense of grammatical correctness, as in the colorful use of double negatives—when someone says, "It ain't none of your business," the speaker doubles the intensity of the negation rather than voiding it.

Though Newman's essay is called "the *Grammar*" for the sake of brevity, Newman did not claim to have written a complete grammar, but only "*An* Essay in Aid of *a* Grammar of Assent." Like a grammar, the essay defines terms, proposes syntax, and discusses rules and exceptions to rules, but does so with implicit deference to a more definitive work. Just as a grammar concentrates on the conditions of correct speech, the essay focuses on the question of the conditions of correct assent to a proposition.

In order to clarify these conditions, Newman defined terms and laid down certain guidelines for correct assent. In Part One of the *Grammar*, Newman intended to show that one may legitimately assent even to what one does *not* understand,[59] on the assumption that one may trust another's testimony about what is the case. In the first four chapters, this is dealt with in principle, while in the fifth chapter, Newman applied this understanding of assent to three test cases of religious belief, in which the one who gives assent relies on the testimony of Revelation in order to accept what is not immediately available for inspection. In Part Two of the *Grammar*, Newman shifted his focus to the paradox of correctly assenting to what *cannot* be proven (*GA* 136).[60] He again devoted four chapters to definition of terms and establishment of general guidelines, then took up the question of Revelation in the final chapter as a persuasive application of his position to religious questions.

---

58. Douglas R. Hofstadter, *Gödel, Escher, Bach: An Eternal Golden Braid* (New York: Random House, 1979), 228–29. No system broad enough to deal with the question of truth can evade Gödel's theorem: ". . . any such system digs its own hole; the system's richness brings about its own downfall. The downfall occurs essentially because the system is powerful enough to have self-referential sentences" (470).

59. Dessain, *Newman*, 148.

60. From this point forward in Chapter I, references to page numbers in the text are to *GA* unless otherwise specified.

Although Newman postponed introduction of the illative sense until the penultimate chapter of the *Grammar*, rhetorically delaying insertion of the keystone until the body of the arch of argumentation had been prepared to receive it, this study will adopt the viewpoint provided by the finished work. Taking this standpoint highlights the connection of the "illative sense" with the other conceptual building blocks that Newman employed, and it may allow the reader to see more clearly how this notion supports all the others. Part One of the *Grammar* shows that one may legitimately assent to religious propositions on the assumption that Revelation is trustworthy; then Part Two shows that one makes the assumption that Revelation is trustworthy on the basis of the illative sense. One believes without understanding everything that is believed because one trusts the person who speaks; one comes to trust the authority of the speaker through the best use of human judgment, which shows many lines of inquiry whose convergence renders the authority of Revelation credible, even though none of them provides absolute proof.

Newman's concern with epistemology derived from the religious conviction that "certitude . . . is essential to the Christian; and if he is to persevere to the end, his certitude must include in it a principle of persistence. This it has . . ." (180). An understanding of when one may legitimately consider oneself to be certain—a grammar of assent—increases one's freedom to act upon faith. "It is assent, pure and simple, which is the motive cause of great achievements" (177). "Sacrifice of wealth, name, or position, faith and hope, self-conquest, communion with the spiritual world, presuppose a real hold and habitual intuition of the objects of Revelation, which is certitude under another name" (193). Misunderstanding the conditions of certitude—an inadequate grammar of assent—can cripple the imagination and weaken the response of the believer to the gift of Revelation.

The structure of the *Grammar* indicates the major misunderstanding that Newman wanted to clear up: that perfect comprehension and complete proof are required for enduring certitude. Part One stresses that partial understanding is sufficient for assent, while Part Two concentrates on the recognition that one must make personal commitments based on formally incomplete lines of thought. Newman's method of attack throughout the essay is to reflect on facts which one does accept as certain and to draw modest conclusions from these facts about when and how one may assent unreservedly: "To arrive at the fact of any matter, we must eschew generalities, and take things as they stand, with all their circumstances" (243).

In this emphasis on "the world of facts" (272) Newman showed himself to be an empiricist, though in his criticism of Locke and Hume he rejected the classical paradigms of British empiricism; Lyons makes the case that Newman is more empirical than the empiricists, who often overlook the facts of how the mind actually operates in favor of their a priori assumptions about how it should function.[61] The aim of the *Grammar* is to "go by facts" (136) because "things concrete" (87) give the highest meaning and greatest freedom to human life. The goal is not a complete theory of assent but a determination of "what is the matter of fact" (270) about the fundamental operations of the mind.

Newman assumed that there are many certitudes, recognized and accepted as such by all. Even though one cannot specify completely *how* it is that certitude developed, one may know *that* one knows—"for me it is sufficient that certitude is felt. This is what the schoolmen, I believe, call treating a subject *in facto esse*, in contrast with *in fieri*" (270–71). Newman opposed his approach to Locke, Hume, and Kant, among others, whose "grammars of assent" would rule out in principle this kind of informal, personal certitude:

Such is what may be called the *à priori* method of regarding assent in its relation to inference. It condemns an unconditional assent in concrete matters on what may be called the nature of the case. Assent cannot rise higher than its source, inference in such matters is at best conditional, therefore assent is conditional also. (136)

He went on to scorn the "pretentious axiom that probable reasoning can never lead to certitude," naming Locke as one in particular who refuses to accept the significance of unconditionally accepted, though undemonstrated, truths (136).

The a priori skeptics create a standard which they themselves cannot live up to: in spite of Locke's determination to grant assent to a proposition only in strict proportion to proof in its favor, he "is obliged to make exceptions to his general principle,—exceptions, unintelligible on his abstract doctrine, but demanded by the logic of facts" (137). Extending the same criticism to "the class of writers" like Locke, Newman

61. Lyons, *Dialogues*, 10, 15, 33.

observed: "Having made their protest, they subside without scruple into that same absolute assurance of only partially-proved truths, which is natural to the illogical imagination of the multitude" (151–52).

Newman did not mean to run to the other extreme of mindlessly absorbing everything that is suggested by the world-at-large or by a religious tradition. He acknowledged that there can be a "reasonable skepticism" (294), but held that one progresses in knowledge by learning from one's mistakes in judgment:

Errors in reasoning are lessons and warnings, not to give up reasoning, but to reason with greater caution. It is absurd to break up the whole structure of our knowledge, which is the glory of the human intellect, because the intellect is not infallible in its conclusions. (187)

In religious matters, assent is prevented from falling into the errors of enthusiasm by the continued check of reason (109). One makes the best of what has actually been given in human nature, even if it is not the "best" from an idealistic or a priori standpoint. The thoroughgoing skeptic looks at the history of human errors and the inability of reason to reach more than probabilities when dealing with concrete matters, and judges that "certitude is ever a mistake" (270); Newman contemplated the same circumstances, and decided that we are meant to learn from our mistakes:

Whatever be the legitimate weight of the fact of that mistake in our inquiry, justice has been done to it, before we have allowed ourselves to be certain again. . . . Am I not to indulge my second certitude, because I was wrong in my first? does not any objection, which lies against my second from the failure of my first, fade away before the evidence on which my second is founded? . . . Because I have been mistaken in my certitude, may I not at least be certain that I have been mistaken? (188)

It would be much nicer if the mind were either wholly infallible or completely untrustworthy. The responsibility of continuing to assess one's judgments to determine whether they are well-formed is hard work under the best of circumstances. Newman's essay in criticism of unrealistic "grammars of assent" can help us accept this responsibility without suffering from fruitless anxiety caused by unreasonable standards of reason.

The Line of Argument in Part One: Making up Our Minds about Ideas and Things

The first part of the *Grammar* is dedicated to the study of "Assent and Apprehension." In this section, Newman wanted to show that, although apprehension plays a role in giving rise to assent, the two are not identical and do not vary directly with one another—we do not necessarily commit ourselves to a position in proportion to our "direct experience"[62] of it. In the conduct of this argument, Newman also defined key terms which play a role throughout the essay:

1. Assent: unconditional acceptance of a proposition.
2. Inference: conditional acceptance of a proposition.
3. Notional apprehension: grasping an idea.
4. Notional assent: deciding whether to accept or reject an idea.
5. Real apprehension: grasping a reality.
6. Real assent: deciding how to respond to a reality.

Notional apprehension and notional assent deal with the world of abstractions; real apprehension and real assent deal with things. Apprehension is generally passive and receptive in nature, even though it may take great effort to place oneself in a position to perceive an idea or a reality, while assent is more active and necessarily engages the will. Because these last four terms are so central to the rest of this essay, I would like to show how they work in four different examples.

1. The basic idea of a hamburger is a portion of cooked ground beef served on a bun. To recognize this definition is an act of notional apprehension; to agree or disagree with this definition is an act of notional assent. To cook, purchase, or accept a hamburger and then to take a bite of it are acts of real assent, which then give rise to the personal experience (real apprehension) of what this kind of food is like. One can also have apprehension of this reality by sight and smell, which require much less of a commitment than the decision to eat the burger. When one is hungry, there is a world of difference between meditating on the recipe for a hamburger (notional apprehension) and actually eating one (real assent and real apprehension combined in a single action).

2. To apprehend a building notionally is to consider it in the ab-

62. Trevor, *Light,* 487.

stract. The Temple in Jerusalem, for example, might be defined as the central place for Israelite worship built by David's son in the tenth century B.C. A historian, an archeologist, or a biblical scholar might exercise notional assent by rejecting or qualifying this definition of the Temple. The only avenue to real apprehension of the Temple at present is through historical testimony. The building itself, except for ruins of a retaining wall and perhaps some other foundations lost underneath a Muslim mosque, has ceased to exist. Some blueprints and models have been created to help us to imagine the past reality and make it accessible to our minds. If the ultra-Orthodox in Israel have their way, those plans will be turned into a new Temple some day by an act of assent which calls that reality into being. When and if the Temple is reconstructed, it will be the object of real apprehension again as it was in the past.

3. Science is a vast series of interlinked ideas about reality. Understanding formulas such as $e = mc^2$ or $f = ma$ is an act of notional apprehension. Only after grasping the ideas proposed by a scientist can critics render a judgment on the value of the theories (notional assent). The fundamental art in science is knowing how to bring these theories to bear on the data provided by the perception of realities (real apprehension). To this end, the scientists must make a fundamental disposition of themselves through acts of real assent so that they can attend to their observations and experiments.

4. For Newman, religion is primarily located in the area of experience of supernatural realities (real apprehension) and religious actions (real assent). Grasping and judging ideas about religious realities (notional apprehension and assent) is the work of theology. As in the case of Moses' experience at the burning bush or Saul's experience on the road to Damascus, apprehension of the divine reality may burst into a person's life unexpectedly, calling forth assent to that reality prior to any reflective understanding or judgment. At the other end of the spectrum is a conversion like Newman's, in which an idea (specifically, the idea that the primitive Church may have developed into the Roman Catholic Church) takes root in the imagination and gradually discloses a religious reality that wins the assent of the heart.

The first chapter of the *Grammar* clarifies the nature of assent by analyzing the use of propositions. Newman indicated that he has two "main subjects": (1) "the distinctions in the use of propositions" and (2) "the questions which those distinctions involve" (31). In one sentence, Newman defined what a proposition is and categorized the three states it may take: "Propositions (consisting of a subject and predicate united by the copula) may take a categorical, conditional, or interrogative form" (25). The grammatical form of the propositions indicates the attitude of the speaker toward the object of the proposition—disagreement, conditional acceptance, or unconditional acceptance (26). These three categories of "Doubt, Inference, and Assent" can really be collapsed into two, because the act of doubting may be considered as an assent to a contrary proposition.[63] There is, however, another kind of doubt, which suggests openness to new ideas and a willingness to continue raising questions before coming to a final judgment. Skipping over the role of questioning as part of the process of making new discoveries allowed Newman to focus his attention on the distinction between inference and assent, which he considered the key to the development of the essay, but it may have distorted his dialogue with Froude, who felt that the principle of doubt was the source of progress in science, technology, politics, and religion.[64] If Newman had named the third state of mind "questioning" or "investigating" rather than "doubt," he might have been able to indicate more clearly where and how he disagreed with Froude. As we shall see when we consider Newman's view of presumption, Newman did not believe that the success of scientific investigations came from doubt per se but from the structure of apprehension and assent.

Assent, said Newman, differs from inference in two key points (28). The first distinction is that assent is unconditional, while inference is not: assent "is in itself the absolute acceptance of a proposition without any condition" (32). In the act of assent, one accepts a proposition as true ("It is raining now"), while in an inference, one makes a commitment to a conclusion only insofar as its antecedent may be true ("If the wind continues from the northeast, the rain will turn to snow tomorrow").

The second distinction between assent and inference is that assent

63. GA 28: "I dismiss Doubt with one observation"—namely, that it is really just an assent to a contrary proposition.
64. Froude to Newman, December 29, 1859, in Harper, Newman and Froude, 122.

requires "some concomitant apprehension" of the meaning of the terms involved in the proposition (32), while inference may depend solely upon the formal manipulation of the terms, without regard to their content. This observation constitutes the main point of Chapter Two, "Assent Considered as Apprehensive." Newman defined "apprehension of propositions" as "imposition of a sense on the terms of which they are composed" (29). The degree to which an assent has an impact on our minds and on the course of our actions varies with the nature of the apprehension involved in forming the assent (47). Inference, on the other hand, depends solely on a formal evaluation of the premises of a proposition (64).

Although apprehension of the predicate is intrinsic to Newman's understanding of assent, he noted that one may come to accept something as true on another's say-so, without understanding what the informant understands. In this "indirect assent" (33–34), one grasps only that what is proposed "is true," but does not personally see the truth of the matter.

In the second half of Chapter One, Newman distinguished two "modes of apprehending propositions": notional and real (29). This, in turn, gave him the distinction between notional and real assents (the title and focus of Chapter Four), depending on which kind of proposition is accepted as true. A "notion," for Newman, is an "aspect of a thing" (60, 57). A "notional proposition" deals with "what is abstract, general, and non-existing," while a "real proposition" refers to "things external to us, unit and individual" (29). Notional propositions present ideas or aspects, while real propositions declare facts (31). The distinction between notional and real propositions is determined according to the capacity of the one who entertains them, not by the grammatical structure of the proposition. The same proposition may be real to one person but merely notional to another, depending on experience, training, imagination, sympathy, or other influences upon perception (30).

The one who apprehends the realities of which the propositions speak brings something different to bear in the act of assent from what is brought to bear on the propositions by the one who considers only a series of abstractions. I have never tasted a truffle, although I understand the proposition that it is a highly valuable, edible fungus that grows in the roots of trees. When I read or think about truffles, I do so only in terms of abstractions, since I lack the concrete experience that would give added meaning to the language used about them. Humans who have eaten truffles may have both notional and real apprehension of them; presumably the pigs that are used to search for truffles have only real apprehension of them, without any further notions about genus, species, market value, or recipes attached to the experience of smelling, tasting, and consuming the truffle.

In his third chapter, Newman extended the notional/real distinction to "the apprehension of propositions" (36). He defined apprehension as "simply an intelligent acceptance of the idea, or of the fact which a proposition enunciates" (36). Newman valued real apprehension more than notional apprehension, though both are essential for the full development of the mind:

> To apprehend notionally is to have breadth of mind, but to be shallow; to apprehend really is to be deep, but to be narrow-minded. The latter is the conservative principle of knowledge, and the former the principle of its advancement. Without the apprehension of notions, we should for ever pace round one small circle of knowledge; without a firm hold upon things, we shall waste ourselves in vague speculations. However, real apprehension has the precedence, as being the scope and end and the test of the notional; and the fuller is the mind's hold upon things or what it considers such, the more fertile is it in its aspects of them, and the more practical in its definitions. (47)

Newman holds that this precedence of fact over idea is what imparts the noticeably different quality to those acts of assent that are related to real objects as opposed to acts of assent to ideas or mental realities (36, 49–50). This corresponds well with the experimental method in science, which prescribes that ideas should be tested against realities.

In his fourth chapter, "Notional and Real Assents," while continuing to develop the vocabulary for his epistemology, Newman began to indicate some of his theological concerns. The purpose of this chapter is "to treat of Assent under this double aspect of its subject-matter,—assent to notions, and assent to things" (48). The first part of the chapter explores five types of notional assent: profession, credence, opinion, presumption, and speculation (52).

These five types of notional assent range from the weakest commitment to the strongest. "Profession" is treated as a practically thoughtless adherence to what others believe:

These are assents so feeble and superficial, as to be little more than assertions. I class them all under the head of Profession. Such are the assents made upon habit and without reflection. . . . Such again are the assents of men of wavering restless minds, who take up and then abandon beliefs so readily, so suddenly, as to make it appear that they had no view (as it is called) on the matter they professed, and did not know to what they assented or why. (52–53)

While pressing home his attack on those who simply adopt a party line without thinking through the issues for themselves, Newman defined what he meant by "mystery" in order to distinguish our acceptance of a mystery from mere assertion of an incomprehensible position:

A mystery is a proposition conveying incompatible notions, or is a statement of the inconceivable. Now we can assent to propositions (and a mystery is a proposition), provided we can apprehend them; therefore we can assent to a mystery, for, unless we in some sense apprehended it, we should not recognize it to be a mystery, that is, a statement uniting incompatible notions. The same act, then, which enables us to discern that the words of the proposition express a mystery, capacitates us for assenting to it. Words which make nonsense, do not make a mystery. (55)

Newman compared the use of language in the declaration of mysteries to the use of metaphors in language and to the use of "practical approximation" in the sciences, calling such inexact-but-sufficient constructions "an economy" (56). Although we do not *understand* everything about the object of our thoughts in a dogmatic proposition, "we *apprehend sufficiently* to be able to assent to these theological truths as mysteries" (60; italics mine). Like the scientist who disregards imperfections in his model or like the poet who overlooks peripheral incongruities in a metaphor, the believer senses that the statement of a mystery is full of meaning, even if it is entangled in perplexities. We know enough to know we should cling to the reality indicated by the religious language, even though we cannot spell out all of the relationships involved—we know enough to know how little we know.

The second class of notional assents, "credence," are those commonplace assumptions that we take for granted. Such assents provide the intellectual background one needs to begin to function as a mature thinker:

What I mean by giving credence to propositions is pretty much the same as having "no doubt" about them. It is the sort of assent which we give to those opinions and professed facts which are ever presenting themselves to us without any effort of ours, and which we commonly take for granted, thereby obtaining a broad foundation of thought for ourselves, and a medium of intercourse between ourselves and others. [These are] . . . the furniture of the mind. . . . a rich and living clothing. . . . ungrudging, prompt assents . . . [the result of a] liberal education . . . standards of thought and action . . . moral language . . . national characteristics. (60–61)

Newman made a distinction here between "theology" and "religion." Theology is a kind of credence, since it provides a notional background for dialogue: "Theology as such, always is notional, as being scientific: religion, as being personal, should be real" (62). To engage in dialogue with other believers, we need to be somewhat fluent in the language of theology, but to be in contact with God, we need to turn toward a reality that is before, behind, and beyond all of our notions of "God."

Newman defined the third category of notional assents by way of contrast with the second. Where credence is "a spontaneous acceptance of the various informations" (64) given to us in our culture, "opinion" is marked by a greater degree of reflection and by an awareness that one assents to a probability rather than to a certainty:

It differs from Credence in these two points, viz. that, while Opinion explicitly assents to the probability of a given proposition, Credence is an implicit assent to its truth. It differs from Credence in a third respect, viz. in being a reflex act;— when we take a thing for granted, we have credence in it; when we begin to reflect upon our credence, and to measure, estimate, and modify it, then we are forming an opinion. (65)

The insistence on the reflex and personal character of this process sets Newman's usage of the term slightly apart from the ordinary language about "opinion," but corresponds to the tradition of giving respect to "theological opinion, in contrast with faith in dogma" (64, 65).

"Presumption" is the fourth kind of notional assent: "By presumption I mean an assent to first principles; and by first principles I mean the propositions with which we start in reasoning on any given subject-matter" (66). There is a sense in which one might construe the purpose of the *Grammar* as the advocacy of Newman's own personal first principles of thought. Only those who adopt his view will see how he comes to his conclusions. Those who operate with a different set of fundamental options, like William Froude and his commentator, Gordon Harper, will not be able to make sense out of the argument, no matter how many different ways it is stated. In Harper's description of the differences between Newman and Froude, he seems much more sympathetic to the scientist:

To Froude the truth was something external to the mind but discernible if sought intelligently, honestly, and in the proper manner, that is, by a judicial and entirely unprejudiced weighing of evidence. And the evidence for arriving at true conclusions was, he maintained, equally open to all men to see and to evaluate. Newman held entirely different principles. The cardinal point in his philosophy was that a special disposition of mind was indispensable to the discovery of special truths; to discover religious truth one had to be religiously minded. The evidence was not, he believed, open alike to all men, and the reason why an irreligious man could not perceive religious truth was that, in the first place, much of the evidence for religion was hidden from him; he had not the proper intellectual equipment to discover it.[65]

With a greater sympathy for Newman's point of view, one might say that the dispute between Newman and Froude revolved around what "weighing of evidence" might mean in religious questions. In Chapter Ten of the *Grammar*, Newman held that not all thinkers were equally open to the kind of evidence that religion has rather than that the indications were hidden from them (329–30). Harper's statement (or misstatement) of the case clearly illustrates how first principles affect the outcome of an argument.

In keeping with his empiricist temperament, Newman was careful to distinguish such "first principles" from a priori truths: "In themselves they [first principles] are abstractions from facts, not elementary truths prior to reasoning" (69). In contrast to other empiricists, however, Newman insisted that there is no way to evade personal responsibility for the adoption (or presumption) of one's most fundamental beliefs. If we keep questioning our reasons for holding a particular belief, we will find ourselves falling back on "what are called first principles, the recondite sources of all knowledge, as to which logic provides no common measure of minds,—which are accepted by some, rejected by others,—in which, and not in the syllogistic exhibitions, lies the whole problem of attaining to truth,—and which are called self-evident by their respec-

65. Harper, *Newman and Froude,* 78–79.

tive advocates because they are evident in no other way" (216). The "whole problem of attaining to truth," then, lies in presumption of the correct principles; in Chapters Eight and Nine, Newman makes it clear that the only way to take up or modify first principles is by means of the informal operations of the illative sense (282–83).

Newman's view that we are personally responsibility for determining how judgments are to be formed might be characterized by a logician as a vicious circle; it is *formally* incorrect to assume what stands in need of proof. "I know that it is my nature to know because it is my nature to know" does not pass muster as a logical proof. Nevertheless, this is the view which Newman adopted and advocated as a first principle of reason:

I am what I am, or I am nothing. I cannot think, reflect, or judge about my being, without starting from the very point which I aim at concluding. My ideas are all assumptions, and I am ever moving in a circle. I cannot avoid being sufficient for myself, for I cannot make myself anything else, and to change me is to destroy me. If I do not use myself, I have no other self to use. My only business is to ascertain what I am, in order to put it to use. (272–73)

Those who refuse to respect this circular position are cut off from dialogue with Newman: "I cannot convert men, when I ask for assumptions which they refuse to grant to me; and without assumptions no one can prove anything about anything" (319). Three of Newman's fundamental presumptions concerned his own existence as a rational being (323), the presence of God in conscience (97, 324), and an awareness of guilt as an indicator of a need for salvation (325); he also assumed that God's providence would make up for the weakness of human reason (275, 321).

Newman sharply criticized the fundamental assumption of both the empiricists and the evidentialists that one must "doubt everything" as the method of determining the legitimacy of an assent: "to forbid assumptions universally is to forbid this one in particular" (294). Newman took a stance diametrically opposed to the empiricists' view of how one should approach the crucial issues in life: "Of the two, I would rather have to maintain that we ought to begin with believing everything that is offered to our acceptance, than that it is our duty to doubt everything" (294; cf. 90–91, 272).

Aligning himself with Froude, Harper characterized Newman's view as a "repulsive" attitude, since it seems to abandon the "scientific" method of proof[66] and the "fundamental principle of universal doubt."[67] Harper's criticism that Newman blinded himself by operating on the basis of his presumptions reflects Harper's implicit belief that scientists operate from a presuppositionless standpoint:

Froude's mind reacted to evidence with a precision from which every trace of emotion, prejudice, or preconception had been rigidly excluded. Newman on the contrary deviated from this clear line and brought from his own mind certain additional elements, and those quite imponderable, which frequently became the ruling factors in his decisions. Thus, though relying upon probabilities, he used them to support what his prejudice (he would have said his insight or cast of mind) secretly favored. He started with definite assumptions and his selection of probabilities was made on the basis of whether or not they tended to support his assumption.[68]

Harper honors the scientific method so much that he overlooks the fact that scientists also start with "definite assumptions" and select probabilities on the degree to which they support those first principles. As we shall see below (130–35), Polanyi's analysis of commitment supports Newman's assertion that all thought depends upon presumptions that are incapable of proof.

The fifth category of notional assent is "speculation," not in the common sense of idle daydreaming or tentative and half-hearted musings, but in the sense of "the firm, conscious acceptance of propositions as true. This kind of assent includes the assent to all reasoning and its conclusions, to all general propositions, to all rules of conduct, to all proverbs, aphorisms, sayings, and reflections on men and society" (75). In this category, Newman located the fields of mathematics, legal judgments, constitutional maxims, the general determinations of science, and "the principles, disputations, and doctrines of theology" (75).

The second part of Chapter Four is devoted to a consideration of "real assent." As indicated above in distinguishing real and notional apprehension, the distinction between notional and real assent is found not in the grammatical construction of the propositions express-

66. Harper, *Newman and Froude*, 78.
67. Letter from Froude, December 29, 1859, in Harper, *Newman and Froude*, 123.
68. Harper, *Newman and Froude*, 125.

ing the apprehension or the assent, but is, so to speak, in the eye of the beholder:[69]

[Some students who struggled with notions] are suddenly found to have what is called an eye for that work—an eye for trade matters, or for engineering, or a special taste for literature—which no one expected from them at school, while they were engaged on notions. Minds of this stamp not only know the received rules of their profession, but enter into them, and even anticipate them, or dispense with them, or substitute other rules instead. And when new questions are opened, and arguments are drawn up on one side and the other in long array, they with a natural ease and promptness form their views and give their decision as if they had no need to reason, from their clear apprehension of the lie and issue of the whole matter in dispute, as if it were drawn out in a map before them. These are the reformers, systematizers, inventors, in various departments of thought, speculative and practical; in education, in administration, in social and political matters, in science. (77)

Assents founded on such a grasp of concrete realities—founded on real apprehension—have a much stronger hold on the life of the person than those founded on a series of ideas and inferences. The one who contemplates the realities to which language refers is able to use language with a freedom, directness, and individuality that those who deal only in notions cannot follow. Because the power of apprehension is in the person and not in the propositions used to express the apprehension, judgments based on the person's vision of reality are not directly transferable from one person to another:

[Real assents] are of a personal character, each individual having his own, and being known by them. It is otherwise with notions; notional apprehension is in itself an ordinary act of our common nature. . . . But we cannot make sure, for ourselves or others, of real apprehension and assent, because we have to secure first the images which are their objects, and these are often peculiar and special. They depend on personal experience; and the experience of one man is not the experience of another. Real assent, then, as the experience which it presupposes, is proper to the individual, and, as such, thwarts rather than promotes the intercourse of man with man. It shuts itself up, as it were, in its own home, or at least it is its own witness and its own standard; and, as in the instances above given, it cannot be reckoned on, anticipated, accounted for, inasmuch as it is the accident of this man or that. (82)

69. As real apprehension is in the one who apprehends, so the certitude based on it is in the mind of the knower and not in the proposition itself: "It follows that what to one intellect is a proof is not so to another, and that the certainty of a proposition does properly consist in the certitude of the mind which contemplates it" (GA 233).

The capacity to *see* into the heart of the matter is a gift or accomplishment of a person, an intensely private property that never passes into the public domain. Certitude is therefore always "personal certitude" (259): "Every one who reasons, is his own center; and no expedient for attaining a common measure of minds can reverse this truth" (271). Others may follow the lead of the one who first catches sight of a new aspect of reality and come to see for themselves what the pioneer had seen, but each one who does so undergoes a "personal formation" (85) in order to do so. In other words, the "personal character" of real apprehension and assent is not diminished by the number of people who acquire the same experience and who adopt the same standpoint toward it. No matter how many people experience the thrill of hang gliding or bungee jumping, and no matter how much they try to put the experience into words, in the end the rule for each newcomer is "See for yourself." After joining the circle of initiates by taking the first flight or the first jump, a newcomer will often say, "Now I see what you mean." Every field of knowledge of sufficient depth presents similar initiatory experiences to neophytes. Unless they come to see for themselves how the methods of the discipline work, they cannot make a worthwhile contribution to it; and unless they adopt (by acts of real assent) the same stance toward reality as that taken by the masters of the discipline, they cannot enter into the eye-opening experiences that make it possible for them to become masters themselves.

There are times in life when we must force ourselves to accept realities. Some events seem too good to be true; others, too horrible. In religion, realization implies a transition from discussion of theological notions to personal involvement in the underlying realities. "To the devout and spiritual, the Divine Word speaks of things, not merely of notions. . . . The purpose, then, of meditation is to realize them; to make the facts which they relate stand out before our mind as objects, such as may be appropriated by a faith as living as the imagination which apprehends them" (79). It is not just in religion that real apprehension and assent must be "sought after in order to be found, and encouraged and cultivated in order to be appropriated" (85). The ability to "take a view" of a field and to know for oneself what really matters is at the heart of all human accomplishments. Until we make "moral objects" real to ourselves by a constructive act of the imagination, "we have no intellectual moorings, and are at the mercy of impulses, fancies and wandering lights, whether as regards personal conduct, social and political action, or religion. [Real assents] create, as the case may be, heroes and saints, great leaders, statesmen, preachers and reformers, the pioneers of discovery in science, visionaries, fanatics, knight-errants, demagogues, and adventurers" (85–86). The wellsprings of action, both for good and for ill, lie in the personal view of reality: "The heart is commonly reached, not through the reason, but through the imagination, by means of direct impressions, by the testimony of facts and events, by history, by description" (89). In the final section of the fourth chapter, Newman showed that grammars of assent which focus solely on the public and notional dimensions of the mind overlook the importance of this individual contact with reality, and therefore undermine the foundation of religious belief.

Some have sought relief from the burden of personal responsibility for assent by turning to the beautiful impersonalities of logic, the science of inference (211–12). Newman accepted the fact that logic plays a major role in the development and preservation of certitude, but rejected the notion that in and of itself logic can strictly determine when assent is to be given or withheld. It is a *categorical* mistake to ask logic to settle matters of fact, and a correct grammar of assent would rule against such confusion of categories, because the power of apprehension on which such matters are settled is inadequately reflected in the narrow terms required for formal operations (87). No matter how hard one presses the science of inference to extend its services to the key questions of fact which one needs to decide, it cannot be other than what it is: an ordering of abstractions. The value of such logical ordering in the settlement of any particular question will be determined by the illative sense, not by logic itself. Logic does not apprehend realities; people do.

In the fifth chapter, "Apprehension and Assent in the Matter of Religion," Newman suspended the development of his epistemological observations in order to demonstrate their theological application:

We are now able to determine what a dogma of faith is, and what it is to believe it. A dogma is a proposition; it stands for a notion or a thing; and to believe it is to give the assent of the mind to it, as it stands for the one or the other. To give a real assent to it is an act of religion; to give a notional, is a theological act. It is discerned, rested in, and appropriated as a reality, by the religious imagination; it is held as a truth, by the theological intellect. (93)

Newman's objective in this chapter is not to show *why* one should believe in any dogmas concerning God, but "to investigate what it is to
believe in them, what the mind does, what it contemplates, when it
makes an act of faith" (93–94). In Chapter IV we will return to the particular questions Newman raises about belief in God and belief in the
Trinity.

The Line of Argument in Part Two:
The Informal Foundations of Certitude

The second part of the *Grammar* concerns itself with the difference
between assent ("adhesion without reserve or doubt to the proposition
to which it is given" [145]) and inference ("conditional acceptance of a
proposition" [209] based on the assumption of premises and the operations of formal logic [28, 64]). The central concern is how one comes
to unqualified adhesion when a proposition does not have a strict logical proof (135); Newman characterized this as "assent on reasonings
not demonstrative" (150). In Chapter Six, "Assent Considered as Unconditional," Newman took special pains to rule out Locke's rule that
assent should be strictly governed by inference (138). For Locke, "assent cannot rise higher than its source, inference in such matters is at
best conditional, therefore assent is conditional also" (136). The appeal of Locke's position is obvious: if our fundamental positions are not
governed by the most rigorous standards of thought, what is to protect
us from the unconditional adoption of absurdities that fly in the face of
reason? It may seem better to restrict the field of knowledge to the
bounds of strict proof rather than to open the gates of the mind to un-
reason.

Newman responded to the challenge by pointing out two kinds of
assent with which we are all familiar. In the first instance, there are
"simple assents" that all people live by without realizing that they are
attached to them unconditionally (157, 173). If these relatively unconscious convictions are challenged, it is possible that we may deliberately assent to our "previous assenting," which yields "reflex or complex
assent" (158). In either case, Newman held that our capacity to grasp
facts goes far beyond our ability to prove them. We must not cripple
ourselves with a specious humility and "a rule which will not work for

a day" (150). Locke's effort to restrict belief to that which is demonstrably true is a theory which "cannot be carried out in practice":

> It may be rightly said to prove too much; for it debars us from unconditional assent in cases in which the common voice of mankind, the advocates of this theory included, would protest against the prohibition. There are many truths in concrete matter, which no one can demonstrate, yet every one unconditionally accepts; and though of course there are innumerable propositions to which it would be absurd to give an absolute assent, still the absurdity lies in the circumstances of each particular case, as it is taken by itself, not in their common violation of the pretentious axiom that probable reasoning can never lead to certitude. (136)

In this last phrase we have the inversion of the theme of the second part of the *Grammar,* that probable reasoning (ultimately based on the illative sense) *can* lead to certitude both in secular and in religious matters. Newman's criticism of the empiricists uses an empirical standard of judgment: their theory of knowledge simply does not fit the facts which they themselves acknowledge. No matter how messy, incomplete, and uncontrollable the notion of the illative sense may prove to be when compared to the idealizations of the empiricists, it has the advantage of corresponding better to the way the mind really operates.

The seventh chapter is devoted to clarifying what is meant by "certitude." Newman spelled out the meaning of his terms in the preceding chapter while illustrating the difference between simple and complex assent:

> I have one step farther to make—let the proposition to which the assent is given be as absolutely true as the reflex act pronounces it to be, that is, objectively true as well as subjectively:—then the assent may be called a *perception,* the conviction a *certitude,* the proposition or truth a *certainty,* or thing known, or a matter of *knowledge,* and to assent to it is to *know.* . . .
> . . . Certitude, as I have said, is the perception of a truth with the perception that it is a truth, or the consciousness of knowing, as expressed in the phrase, "I know that I know," or "I know that I know that I know,"—or simply, "I know;" for one reflex assertion of the mind about self sums up the series of self-consciousness without the need of any actual evolution of them. (162, 163)

Notice that Newman was speaking hypothetically here. *If* the proposition is "as absolutely true as the reflex act pronounces it to be," then one may be said to be certain. He did not yet tackle the difficult question of *how* we know that we know the truth; his only purpose was to develop the vocabulary that would be needed to address that question in the eighth and ninth chapters of the book.

The purpose of the seventh chapter is to clear away a number of misconceptions about the nature of certitude. Newman first contrasted assent and certitude in order to show that while all certitudes are complex assents, not all assents are certitudes. "Assents may and do change; certitudes endure" (180). It is important to notice the difference so that we do not poison the notion of certitude with associations drawn from the changeable nature of other kinds of assent:

> The multitude of men confuse together the probable, the possible, and the certain, and apply these terms to doctrines and statements almost at random. They have no clear view what it is they know, what they presume, what they suppose, and what they only assert. They make little distinction between credence, opinion, and profession; at various times they give them all perhaps the name of certitude, and accordingly, when they change their minds, they fancy they have given up points of which they had a true conviction. Or at least bystanders thus speak of them, and the very idea of certitude falls into disrepute. (190–91)

In contrast to this muddled, popular view of certitude, Newman proposed that certitude is a reflex assent to a truth, "a deliberate assent given expressly after reasoning" (186–87), and therefore is "indefectible":

> It is the characteristic of certitude that its object is a truth, a truth as such, a proposition as true. There are right and wrong convictions, and certitude is a right conviction; if it is not right with a consciousness of being right, it is not certitude. Now truth cannot change; what is once truth is always truth; and the human mind is made for truth, and so rests in truth, as it cannot rest in falsehood. When then it once becomes possessed of a truth, what is to dispossess it? but this is to be certain; therefore, once certitude, always certitude. (181)

The great crisis of our age, caused in large measure by the restless overthrow of one scientific conviction after another, is to decide whether there are any unchanging truths by which life may be illuminated and directed. Many might agree that Newman has correctly defined the notion of certitude—being right with a consciousness of being right—but deny that we shall ever possess that kind of knowledge.

As Newman explored the notion of certitude, attempting to disengage its true nature from the host of misconceptions that are attached to it in the popular mind, he argued that no recitation of errors of judgment could ever lead properly to the conclusion that we should abstain from all acts of assent:

An act, viewed in itself, is not wrong because it is done wrongly. False certitudes are faulty because they are false, not because they are (supposed) certitudes. They are, or may be, the attempts and the failures of an intellect insufficiently trained, or off its guard. Assent is an act of the mind, congenial to its nature; and it, as other acts, may be made both when it ought to be made, and when it ought not. It is a free act, a personal act for which the doer is responsible, and the actual mistakes in making it, be they ever so numerous or serious, have no force whatever to prohibit the act itself. (189)

If an opponent presented an example of a false claim to certitude, Newman was prepared to lay the blame for the error on the shoulders of the one who made the claim rather than on the notion of certitude itself: "No instances then whatever of mistaken certitude are sufficient to constitute a proof, that certitude itself is a perversion or an extravagance of his nature" (189). In Newman's view, knowing is a kind of doing, and knowers may therefore be held responsible for the quality of their cognitive actions. The failure of others to act well intellectually does not absolve us from our obligation to act conscientiously in our intellectual lives.

Newman did not think that there was any simple method of telling truth from falsehood:

Certitude does not admit of an interior, immediate test, sufficient to discriminate it from false certitude. Such a test is rendered impossible from the circumstance that, when we make the mental act expressed by 'I know,' we sum up the whole series of reflex judgments which might, each in turn, successively exercise a critical function towards those of the series which precede it. (205–6)

This passage clearly reveals the limits of a grammar of assent. In the last analysis, rules that describe correct conditions of assent do not determine what is to be believed. No grammar determines what is to be said in a given situation; no poem, song, drama, or novel can be deduced from the grammar of the English language; treatises, essays, monographs, and scientific papers may be bound by manuals of style, but their content is radically unaffected by adherence to such standards. The rules of speech, such as they are, create an open field for discourse. For example, the norm for a complete sentence is that there be a subject and a predicate. "God exists" is a complete sentence; but so, of course, is the proposition "God does not exist." The series of judgments needed to uphold one view or the other goes far beyond the bounds of grammar. In Newman's view, no grammar of assent can diminish personal responsibility for the "reflex judgments" that lead to the adoption of a particular position.

Even though there may be no direct interior test to establish truths, as we exercise our illative sense upon the question of whether or not we should grant full assent to a proposition, Newman proposes "three conditions of certitude": "that it follows on an investigation and proof"; "that it is accompanied by a specific sense of intellectual satisfaction and repose"; and "that it is irreversible" (207–8). To those disposed to disagree with Newman, these three conditions of certitude may raise more questions than they answer. What are the limits of investigation and proof necessary to provide grounds for a decision? How long does one wait to obtain the requisite "intellectual satisfaction"? Does it not fly in the face of the history of progress in the nineteenth and twentieth century to hold that assent ought to be "irreversible"? Newman's ultimate answer is that we each decide for ourselves—and if this answer seems to be no answer to the opponent, then perhaps it means that there is no further point in dialogue with each other. It would be completely contrary to the purpose of the *Grammar of Assent* if Newman were to present a purely logical proof that purely logical proofs are inadequate for the conduct of human life; one either catches on to what Newman is pointing at, and learns to view human reality as he views it, or else one finds him more and more exasperating and incomprehensible. The three conditions he suggested are not formulae for the mechanical determination of certitude, but are questions for an intellectual examination of conscience.

In Chapter Eight, "Inference," Newman attempted to show both the power and the weakness of formal logic, and began to sketch an alternative model of rationality based on informal reasoning. The excellence of formal operations is found in "substituting scientific methods, such as all may use, for the action of the individual genius" (210). The explicit structures provided by formalization "may act as a common measure between mind and mind, as a means of joint investigation, and as a recognized intellectual standard,—a standard such as to secure us against hopeless mistakes, and to emancipate us from the capricious *ipse dixit* of authority" (210–11).

Formalization is desirable, though not always possible. In the following passage, Newman imagines what straightjackets have to be fastened on the mind for the sake of logic and inference:

A more ambitious, because a more comprehensive contrivance still, for interpreting the concrete world is the method of logical inference. What we desiderate is something which may supersede the need of personal gifts by a far-reaching and infallible rule. Now, without external symbols to mark out and steady its course, the intellect runs wild; but with the aid of symbols, as in algebra, it advances with precision and effect. Let then our symbols be words; let all thought be arrested and embodied in words. Let language have a monopoly of thought; and thought go for only so much as it can show itself to be worth in language. Let every prompting of the intellect be ignored, every *momentum* of argument be disowned, which is unprovided with an equivalent wording, as its ticket for sharing in the common search after truth. Let the authority of nature, of commonsense, experience, genius, go for nothing. Ratiocination, thus restricted and put into grooves, is what I have called Inference, and the science, which is its regulating principle, is Logic.[70]

Having made a series of suppositions for the sake of showing the meaning of his terms, Newman immediately indicated that the project of objectifying all knowledge can be only a partial success, "succeeding so far as words can in fact be found for representing the countless varieties and subtleties of human thought, failing on account of the fallacy of the original assumption, that whatever can be thought can be adequately expressed in words" (212). Words also fail to do justice to "things"—"matters which do not depend on us for being what they are" (222)—because formal operations demand that the meaning of terms be reduced to "just one unreal aspect of the concrete thing to which it properly belongs," becoming "a common aspect, meager but precise" (214–15).

Even if both thought and things were perfectly reflected in a formal system, there remains the much larger difficulty of deciding the fundamental assumptions or "first principles" of the system. As was noted in the discussion of Chapter Four above, one must presume in order to reason, and the kind of reason based on such acts of presumption cannot fully articulate its own foundation:

70. *GA* 211–12. Newman goes on in the next paragraph to note that he uses "inference" and "logic" as synonyms, "for I shall say nothing about logic which does not in its substance also apply to inference."

We are not able to prove by syllogism that there are any self-evident proposi-tions at all; but supposing there are (as of course I hold there are), still who can determine these by logic? Syllogism, then, though of course it has its use, still does only the minutest and easiest part of the work, in the investigation of truth, for when there is any difficulty, that difficulty commonly lies in determining first principles, not in the arrangement of proofs. (216–17)

Rationality is something greater than logic. By understanding what log-ic can and cannot do, one recognizes that there is something else—explicitly identified as the illative sense in Chapter Nine—at work in the operations of the mind:

Logic then does not really prove; it enables us to join issue with others; it sug-gests ideas; it opens views; it maps out for us the lines of thought; it verifies neg-atively; it determines when differences of opinion are hopeless; and when and how far conclusions are probable; but for genuine proof in concrete matter we require an *organon* more delicate, versatile, and elastic than verbal argumenta-tion. (217)

As excellent as it may be within limits, logic "determines neither our principles, nor our ultimate judgments . . . it is neither the test of truth, nor the adequate basis of assent" (229). Because it cannot govern ei-ther its starting-points or determine the application of its conclusions, logic "hangs loose at both ends" (227).

Newman began his exploration of an alternative model of rationali-ty under the heading "Informal Inference," which is subsequently iden-tified as an operation of the illative sense (283):

It is plain that formal logical sequence is not in fact the method by which we are enabled to become certain of what is concrete; and it is equally plain, from what has been already suggested, what the real and necessary method is. It is the cu-mulation of probabilities, independent of each other, arising out of the nature and circumstances of the particular case which is under review; probabilities too fine to avail separately, too subtle and circuitous to be convertible into syllo-gisms, too numerous and various for such conversion, even were they convert-ible. (230)

That which does this "unwritten summing-up" (232) is "the living mind" (222–23) or "the living intelligence" which uses inferences in a supra-logical fashion (223), or, in other words, the illative sense. It is the illative sense which decides whether the application of logic is worthwhile in a particular case, and if so, which gives logic its starting-points and ultimately determines the bearing of the logical operations on the concrete issues at hand. It is this comprehensive, informal, personal sense of what really matters that is able to follow the paths of thought wherever they may lead. This is the "*organon* more delicate, versatile, and elastic than verbal argumentation" that stands above and below the formal operations of logic and yields "genuine proof" (217).

In the eyes of Newman's adversaries, adopting this standpoint on what knowledge is may look like a relaxation of standards, but in Newman's view it shifts the burden from a logical structure outside the individual to an interior awareness of the obligation to judge for ourselves as best we can—it is a *relocation* of responsibility, not a lowering of standards. Restricting the field of belief to the narrow, artificial, abstract, and rigid field of logical proofs would be a deadly error:

Life is not long enough for a religion of inferences; we shall never have done beginning, if we determine to begin with proof. We shall ever be laying our foundations; we shall turn theology into evidences, and divines into textuaries. We shall never get at our first principles. Resolve to believe nothing, and you must prove your proofs and analyze your elements, sinking farther and farther, and finding "in the lowest depth a lower deep," till you come to the broad bosom of skepticism. I would rather be bound to defend the reasonableness of assuming that Christianity is true, than to demonstrate a moral governance from the physical world. Life is for action. If we insist on proofs for every thing, we shall never come to action: to act you must assume, and that assumption is faith.[71]

"Faith" in this context is not religious faith, but the common human act of assenting to what is not capable of complete proof.

In the conclusion of the section on informal inference in Chapter Eight, Newman summarized his criticism of formal logic—the grammar of inference—and suggested an alternative view of human understanding that depends on the "cumulation of probabilities" (230) rather than strict proof. He took a dispute about authorship of a classical text as an example of the need for the integration of formally incomplete arguments. In making arguments about the identity of the author, one em-

71. GA 90–91. In this passage, Newman is quoting from material first published by him in 1841. This long quotation (pages 88–91) concludes Chapter 4 and provides evidence of the continuity of Newman's thought from 1841 to 1870. He notes that there are "differences in terminology" but judges that the material "suitably illustrates the subject here under discussion" (GA 88).

ploys an "instinctive sense" of what is and is not probable, along with acceptance of others' testimony, in order to come to a decision in the matter (237). This "sense" cannot be replaced by any set of formal operations because so it is rooted in the concrete, the personal, and the nonverbal. Through this sense, "We judge for ourselves, by our own lights, and on our own principles; and our criterion of truth is not so much the manipulation of propositions, as the intellectual and moral character of the person maintaining them, and the ultimate silent effect of his argument or conclusions upon our minds" (240). It is the illative sense which registers such impressions, weighs the worth of the personal dimension in argument, and silently determines the impact that these impressions will have upon our frame of mind.

At the end of Chapter Eight, Newman explicitly defined illative sense as "right judgment in ratiocination" (269) and then devoted the whole of Chapter Nine to examining its nature. The keynote of the illative sense is that it is a reflexive consciousness, a special form of judgment in which the mind evaluates its own operations, and comes to a decision about whether and how to form a judgment on a particular question—it is the power to judge the reliability of our judgments. In his last letter to William Froude, Newman described this faculty as "inductive" (rather than "illative"):

There is a faculty in the mind which I think I have called the inductive sense, which, when properly cultivated and used, answers to Aristotle's *phronesis*, its province being, not virtue, but the "inquisitio veri," which decides for us, beyond any technical rules, when, how, etc. to pass from inference to assent, and when and under what circumstances, etc. etc. not. You seem yourself to admit this faculty, when you speak of the intellect not only as adjusting, but as selecting the results of experience.[72]

The rough draft is dated April 29, 1879; it was never sent because Newman heard of Froude's death before finishing the letter to his satisfaction. In this same draft, Newman granted that this sense may be "rightly or wrongly used." Although the "sole and final judgment on the validity of an inference in concrete matter" comes from the illative sense (271), it is not infallible.

Newman linked his understanding of "illative sense" to his previous

72. Harper, *Newman and Froude*, 203; *LD* XXIX, 115.

discussion of the need for nonformal methods of determining our fundamental view of reality. When discussing how the illative sense operates in every phase of an investigation—setting up the first principles, governing the conduct of the argument, determining when a conclusion may be reached, and assessing the significance of the conclusion—Newman associated his observations on the illative sense with his reflections on informal inference in the preceding chapter (283). Near the end of Chapter Nine, Newman went back to the *Prophetical Office of the Church*, first published in 1837, to retrieve some of his first observations on this aspect of the mind's nature. Seeing reality (real apprehension) takes precedence over speaking of what one sees (notional assent):

Common sense, chance, moral perception, genius, the great discoverers of principles do not reason. They have no arguments, no grounds, they see the truth, but they do not know how they see it; and if at any time they attempt to prove it, it is as much a matter of experiment with them, as if they had to find a road to a distant mountain, which they see with the eye; and they get entangled, embarrassed, and perchance overthrown in the superfluous endeavor. (296–97)

In commenting on this passage, Newman showed that he wished to preserve the epistemology employed in 1837 while discarding the theological conclusions about the use of Scripture: "That is, I considered the assumption *an act of the Illative Sense;*—I should now add, the Illative Sense, acting on mistaken elements of thought" (297; italics mine). This text clearly shows the continuity of Newman's thought about the informal source of certitude while revealing the change in terminology used to express his insight. Further evidence of the close correlation of the notions of the illative sense and informal inference is presented in the final chapter of the *Grammar*, where Newman succinctly describes his apologetic aim in unfolding these observations on how the mind operates; the goal is "to attempt to prove Christianity in the same informal way in which I can prove for certain that I have been born into this world, and that I shall die out of it" (319). Newman had analyzed this particular example of certitude in Chapter Eight and concluded:

If it is difficult to explain how a man knows that he shall die, is it not more difficult for him to satisfy himself how he knows that he was born. . . .

Answers doubtless may be given to some of these questions; but, on the whole, I think it is the fact that many of our most obstinate and most reasonable certitudes depend on proofs which are informal and personal, which baffle our powers of analysis, and cannot be brought under logical rule, because they cannot be submitted to logical statistics. If we must speak of Law, this recognition of a correlation between certitude and implicit proof seems to me a law of our minds. (239)

Whereas formal proof depends on the standards set by the science of logic, informal proof depends on a personal talent for passing judgment by seeing the coalescence of many different strands of thought—that is to say, informal proof depends on the illative sense.

After showing in Chapter Eight the radical incapacity of formal operations to supply what is necessary for the life of the mind, Newman's strategy for demonstrating the reality and the nature of the illative sense as the ground of rationality is to accumulate a number of examples in which there is clearly no substitute for a personal gift of sound judgment. In the first section of Chapter Nine, "The Sanction of the Illative Sense," he suggested that the reader who agrees with his analysis of the examples will accept the illative sense as a "law of our minds . . . whether à priori it ought to be a law or no. Our hoping is a proof that hope, as such, is not an extravagance; and our possession of certitude is a proof that it is not a weakness or an absurdity to be certain" (270–71). Immediately after this, Newman described himself as treating the subject "in facto esse" rather than "in fieri." He was less interested in presenting a complete theory of the illative sense than in securing the agreement of his readers that it is really a matter of fact, an aspect of our nature, always operative whenever we are engaged in thought, and worthy of respect as the supreme standard of judgment in concrete matters. If we are, in fact, so constructed that we can have no higher certitude than that given by the illative sense, then we must submit to that fact as a law of nature: "My first elementary lesson of duty is that of resignation to the laws of my nature, whatever they are; my first disobedience is to be impatient at what I am, and to indulge an ambitious aspiration after what I cannot be, to cherish a distrust of my powers, and to desire to change laws which are identical with myself" (272–73).

If we honestly observe the way in which our minds act, we may recognize that "there is no ultimate test of truth besides the testimony born to truth by the mind itself."[73] Newman hopes that his readers will recognize the "matter of fact . . . that faith, not knowledge or argument, is our principle of action" and resign themselves to this fact despite the unanswered questions that remain about why this should be so.[74] This resignation to a matter of fact about the constitution of the mind is not an act of despair or of intellectual sloth, as if Newman were retreating from a line of inquiry that might yield good results in the hands of a more courageous or vigorous thinker; it is based on the insight that we are what we are and that no amount of investigation will alter our fundamental nature as limited, human knowers.

Action comes from belief, and belief is governed by the illative sense, which decides when assent is appropriate. When confronted with theoretical objections based on a priori models of the mind, Newman responded with a *solvitur ambulando:* despite the paradoxes raised by epistemic analysis, which suggest that we can never come to certitude, we are in fact certain of many things. Newman proposes three examples of such certitudes: that Britain is an island, that the monks of the early middle ages did not compose the classics, and that we shall die (234–39). Instead of abandoning the natural capacity of the mind to assent, one should give up the models that would prohibit this action: "I am not at all insinuating that we are not rational in our certitude; I only mean that we cannot analyze a proof satisfactorily, the result of which good sense actually guarantees to us" (235).

In the second section of Chapter Nine, Newman focuses on "The Nature of the Illative Sense," substantially repeating the definition given at the end of Chapter Eight: "It is the mind that reasons, and that controls its own reasonings, not any technical apparatus of words and propositions. This power of judging and concluding, when in its perfection, I call the Illative Sense . . ." (276–77). The illustrations which fol-

---

73. GA 275. Then again, other honest observers, like Froude, may *not* come to see the structure of the mind as Newman did. There is no way to guarantee that others will come to view reality as he did: "The aspect under which we view things is often intensely personal; nay, even awfully so, considering that, from the nature of the case, it does not bring home its idiosyncrasy either to ourselves or to others. Each of us looks at the world in his own way, and does not know that perhaps it is characteristically his own" (GA 291).

74. GA 91. Newman was quoting his own work from 1841; in the original context of the remark, "all this" refers to Newman's observations on the impossibility of adopting "a religion of inferences" (GA 90–91).

low are inspired by Aristotle's reflections on *"phronesis,* or judgment" and deal with "matters of duty, social intercourse, and taste" (277). After showing a wide range of situations in which the individual must absorb, apply, and/or transcend normal rules of conduct, thereby revealing one's own worth as a person and the quality of one's character, Newman advanced his conclusion in a rhetorical question. Three propositions may be extracted from his question (280):

1. Reason is not "an exception to the general law which attaches to the intellectual exercises of the mind."
2. Reason is not "commensurate with logical science."
3. Logic is not "an instrumental art sufficient for determining every sort of truth."

Later in the chapter, Newman actually gave a very good reason for turning to logic: it provides a method of detaching knowledge from the idiosyncracies of the illative sense and rendering public as far as is possible what is originally a personal possession (283). The central point of Chapters Eight and Nine, however, is that this magnificent instrument of reason is not the same as reason itself and is not, in fact, the fundamental ground of certitude. For logic to make its appropriate contributions to the life of the mind, its "loose ends" (227) must be firmly grasped by the illative sense.

After showing how the illative sense operates in the formation of judgments, Newman made four concluding observations about its nature (281):

1. "it is one and the same in all concrete matters";
2. "it is in fact attached to definite subject-matters";
3. it anticipates its conclusions before obtaining proof;
4. there is no higher criterion to which we can appeal.

A great general and a master painter both rely on the illative sense in making decisions, but their special skills are not interchangeable. The cultural stereotype of the absent-minded professor makes the same point about our inability to apply special gifts to ordinary situations (267). Generals reason like generals, and artists reason like artists. In either case, it is the illative sense that provides a guiding vision for the warrior or the artist. The intuition of what is to be done comes first, then the details fall into place.

In the final section of the chapter, Newman explored "The Range of the Illative Sense." For all practical purposes, the range is coextensive with all the operations of thought, since Newman found a role for the illative sense throughout the process of reasoning:

Thus the Illative Sense, that is, the reasoning faculty, as exercised by gifted, or by educated or otherwise well-prepared minds, has its function in the beginning, middle, and end of all verbal discussion and inquiry, and in every step of the process. It is a rule to itself, and appeals to no judgment beyond its own; and attends upon the whole course of thought from antecedents to consequents, with a minute diligence and unwearied presence, which is impossible to a cumbrous apparatus of verbal reasoning, though, in communicating with others, words are the only instrument we possess, and a serviceable, though imperfect instrument. (283)

It is in this section that Newman praised logic as that which allows some "common measure between mind and mind" in contrast to the illative sense, which ever remains a "personal gift or acquisition" (283). This is an important reminder that the illative sense is not in competition with logic, nor a replacement for it, but provides the personal context—the real apprehension—within which formal operations take on their full meaning and value.

Newman laid great stress on the fact that it is through the illative sense that we adopt the "first principles" of our own thought. The mind is *active* in adapting itself to the standards that guide its own operations:

Nor, lastly, is an action of the mind itself less necessary in relation to those first elements of thought which in all reasoning are assumptions, the principles, tastes, and opinions, very often of a personal character, which are half the battle in the inference with which the reasoning is to terminate. It is the mind itself that detects them in the obscure recesses, illustrates them, establishes them, eliminates them, resolves them into simpler ideas, as the case may be. The mind contemplates them without the use of words, by a process which cannot be analyzed. Thus it was that Bacon separated the physical system of the world from the theological; thus that Butler connected together the moral system with the religious. Logical formulas could never have sustained the reasonings involved in such investigations. (282–83)

The mind determines for itself what will subsequently determine its manner of proceeding. Because presumption is a personal act, adversaries may find themselves isolated by the selection of different first principles, with "no common measure between mind and mind" (283).

Newman did not suppose that there is any possible way to remedy this difficulty by going beyond the framework of personally chosen principles; the law of our being is that we must choose such standards, and nothing can rescue us from the obligation to live by that choice: "All reasoning being from premises, and those premises arising (if it so happen) in their first elements from personal characteristics, in which men are in fact in essential and irremediable variance one with another, the ratiocinative talent can do no more than point out where the difference between them lies, how far it is immaterial, when it is worth while continuing an argument between them, and when not" (283). Later in this section, when comparing the differing approaches of historians to their material, Newman traced "the vague and impalpable notions of 'reasonableness' on his own side as well as on that of others, which both make conclusions possible, and are the pledge of their being contradictory" (287). Here again, one might wish for a less subtle, more definitive, and impersonal *organon*—a philosopher's stone to compel disputants to resolve their differences! It is extremely frustrating to accept the fact that two authors can both be logical, yet contradict each another, and still "not [be] antagonistic because they have no common ground on which they can conflict" (247).

In the absence of a formal method of settling conflicts over fundamental principles, Newman sought "to prove by persuasion rather than persuade by proof."[75] Again quoting from his own earlier work (1841), he spoke of his determination to get at the reasons beyond the reach of reason which alone have the power to change minds: "deductions have no power of persuasion. The heart is commonly reached, not through the reason, but through the imagination, by means of direct impressions, by the testimony of facts and events, by history, by description" (89). It is the illative sense which provides the "personal first principles and judgments" (313) upon which the movement toward certitude takes place.

In illustration of this fact of our nature, Newman followed the

---

75. Lash, introduction to *GA*, 12.

thread of an argument between two historians in order to show how their view of the facts is determined by their personal standpoints, and he noticed how they are forced to make *ad hominem* remarks in the absence of any common standards of judgment: "Men become personal when logic fails; it is their mode of appealing to their own primary elements of thought, and their own illative sense, against the principles and the judgment of another" (288). There is no alternative to this situation; if certitude is always personal certitude, the defense of certainties will always entail vulnerability to personal criticism.

In the tenth and final chapter of the book, Newman described the kind of dialogue partners whom he respected and to whom his exposition of the credentials of Christianity was addressed (323, 329–30). In keeping with his own reflections on the personal foundation of certitude, he did not imagine that he could prove the position to just any sort of person, but only to those who are well-disposed to natural theology, who are active and alert listeners, and who are open to being persuaded by the convergence of many different lines of thought rather than insistent upon "strict proof": "If I am asked to use Paley's argument for my own conversion, I say plainly I do not want to be converted by a smart syllogism; if I am asked to convert others by it, I say plainly I do not care to overcome their reason without touching their hearts. I wish to deal, not with controversialists, but with inquirers" (329–30). The issue is not that the evidence is hidden from some and revealed to others, but rather that some are more willing than others to place the necessary interpretation upon the available evidence that leads them to read it as the vehicle of revelation.

I will postpone discussion of Newman's reading of the evidence for Christianity until the fourth chapter of this essay, when I will criticize and expand his argument by drawing on Polanyi's epistemology.

II. Polanyi's Notion of Tacit Knowledge

The goal of this chapter is to explore how "tacit knowledge" functions as a fundamental notion in Polanyi's epistemology. The phrase is used only rarely in *Personal Knowledge*,[1] but it becomes more prominent in Polanyi's later writings as he developed his view that *"all knowledge is . . . either tacit or rooted in tacit knowing."*[2] This explains why he held that knowledge is always *personal* knowledge; were it not for the tacit dimension of knowing, there would be no bar to the systematic depersonalization of knowledge. Let us first consider how this notion emerged and developed in Polanyi's life and works.

Biographical Context of *Personal Knowledge*

Michael Polanyi was born on March 11, 1891, in Budapest, Hungary.[3] His family was "talented and intellectual:"[4]

1. The phrase Polanyi used most often in *Personal Knowledge* is the "tacit coefficient" of knowing and speaking (86, 169, 250, 257, 259, 336). He also spoke of "tacit assent" (95, 260, 266, 312), "tacit affirmations" (131), "tacit judgments" (205, 206), "tacit endorsements" (207, 268) and "tacit commitments" (251). "Tacit knowledge" (169) or "tacit knowing" (264) serve in Polanyi's later writings and in this study as a useful reminder of all that Polanyi had to say about the "ineffable domain" of knowledge (87). Marjorie Grene noted that tacit knowing is subsidiary to the notion of commitment in *Personal Knowledge* (introduction to Michael Polanyi, *Knowing and Being*, edited by Marjorie Grene [Chicago: University of Chicago Press, 1969; hereafter cited in notes and text as *KB*], xiv).

2. Michael Polanyi, *Meaning*, with Harry Prosch (Chicago: University of Chicago Press, 1975) 61; emphasis added. The same claim appears in nearly identical form in *KB*, 195. In 1964, Polanyi wrote a new introduction to his *Science, Faith and Society* (Chicago: University of Chicago Press, 1946; hereafter cited in notes and text as *SFS*), which had originally been published in 1946 and which has no reference to "tacit knowledge" or the "tacit coefficient" or to any of the parallel expressions that appear in the 1958 *Personal Knowledge*. Polanyi observed that the word "intuition" plays the same role in the earlier work that "tacit coefficient" does in the later, and maintained that "this conception of reality and of the tacit knowing of reality underlies all my writings" (*SFS* 10). If so, the insight remains fundamentally the same, although the language used to express it varies somewhat through Polanyi's philosophical career.

3. Richard Gelwick, *The Way of Discovery: An Introduction to the Thought of Michael Polanyi* (New York: Oxford University Press, 1977), 4.

4. Gelwick, *Discovery*, 31–32.

Polanyi's parents were both of Jewish descent, but by his own account Jewish religion and Jewish nationalism never appealed to him. They evidently played almost no role in the liberal, humanist culture of prewar Budapest in which he grew up.[5]

In 1908, Polanyi entered the university in Budapest to study medicine. While there, he displayed an interest in philosophical questions that foreshadowed his later career:

As a university student in Budapest, Polanyi was a founder and member of a student society known as the Galileo Circle. The group pursued the theme of science above all in its daily discussions of politics and of the existence of God. A progressive-minded student society, the Galileo Circle was imbued with the radical rationalism of revolutionaries. In this setting, Michael Polanyi was a wise and balanced member, anticipating his later concern for traditional rather than radical reforms.[6]

Polanyi graduated with a degree in medicine in 1913.[7] In that same year, he found himself attracted to Christianity:

He declared that it was through reading the *Brothers Karamazov* in 1913 that his religious interests were awakened. He wrote to Karl Mannheim in 1944 "For a time particularly from 1915 to 1920 I was a completely converted Christian on the lines of Tolstoy's confession of faith." In June 1916, when he was searching for a way to do research in chemistry in Karlsruhe, he wrote Kasimir Fajans concerning possible employment as a research assistant that he would gladly join any suggested Christian religion.[8]

As shall be seen below, the question of Polanyi's own religious stance is a matter of some debate (58–60).

In 1914, Polanyi published his first paper on adsorption (how gas molecules adhere to the surface of solids and liquids) and joined the Austro-Hungarian army as a medical officer (*KB* 87–89). He continued to work on this topic while recovering from diphtheria.[9] In 1917 his theory of adsorption was accepted as a Ph.D. thesis at the University of Budapest, thanks to the "complete ignorance of the professor of theoretical physics" (*KB* 93):

The turmoil of war had protected his theory from the knowledge of experiments that would have made it untenable. . . . Both Haber and Einstein opposed

5. William T. Scott, "The Question of Religious Reality: Commentary on the Polanyi Papers," *Zygon* 17 (1982): 85.

6. Gelwick, *Discovery*, 30.   7. Gelwick, *Discovery*, 32.

8. Scott, "Religious Reality," 85–86.   9. Gelwick, *Discovery*, 32.

Polanyi's theory on the grounds that he had displayed a total disregard for the new knowledge of the electrical concept of interatomic forces. Polanyi persisted with further evidence at a later meeting, but his theory was rejected again as a failure. If Polanyi had not gone on immediately to prove himself in other work in physical chemistry, the opposition to his theory would have ended his scientific career. Still, the most striking point to the story is the fact that Polanyi's theory was right and is in use today. The evidence to confirm the theory began to appear in 1930, and others went on to establish what Polanyi had begun. Far from teaching that science is practiced by a strict code of impartiality and openness, the episode discloses the role of authority in the work of science.[10]

Although it must have been a painful experience to be publicly criticized by Einstein, Polanyi displayed no rancor in his reflections on this event.

According to his wife, who produced a baptismal certificate to authenticate the story, Polanyi converted to Catholicism in 1919:

On October 18, 1919, he was baptized a Catholic, several weeks before he met his bride-to-be, the Catholic Magda Kemeny. She later reported that she did not know how long he remained a Catholic, for his later involvement in Christianity was clearly on the Protestant side. His fondness for the British conception of liberty with its tacit grounding in a Protestant religious outlook led him to considerable appreciation of that outlook. However, as he wrote to an inquirer in 1969, he had never been a communicant of a church.[11]

Polanyi and Kemeny were married in 1921.[12]

After the war, Polanyi abandoned medicine in favor of physical chemistry. In 1920, he joined the Institute of Fibre Chemistry in Berlin-Dahlem, working on X-ray diffraction and crystals (*KB* 97). Success in this area led to promotion to the Institute of Physical Chemistry, where his main interest was reaction kinetics (*KB* 104). In 1929, he was made a Life Member of the Institute.[13] However, only four years later he resigned "in protest against Hitler's policies," and accepted a chair in physical chemistry at the University of Manchester in England.[14]

10. Gelwick, *Discovery*, 32–33.

11. Scott, "Religious Reality," 86. Scott makes two interesting remarks in footnotes attached to this passage: (1) "From Hugh O'Neill I learned that Polanyi's connection with Protestantism must have begun after the summer of 1934." (2) "Whether this [declaration that he had never been a communicant] referred only to the Protestant church he had been attending or also to his Catholic status is not clear."

12. Richard Lee Gelwick, "Science and Reality, Religion and God: A Reply to Harry Prosch," *Zygon* 17 (1982): 26.

13. Michael Polanyi, *The Tacit Dimension* (New York: Doubleday and Company, 1966; hereafter cited in notes and text as *TD*), ii.

14. Gelwick, *Discovery*, 35.

As in his student days, Polanyi continued to reflect on the cultural context of science: "Always aware of the interactions of science and society, he formed in 1928 with Leo Szilard, Eugene Wigner, and John von Neumann a discussion group on Soviet affairs."[15] This interest led him to visit Moscow at Easter time in 1935, where he "came up against the Soviet ideology under Stalin which denied justification to the pursuit of science" (*TD* 3; *SFS* 8–9).

The political turmoil of Europe continued to press upon Polanyi in his new position. The conflicts between rival systems began to alert him to the deeper philosophical problems that were involved. The conflicts were about ideas and values, not power only. In 1935 a conversation with Bukharin, a leading Communist theoretician, in Russia gave him a decisive clue to the problem. . . . Polanyi was struck by the fact that independent scientific thought was being denied by a socialist theory that based itself upon its scientific appeal. To Polanyi it seemed that paradoxically the scientific outlook had produced a mechanical conception of human nature and history in which there were no grounds for science itself.[16]

Polanyi found himself forced to delve more deeply into the philosophy of science in order to articulate the case for the free pursuit of science. In the process, he (reluctantly at first?) came to recognize the role of authority in science:

My writings and those of J. R. Baker which, from 1943 on, exposed this persecution [of biologists in Soviet Russia] were brushed aside as anti-Communist propaganda. The way in which scientific research was organized in Soviet Russia was held up as an example to be followed. Public meetings, attended by distinguished British scientists, gave currency to this appeal.

It was in facing these events that I became aware of the weakness of the position I was defending. When I read that Vavilov's last defence against Lysenko's theories, in 1939, was to evoke the authority of Western scientists, I had to acknowledge that he was appealing to one authority against another: to the authority accepted in the West against the authority accepted in Soviet Russia. (*SFS* 9)

In 1938, Polanyi helped found the Society for the Freedom of Science "in opposition to the centralization of scientific planning" proposed on "utilitarian and positivistic assumptions."[17] The following year, he was

---

15. Gelwick, *Discovery*, 35.   16. Gelwick, *Discovery*, 35.
17. Gelwick, *Discovery*, 38.

invited to participate in still another group, "The Moot," devoted to discussion of social and religious questions:[18]

Polanyi participated ecumenically as a leading intellectual in the Christian community. One example of this ecumenical participation was his years of meeting with the Moot, which was founded by Joseph Oldham (head of International Missionary Council) and who was in many ways a pioneer of the World Council of Churches.[19]

Polanyi says that he "turned to philosophy as an afterthought to my career as a scientist" (*TD* 3), but it is clear that he was exploring philosophical issues all through his scientific career.

In 1946, Polanyi published *Science, Faith and Society*, his first lengthy examination in print of the issues that had occupied him so often in dialogue with his friends and fellow scientists. When the book was re-issued in 1963, Polanyi added an introduction, "Background and Prospect," in which he summarizes the purpose of the book as follows:

Marxism has challenged me to answer these questions: the essays republished here were written in reply to them. Like the Marxist theory, my account of the nature and justification of science includes the whole life of thought in society. In my later writings it is extended to a cosmic picture. But the ultimate justification of my scientific convictions lies always in myself. At some point I can only answer, "For I believe so." This is why I speak of Science, Faith and Society. (*SFS* 9)

Although Polanyi saw the continuity between his first and later writings, he acknowledged a shift away from speaking about "spiritual reality" in 1946 to discussion of "a belief in the reality of emergent meaning and truth" in 1963 (*SFS* 17).

---

18. "In 1939, Joseph Oldham, a distinguished ecumenical leader, invited Polanyi to join the company of other leading thinkers to discuss the basic questions facing our civilization. Numbered among this group called 'The Moot' were Karl Mannheim, Sir Walter Moberly, T. S. Eliot, H. A. Hodges, Kathleen Bliss, A. R. Vidler, D. M. MacKinnon, and John Baillie. Apart from his personal experience as a scientist and thinker, Polanyi regarded the biannual meetings of this society as a major intellectual influence on his thought" (Gelwick, *Discovery*, 41).

19. Gelwick, "Science and Reality," 26. In a footnote, Gelwick claims that "a full reading of the correspondence between Polanyi and Oldham until Oldham's death in 1969 discloses a long friendship in which they saw each other as allies in the struggle for faith and the affirmation of the reality of God."

Polanyi also noted a change in the terminology he used to describe the process of discovery:

> *Scientific knowing consists in discerning Gestalten that are aspects of reality.* I have here called this "intuition"; in later writings I have described as the tacit coefficient of a scientific theory, by which it bears on experience, as a token of reality. Thus it foresees yet indeterminate manifestations of the experience on which it bears. (*SFS* 10)

This definition of scientific knowing clearly shows Polanyi's debt to Gestalt psychology. In the 1963 introduction, Polanyi claims that his approach to the philosophy of science is much like that of A. D. Ritchie, W. I. Beveridge, J. D. Bronowski, Stephen Toulmin, N. R. Hanson, Konrad Lorenz, Thomas Kuhn, Gerald Holton, Ch. Perelman, and A. I. Wittenberg (*SFS* 12–13). In 1948, two years after the publication of *Science, Faith and Society,* he "retired from the professional pursuit of science to take up philosophy" (*KB* 87).

In *The Logic of Liberty,* Polanyi collected some essays on science, academic freedom, and social-economic questions that he had published from 1942 to 1950. It is clear from his preface that he had begun by then to take the first steps toward composing *Personal Knowledge:*

> These pieces were written in the course of the last eight years. They represent my consistently renewed efforts to clarify the position of liberty in response to a number of questions raised by our troubled period of history. . . . I have thought of melting down the material and casting it into a mould of a comprehensive system, but this seemed premature. It cannot be attempted without establishing first a better foundation than we possess today for the holding of our beliefs.
>
> But I hope that my collection may supply some elements of a future coherent doctrine, since it expresses throughout a consistent line of thought. I take more seriously here than was done in the past the fiduciary presuppositions of science; that is the fact that our discovery and acceptance of scientific knowledge is a commitment to certain beliefs which we hold, but which others may refuse to share.[20]

It is clear that *Personal Knowledge* supplies the "comprehensive system" and "coherent doctrine" that Polanyi felt was required as the framework for understanding the full import of these essays.

---

20. Michael Polanyi, *The Logic of Liberty: Reflections and Rejoinders* (London: Routledge and Kegan Paul, 1951; hereafter cited in notes and text as *LL*), v.

Polanyi dated the origins of *Personal Knowledge* to a work that he published in 1939:

The enquiry of which this volume forms part started in 1939 with a review article on J. D. Bernal's *The Social Functions of Science.* I opposed his view, derived from Soviet Marxism, that the pursuit of science should be directed by the public authorities to serve the welfare of society. I held that the power of thought to seek the truth must be accepted as our guide, rather than be curbed to the service of material interests. A defence of intellectual freedom on such metaphysical grounds was no more acceptable to the dominant schools of Western philosophy than to the Marxists. Believing it to be both right and important, I set out in search of its justification. (*PK* ix)

Personal Knowledge was nine years in the writing, from 1948 to 1957:

Manchester University has made it possible for me to accept the invitation of Aberdeen and to spend nine years almost exclusively on the preparation of this book. The generosity of Senate and Council [allowed] me to exchange my Chair of Physical Chemistry for a Professorial appointment without lecturing duties. (*PK* ix)

Polanyi praised Marjorie Grene for her assistance over seven years in developing his philosophy:

This work owes much to Dr. Marjorie Grene. The moment we first talked about it in Chicago in 1950 she seemed to have guessed my whole purpose, and ever since she has never ceased to help its pursuit. Setting aside her own work as a philosopher, she has devoted herself for years to the service of the present enquiry. Our discussions have catalyzed its progress at every stage and there is hardly a page that has not benefitted from her criticism. She has a share in anything that I may have achieved here. (*PK* ix)

Polanyi first presented the material as a whole in the Gifford Lectures of 1951–52 at the University of Aberdeen (*PK* ix). After the appearance of *Personal Knowledge,* Polanyi "lectured . . . as Visiting Professor or Senior Fellow, at the universities of Chicago, Aberdeen, Virginia, Stanford, and Merton College, Oxford" (*TD,* ii).

In 1958, Polanyi was chosen to give the Lindsay Memorial Lectures at the University College of North Staffordshire; these were published in 1959 as *The Study of Man.* In his preface, Polanyi called the lectures "an introduction to *Personal Knowledge*"; he later described them as "a theory of historiography" (*TD* ix). In the first lecture, he gave a clear description of what he meant by "tacit knowledge":

Human knowledge is of two kinds. What is usually described as knowledge, as set out in written words or maps, or mathematical formulae, is only one kind of knowledge; while unformulated knowledge, such we have of something we are in the act of doing, is another form of knowledge. If we call the first kind explicit knowledge, and the second, tacit knowledge, we may say that *we always know tacitly that we are holding our explicit knowledge to be true*. If, therefore, we are satisfied to hold part of our knowledge tacitly, the vain pursuit of reflecting ever again on our own reflections never arises. (*PK* viii)

In *Personal Knowledge*, the tacit act of "holding our explicit knowledge to be true" is the act of commitment: "Personal knowledge is an intellectual commitment, and as such inherently hazardous" (*TD* ix).

Like *Personal Knowledge*, *The Tacit Dimension* is the fruit of nine years of reflection (1957 to 1966):

The present volume is the first account in book form of the work done during these nine years. The delay was caused by hope and by fear. The lure of the next bend behind which new sights might appear distracts us from the labor of taking stock, and the effect of this distraction is reinforced by the anxiety that our theories might be defeated at the next turn. (*TD* 4)

The theme of this book is succinctly stated in Polanyi's opening remarks on "tacit knowing": "I shall reconsider human knowledge by starting from the fact that *we know more than we can tell*" (*TD* iii). Polanyi first lectured on the substance of this book at the University of Virginia in 1961 and developed the ideas further in the 1962 Terry Lectures at Yale (*TD* iii). In 1964, Polanyi spent the summer at the Center for Advanced Studies in the Behavioral Sciences in Palo Alto and at Duke University (*TD* ii). The next year he was named a Senior Fellow at the Center for Advanced Studies at Wesleyan University (*TD* x). In his introduction to this book, Polanyi noted another fundamental development in his thought:

Viewing the content of these pages from the position reached in *Personal Knowledge* and *The Study of Man* eight years ago, I see that my reliance on the necessity of commitment has been reduced by working out the structure of tacit knowing. This structure shows that all thought contains components of which we are subsidiarily aware in the focal content of our thinking, and that all thought dwells in its subsidiaries, as if they were parts of our body. Hence thinking is not only necessarily intentional, as Brentano has taught: it is also necessarily fraught with the roots it embodies. It has a *from-to* structure. (*TD* x)

The shift in emphasis is somewhat disquieting, as "commitment" forms the backbone of the analysis in *Personal Knowledge*.[21] Polanyi did not say that the notion of "commitment" was wrong, only that it is of "reduced" importance in his current understanding of knowledge. The development of his understanding of tacit knowledge seems to have modified Polanyi's understanding of the "inherently hazardous" nature of commitment (*PK* viii). "Commitment" appears at least eight times in *The Tacit Dimension*.[22] In every case, Polanyi continues to use the concept very much as he had in *Personal Knowledge*. For example, in the concluding paragraphs of the first lecture, "Tacit Knowing," Polanyi correlates tacit knowledge with the act of commitment:

> To hold such knowledge is an act deeply committed to the conviction that there is something there to be discovered. . . . To accept the pursuit of science as a reasonable and successful enterprise is to share the kind of commitments on which scientists enter by undertaking this enterprise. You cannot formalize the act of commitment, for you cannot express your commitment non-committally. To attempt this is to exercise the kind of lucidity which destroys its subject matter. (*TD* 25)

It is important not to create a false dichotomy between the act of commitment and the tacit subsidiaries on which commitment rests. In 1969, Marjorie Grene edited a collection of Polanyi's previously published essays (composed from 1959 to 1968). In her introduction to *Knowing and Being*, Grene underscored the centrality of the notion of "commitment" in Polanyi's earlier work and considered it as correlative to, not in competition with, the notion of "tacit knowledge":

> *Personal Knowledge* was directed not so much to tacit knowing as to the problem of intellectual commitment, the question how I can justify the holding of dubitable beliefs. The theory of tacit knowing is indeed the foundation of the doc-

21. "It is the act of commitment in its full structure that saves personal knowledge from being merely subjective" (*PK* 65); the tenth chapter of *PK* is devoted to illuminating the structure of commitment. In the 1974 "Preface to the Torchbook Edition," Polanyi gives a very straightforward report of how the notion functions in this work: "Any particular commitment can be challenged, but only on the grounds of a rival commitment. The only question is then, how a particular set of beliefs can be justified. Three-quarters of this book serves to introduce my answer, stated within a framework declared to be my own commitment. I claim that no more than such a responsible personal knowledge can be required of us" (x). Toward the end of this preface, he remarks, "My later writings, including a new book on press, are less occupied with the justification of our ultimate commitments and concentrate instead on working out precisely the operations of tacit knowing" (xi).

22. *TD* x, 23, 25, 77, 78, 79, 80, 87.

trine of commitment, but while the latter probes deeper into the foundation of human personality, the former is more far-ranging. It reveals a pervasive substructure of all intelligent behavior. (*KB* xiv)

To her eye, the essays in this volume "exemplify [the] development" of Polanyi's thought since the publication of *Personal Knowledge* (*KB* xii).

In 1975, Polanyi collaborated with Harry Prosch on *Meaning*. The material in this book was derived from lectures at the University of Texas and at the University of Chicago in 1969, and other lectures in 1970 and 1971; Polanyi started working to publish them in 1972 and had a draft done by 1973–74 (*Meaning* ix). While the book is completely consistent with Polanyi's previous epistemology, exploring the fact that *"All* knowing is personal knowing—participation through indwelling" (*Meaning* 44), its apparent reduction of religion to the status of fiction and art caused some to interpret it as a major break from the ontology of *Personal Knowledge:*

[*Meaning*] focuses on the discontinuities between art and science; yet it seems a natural inference from earlier Polanyi publications to argue for certain close affinities between scientific and artistic meaning. In the same way, Hall argues, the account of religion in *Meaning* is unbalanced: Polanyi identifies religious meaning as predominantly abstract and aesthetic; this claim ignores the existential focus of historical religions.[23]

Polanyi died on February 22, 1976,[24] before the critical questions raised by *Meaning* developed full force. Prior to the publication of *Meaning,* theologians felt relatively comfortable in the assumption that Polanyi saw science and religion as dealing with two different aspects of reality; afterward, a major debate arose about whether this assumption was correct. In *Personal Knowledge,* Polanyi seemed to align himself with Protestantism: "I find my own conception of the scope and method of a progressive Protestant theology confirmed by many passages in the writings of Paul Tillich" (*PK* 283n1). Prosch, however, argues that Polanyi was not a Christian at all and that the derogation of the status of religion as compared to science in *Meaning* is completely consistent with Polanyi's earlier work:

---

23. Phil Mullins, "The Spectrum of Meaning—Polanyian Perspectives on Science and Religion," *Zygon* 17 (1982): 6.

24. Gelwick, *Discovery,* 52.

The only other scholar I know to have made this point about Polanyi is Terence Kennedy, who says that "honesty demands that we acknowledge that Polanyi was not religiously committed nor did he have religious faith as this is understood in Christian theology."[25]

Was Polanyi really a Christian? What defines a Christian? He was not, of course, as Kennedy defines a Christian. At one point Polanyi did seem to think of himself as a fully practicing Christian. When I knew him he obviously was not one.[26]

Colin Weightman, in a careful and persuasive survey of the issue, concludes, "It is possible that Polanyi affirmed the independent existence of God in his early period but it is clear, from *Personal Knowledge* onwards, that he did not do so in later life."[27]

William T. Scott, who worked for sixteen years on a biography of Polanyi, sees a number of possible explanations for Polanyi's apparent relapse into a positivistic view of religion:

A second possibility is that the writing reflects Polanyi's diffidence in expressing to friends and acquaintances his religious commitments. Several persons who had extensive conversations with him on religious matters reported that he had never revealed where he stood himself.

A third possibility is that Polanyi actually changed his mind from the time when he regularly attended Anglican worship in the late 1940's to the time of his lectures on "Meaning" and the publication of the book.[28]

Even though Scott has found that Polanyi "only rarely was . . . able to believe in the divinity of Christ,"[29] he nevertheless concludes that Polanyi ultimately did intend to assert the reality of a divine being:

With all his charm and conviviality, Michael Polanyi was at heart a secret person, as a close friend of the years 1913–16 already had observed. Especially he was not a person to share his convictions in a religious community or to participate actively in corporate religious life. I am convinced both that he considered the Christian religion at its best to involve an encounter with and surrender to a

25. Prosch refers the reader to Terence Kennedy, *The Morality of Knowledge* (Rome: Pontifica Universitas Lateranensis, 1979), 138–40.

26. Harry Prosch, "Polanyi's View of Religion in *Personal Knowledge*: A Response to Richard Gelwick," *Zygon* 17 (1982): 46–47.

27. Colin Weightman, *Theology in a Polanyian Universe: The Theology of Thomas Torrance*, volume 174 in American University Studies: Series VII, Theology and Religion (New York: Peter Lang Publishing, 1994), 9.

28. Scott, "Religious Reality," 85.

29. Scott, "Religious Reality," 86.

preexisting reality and that he must have had some visions himself, however in-effable, of this reality.[30]

It is somewhat paradoxical that the man who wanted to restore the dig-nity of making an act of commitment to unproven realities himself hes-itated to say clearly where he stood on the question of God.

Purpose and Structure of *Personal Knowledge*

Polanyi wrote this book to advocate the paradigm of "personal knowledge" as the best alternative to the "ideal of scientific detach-ment" (*PK* vii)[31] that is so deeply ingrained in modern culture. He in-tended "to show that complete objectivity as usually attributed to the exact sciences is a delusion and is in fact a false ideal" (18). Where the ideal of strict objectivity counsels holding as true only what has been demonstrated to be true, Polanyi argued that one must learn to accept what one "might conceivably doubt" (109): "The principal purpose of this book is to achieve a frame of mind in which I may hold firmly to what I believe to be true, even though I know that it might conceivably be false" (214).

Polanyi conceded to skeptics that our knowledge is always based on such incompletely demonstrated beliefs. Instead of joining the ob-jectivists in their attempt to build a system of impersonal procedures that would guarantee some kind of absolute knowledge, Polanyi ac-cepted the limitations of the human mind as a fact of life: "Our duty lies in the service of ideals which we cannot possibly achieve" (245). Polanyi described the adoption of this viewpoint as an act of "ultimate self-reliance, to which this entire book shall bear witness" (265). The skeptic focuses on the fact that there is no access to reality unmediated by belief, and declares that therefore there is no knowledge; objec-tivists grant that there is knowledge, but define the conditions of justi-fied belief so narrowly that very little passes their stringent tests. Polanyi saw the same central role of belief in knowledge, and accepted it as a condition of our existence over which one does not have and can never have complete control:

---

30. Scott, "Religious Reality," 86.

31. From this point forward in Chapter II, page references in the text belong to *PK* unless otherwise specified.

"I believe that in spite of the hazards involved, I am called upon to search for the truth and state my findings." This sentence, summarizing my fiduciary program, conveys an ultimate belief which I find myself holding. Its assertion must therefore prove consistent with its content by practicing what it authorizes. This is indeed true. For in uttering this sentence I both say that I must commit myself by thought and speech, and do so at the same time. Any enquiry into our ultimate beliefs can be consistent only if it presupposes its own conclusions. It must be intentionally circular. (299)

Taken out of context, this program may seem to license solipsism, as when Polanyi remarked that "man stands at the beginning and the end, as begetter and child of his own thought" (265). This remark is made in Chapter Eight, in the section entitled "The Fiduciary Program." In Chapter Ten, Polanyi admits, "It threatens to sink into subjectivism; for by limiting himself to the expression of his own beliefs, the philosopher may be taken to talk only about himself" (299); but later in that chapter he argues, "This position is not solipsistic, since it is based on a belief in an external reality and implies the existence of other persons who can likewise approach the same reality. Nor is it relativistic" (316).

The conscious acceptance of "intentional circularity" is balanced by Polanyi's insistence that we must and do make contact with a reality other than ourselves that has the capacity to reveal itself to us in "an indefinite number of unpredictable ways" (311). This contact with reality is made primarily in the "tacit dimension" by unspecifiable acts of the individual mind; it is only after such contact is achieved that we can make some of the connections explicit in reflection and articulation. Despite the limitations that this places on our desire to clarify what we know, Polanyi insisted that the "personal coefficient" of knowledge is "no mere imperfection but a vital component" of knowing (vii). Understanding this participation of the knower in all that is known[32] causes a profound revision in what we mean by "objectivity":

Such knowing is indeed *objective* in the sense of establishing contact with a hidden reality; a contact that is defined as the condition for anticipating an indeterminate range of yet unknown (and perhaps yet inconceivable) true implications. It seems reasonable to describe this fusion of the personal and the objective as Personal Knowledge. (Vii–viii)

32. I am echoing the title of Marjorie Grene's essay on epistemology, *The Knower and the Known* (New York: Basic Books, 1966).

It is his assumption that we are able to make such contact with reality that gives Polanyi a line of defense against the charge of unrestrained subjectivity. Faced with the question of whether we really know things, as opposed to knowing only our ideas of things, Polanyi chooses to believe that we know things. Objectivists may complain that this fuzzy, quasi-mystical assumption is precisely what stands in need of proof, since showing the coherence of a belief with practice does not necessarily justify the belief. To them, the following affirmation would be a vicious circle: "Throughout this book I am affirming my own beliefs, and more particularly so when I insist, as I do here, that such personal affirmations and choices are inescapable, and, when I argue, as I shall do, that this is all that can be required of me" (209). For Polanyi, the belief that we know *things* and not just the figments of our imagination is one of the many indemonstrable truths to which he is personally and passionately committed, even though the clues which sustain his vision never become proofs: "And around this central fact [the passionate contribution of the person knowing what is being known] I have tried to construct a system of correlative beliefs which I can sincerely hold, and to which I can see no acceptable alternatives" (viii).

Polanyi's strategy in this book, then, is to discredit "a mistaken ideal of objectivity" (7) and accredit, as the subtitle of the work suggests (265–66), a different ideal of objectivity based on a "post-critical philosophy" (vii). Polanyi divides the work into four parts. In Part One, "The Art of Knowing," he launches an attack on models of objectivity derived from the "exact sciences" (18–19) and begins to sketch the "ubiquitous participation of the scientist in upholding the affirmations of science" (132). In Part Two, "The Tacit Component," evidence is developed to support three key facts on which Polanyi's case for the post-objectivist viewpoint rests:

(1) Nearly all knowledge by which man surpasses the animals is acquired by the use of language.

(2) The operations of language rely ultimately on our tacit intellectual powers which are continuous with those of the animals.

(3) These inarticulate acts of intelligence strive to satisfy self-set standards and reach their conclusions by accrediting their own success. (95)

Part Three, "The Justification of Personal Knowledge," explores Polanyi's understanding of the structure of personal knowledge and argues that the only stable and consistent epistemology is that of commitment to fundamental beliefs. Part Four develops an ontology of personal knowledge, exploring some of its ramifications for an understanding of the evolution of life in the universe. In the discussion that follows, I will concentrate on just the first three parts of the book, since they constitute the core of his analysis of personal knowledge.

The Line of Argument in Part One: The Art of Knowing

Polanyi's primary purpose in the first part of *Personal Knowledge* is to collect "facts . . . which demonstrate the pervasive participation of the knowing person in the act of knowing by virtue of an art which is essentially inarticulate" (70). In this section he claimed to have "demonstrated everywhere the limits of formalization. These observations show that strictly speaking nothing that we know can be said precisely" (87–88). Chapter One, "Objectivity," considers several turning points in the history of science from the Copernican revolution to modern physics in order to show that the attainment of objective results always takes place within a subjective framework. Objectivity is portrayed as the accomplishment of a person "striving passionately to fulfill his personal obligations to universal standards" (17). As Polanyi sampled the progress of science over the last five centuries, he called attention to the personal act of appraisal lying at the heart of each advance in understanding. Although he ran the risk of being mocked for his "out-dated Platonism," he nevertheless proposed a trans-empirical model of discovery:

1. "A discovery of objective truth in science consists in the apprehension of a rationality which commands our respect and arouses our contemplative admiration."

2. "Such discovery, while using the experience of our senses as clues, transcends this experience by embracing the vision of a reality beyond the impressions of our senses."

3. The vision of reality "speaks for itself in guiding us to an ever deeper understanding of reality." (5–6)

The key to Polanyi's understanding of objectivity is the personal "apprehension of a rationality" through the integration and interpretation of clues. Without a central vision "grounded in reason and transcending the senses" (12) to hold everything together, there are only meaningless pieces of a puzzle.

In saying that objectivity is the accomplishment of subjects, Polanyi did not mean that objectivity *is* subjectivity. After one has seen how the pieces fit together to form a whole, one may construct a *theory* which intentionally leaves the role of the knower out of the focus of the account:

> A theory is something other than myself. It may be set out on paper as a system of rules, and it is the more truly a theory the more completely it can be put down in such terms. Mathematical theory reaches the highest perfection in this respect. But even a geographical map fully embodies in itself a set of strict rules for finding one's way through a region of otherwise uncharted experience. Indeed, all theory may be regarded as a kind of map extended over space and time. It seems obvious that a map can be correct or mistaken, so that to the extent to which I have relied on my map I shall attribute to it any mistakes that I made by doing so. A theory on which I rely is therefore objective knowledge in so far as it is not I, but the theory, which is proved right or wrong when I use such knowledge. (4)

Polanyi adds two further observations on this same page about how a theory functions: that it is not affected by "my personal illusions" and that it "may be constructed without regard to one's normal approach to experience." Both of these points reinforce his first point that a theory is "something other than myself."

When we rely on a theory, it determines what kind of information is considered significant: "Facts which are not described by the theory create no difficulty for the theory, for it regards them as irrelevant to itself. Such a theory functions as a comprehensive idiom which consolidates that experience to which it is apposite and leaves unheeded whatever is not comprehended by it" (47). For example, in the field of psychology, "not until the concept of hypnosis was established as a framework for the facts, could these facts eventually be admitted to be true" (52).

Development of an objective theory does not determine all of the meanings or applications of the theory itself; it is the beginning of a new process of investigation even if it comes at the end of another. A theory that has made contact with reality possesses "prophetic powers" because of the "wholly indeterminate scope of its true implications" (5). The one who sees a new level of rationality in the universe does not thereby gain complete control over what is grasped, yet the lack of control over the meaning of the vision does not diminish the objectivity of the understanding. In Polanyi's view, the inability to exhaust an insight is one of the indications that one is in touch with reality (37). There is room for others to build on the pattern *(Gestalt)* recognized by the first to see it because "a scientific theory, when it conforms to reality, gets hold of a truth that is far deeper than its author's understanding of it" (43).

Polanyi opposes his view of objectivity to that of Locke, Hume, Mach, and other philosophers inclined toward "a mistaken ideal of objectivity" (7–9). He faulted them for attending to only part of the story of the development of science:

Any critical verification of a scientific statement requires the same powers for recognizing rationality in nature as does the process of scientific discovery, even though it exercises these at a lower level. When philosophers analyze the verification of scientific laws, they invariably choose as specimens such laws as are not in doubt, and thus inevitably overlook the intervention of these powers. They are describing the practical demonstration of scientific law, and not its critical verification. As a result we are given an account of the scientific method, which having left out the process of discovery on the grounds that it follows no definite method, overlooks the process of verification as well, by referring only to examples where no real verification takes place. (13–14)

Our "powers for recognizing rationality" give rise to objectivity, but are not objective themselves. Enchanted by the enormous success of scientific objectivity, positivist philosophers neglect the important role of scientific subjectivity and envision a process of coming to know that is as clear and distinct as what is known. They systematically overlook the "passionate, personal, human appraisals of theories" and "the intuition of rationality in nature" which Polanyi holds are "a justifiable and indeed essential part of scientific theory" (15–16). This systematic neglect of the personal ground of science does not reduce the role of the knower in the known—it does not make scientists more objective in fact. It is simply a coverup. The positivist relies on a personal appraisal of facts no less than the post-critical thinker.

In Chapter Two, Polanyi's main purpose is to examine the role of personal appraisal in the evaluation of probabilities. To the uninitiated, the field of probability may seem to be a paradigm of objectivity: it is all numbers, and numbers do not lie. The problem is that they may not tell the truth, either. The art of the scientist lies in knowing which numbers to consider, and which to neglect, so that a meaningful pattern emerges from a cluttered background of quanitifiable events. In this selective concentration of attention there are no rules to replace the "personal skill" of the scientist (19). Because there is never a perfect fit between theory and experimental measurement, "there are always some conceivable scruples which scientists customarily set aside in the process of verifying an exact theory. Such acts of personal judgment form an essential part of science" (20).

The ideal of developing "precise rules which can be formally set out and empirically tested" (18) has had to give way on two quite different grounds. Even while classical mechanics governed the conduct of science, it had to be admitted that verification of theory depended on the judgment that experimental results were close enough and that "residual indeterminacies" really were not significant (20). When quantum mechanics became established, a quite different kind of indeterminacy had to be accepted and handled through the probabilistic interpretation of laws (21). In 1921, J. M. Keynes attempted to codify strict rules of evidence for the determination of probability, so that the ideal of objectivity might be preserved even in this new context (24). Polanyi refused to accept Keynes's fundamental assumption that scientific propositions are only about other propositions, and therefore may be strictly controlled by formal rules. In Polanyi's view, language refers to realities, not just to other linguistic structures. Probabilities are *statements about probable events* and *not probable statements about events*" (25). At the end of the chapter, Polanyi conceded that Keynes's reflections have "some value" as a set of maxims or "rules of art" that may be helpful to one who has some personal knowledge of the field, but not as a substitute for that personal knowledge: "Maxims can function only—as I have said—within a framework of personal judgment" (31). If we have sufficient personal knowledge to place the correct interpretation on them, we may profit from the maxims of an art; if we lack the personal knowledge, the maxims will lead us nowhere (50).

Polanyi does not prove that Keynes is wrong. Instead, he argues that there is a more *satisfying* way of accounting for what scientists do. "Satisfaction" is an informal, unquantifiable, and uncontrollable notion. In Polanyi's discussion of "The Nature of Assertions," (the fifth section of Chapter Two), it is also the heart of the matter: "No sincere assertion of fact is essentially unaccompanied by feelings of intellectual satisfaction or of a persuasive desire and a sense of personal responsibility" (27). To put Polanyi's point in its most offensive form, one might say that science is fundamentally a matter of feelings. It is true that those feelings are highly refined, intellectual passions, not random whims or passing moods. It is also true that even these educated feelings would be practically worthless without the tools provided by modern instrumentation and the wealth of data acquired by scientists through the centuries; but the instruments and data are just as worthless without the intellectual passions of the scientists that guide the construction and correction of images or models of reality.

Polanyi's conclusion about the nature of assertions is that there is an implicit, passionate commitment of the speaker involved in every affirmation of fact (27–28). Polanyi devoted the whole of Chapter Six to an examination of the role of intellectual passions in personal knowledge. He anticipated that discussion in Chapter Two in order to make it clear that this "fiduciary act" cannot be translated into other terms. Taking a position is always "a personal act of my own" (29). Those who recognize the development of their own passionate commitment as the substratum of their intellectual life may follow Polanyi in rejecting other ideals of objectivity; those who reject Polanyi's fusion of subjectivity and objectivity might say that Polanyi has misunderstood what makes science *scientific* and that the attempted fusion results only in confusion about real knowledge.

Chapter Three takes up the question of whether order or disorder is fundamental to the structure of the universe. The adoption of one standpoint or the other is like the central assumption of Chapter One that everyone makes contact with reality: it is a choice that determines one's "vision of reality"[33] and that sets a standard of judgment for all subsequent discussion of what is and is not rational. From Polanyi's standpoint, the decision to view disorder as fundamental is "a logical muddle" (35). To those who adopt the opposite mindset, there is no "logical muddle" at all, because their understanding of logic is conditioned by their presupposition that random events can and do give rise

33. I will return to this central notion of "vision of reality" when considering the material in Chapter Six. One's vision of reality is the ultimate interpretative framework from which all other articulate frameworks are derived.

to order. The argument is not so much over the statistical analysis of the probability of life appearing by chance, but over how to *assess* the meaning of the number. To Polanyi, the extreme odds are a clue that there must be a higher, ordering principle at work in the emergence of life. To other scientists, the chances against life appearing only mean that it will not occur frequently throughout the universe.

A second assumption that Polanyi explored in this chapter is that the order discerned by science is not just a projection of the mind, but belongs to the universe itself. Polanyi used crystallography as a prime example of an order in nature corresponding to an ordered conceptual construction. In this instance, the recognition of certain patterns in crystals suggested a purely mathematical model of "all distinct kinds of crystal symmetry," which were in turn correlated with a theory of atomic regularities (44–45). The order in nature gave rise to an ordered understanding. The abstract mathematical model, inspired by the "hidden principles of the experienced world" (46) may be used to criticize things and events "to the extent to which they fall short of the standards which the theory sets for nature" (48). It is part of the unspecifiable art of science to know when to use theory to criticize data and when to use data to criticize a theory (135, 138).

The first three chapters of Part One are primarily critical of false or misleading interpretations of objectivity, probability, and order. In each case, Polanyi suggested that there is another way of viewing the issue so as to include the person of the knower in what is known. Chapter Four, "Skills," begins to sketch a constructive view of this personal participation in knowledge. Polanyi knew that his emphasis on personal knowledge might seem contrary to the nature of science itself. In this chapter, he emphasized that personal knowledge is not a license to indulge in superstition and specious practices: "It is the act of commitment *in its full structure* that saves personal knowledge from being merely subjective."[34]

Polanyi's fundamental assumption was that the conduct of science is a skillful activity. It is this assumption which licensed him to transfer the conclusions derived from consideration of bodily skills to the domain of conceptual skills (49). From this point of view, science is highly unscientific. In a sense, the personal skill with which the formulae of

---

34. *PK* 65; emphasis added. Chapter Ten, "Commitment," is devoted to an exploration of the structure of commitment.

science are interpreted and applied matters more than the formulae themselves. Science depends upon "an art which cannot be specified in detail" and which therefore "cannot be transmitted by prescription, since no prescription for it exists. It can be passed on only by example from master to apprentice" (53). Memorizing the results of scientific research does not make one a research scientist. All of the splendidly precise accomplishments of science become meaningless if one cannot see for oneself how the facts fit together.

Polanyi invited his readers to consider their own experiences of acquiring skills in order to recognize "the well-known fact *that the aim of a skillful performance is achieved by the observance of a set of rules which are not known as such to the person following them*" (49). Knowledge of a skill is demonstrated by performance rather than by listing the correct rules; his initial examples are things like riding a bicycle (50), operating a glass-blowing machine (52), building a violin (53), and assessing works of art (55). From these examples, he proceeds to the claim in the next chapter that articulation is a skillful performance that builds on a foundation of "mute abilities" (70).

Since the requisite knowledge resides in the person and cannot be fully expressed in language, the communication of this knowledge to another takes place in the tacit dimension:

To learn by example is to submit to authority. You follow your master because you trust his manner of doing things even when you cannot analyze and account in detail for its effectiveness. By watching the master and emulating his efforts in the presence of his example, the apprentice unconsciously picks up the rules of the art, including those which are not explicitly known to the master himself. These hidden rules can be assimilated only by a person who surrenders himself to that extent uncritically to the imitation of another. A society which wants to preserve a fund of personal knowledge must submit to tradition. (53)

Polanyi also used common law and connoisseurship as outstanding examples of fields in which "practical wisdom is more truly embodied in action than expressed in rules of action" (54). In these, as in many other examples, he showed that action speaks louder than words. The paradox that emerges, however, is that even when action speaks, it remains a matter of the tacit dimension; the meaningful effects of the action have more impact than mere words because the action touches us at a level of personal understanding that is too deep for words. The clue that scientists also function like judges rendering a verdict or like connoisseurs evaluating a work of art is found in the lab requirements of the sciences:

> The large amount of time spent by students of chemistry, biology and medicine in their practical courses shows how greatly these sciences rely on the transmission of skills and connoisseurship from master to apprentice. It offers an impressive demonstration of the extent to which the art of knowing has remained unspecifiable at the very heart of science. (55)

Modern science, then, has not done away with the authority of masters over their disciples, although it has dramatically altered the contents of the process of tradition, and it has erected vast theoretical structures that can cause one to overlook the personal foundation upon which they rise.

Having shown how important the tacit dimension is to the art of knowing, Polanyi then called attention to "two kinds of awareness" that play key roles in the structure of personal knowledge: subsidiary and focal awareness. The art of knowing lies in the skill of bringing subsidiary awareness to bear on a meaningful focus of attention. The tacit presuppositions of a science are brought together by the knower to bestow meaning on the question that stands at the center of attention, but *without* a complete consciousness of the act of integration that supplies the "interpretative framework" (59):

> The curious thing is that we have no clear knowledge of what our presuppositions are and when we try to formulate them they appear quite unconvincing. . . .
>
> I suggest now that the supposed pre-suppositions of science are so futile because the actual foundations of our scientific beliefs cannot be asserted at all. When we accept a certain set of pre-suppositions and use them as our interpretative framework, we may be said to dwell in them as we do in our own body. Their uncritical acceptance for the time being consists in a process of assimilation by which we identify ourselves with them. They are not asserted and cannot be asserted, for assertion can be made only *within* a framework with which we have identified ourselves for the time being; as they are themselves our ultimate framework, they are essentially inarticulable. (59, 60)

It is possible to bring some parts of an interpretative framework into focus one at a time, but while this or that aspect of the whole is dominating our focal awareness, it no longer plays its role as a subsidiary, and hence appears in quite a different light: "Our attention can hold only one focus at a time. . . . It would hence be self-contradictory to be both subsidiarily and focally aware of the same particulars at the same time" (57).

The evidence for this assertion of the distinction between subsidiary and focal awareness must be developed by experimentation with one's own set of skills and integrated understandings, recognizing for oneself how the skill or understanding falls apart when attention is shifted from the center to the underpinnings of the act. It is by such thought experiments that we may get a feel for what Polanyi meant by the "logical unspecifiability" of the relations between subsidiary and focal awareness:

All these curious properties and implications of personal knowledge go back to what I have previously described as its logical unspecifiability; that is to the disorganizing effect caused by switching our attention to the parts of a whole. . . . Such dismemberment leaves us with the bare, relatively objective facts, which had formed the clues for a supervening personal fact. It is a destructive analysis of personal knowledge in terms of the underlying relatively objective knowledge. (63)

To be a disciple of Polanyi one must see for oneself that this is how the mind functions. His epistemology is verified primarily by experience tacitly grasped and not by any formal demonstration or linguistic analysis.

Polanyi correlated his notion of "personal commitment" with the distinction between subsidiary and focal awareness:

Like the tool, the sign or symbol can be conceived as such only in the eyes of a person who *relies on them* to achieve or to signify something. *This reliance is a personal commitment which is involved in all acts of intelligence by which we integrate some things subsidiarily to the center of our focal attention.* Every act of personal assimilation by which we make a thing form an extension of ourselves through our subsidiary awareness of it, is a commitment of ourselves; a manner of disposing of ourselves. (61)

Notice how odd it is that the act of commitment is both to what we do not see (the subsidiaries) as well as what can be seen (the focus of attention). At the beginning of our apprenticeship, we often pay attention to the wrong aspects of the art that is to be acquired. In order to master the art, these obstacles to understanding must sink to the level of subsidiaries, becoming *practically* unknown in order to allow the focus of the performance to dominate the field of our attention:

As we learn to handle a hammer, a tennis racket or a motor car in terms of the situation which we are striving to master, we become unconscious of the actions by which we achieve this result. This lapse into unconsciousness is accompanied by a newly acquired consciousness of the experiences in question, on the operational plane. It is misleading, therefore, to describe this as the mere result of repetition; it is a structural change achieved by a repeated mental effort aiming at the instrumentalization of certain things and actions in the service of some purpose. (61–62)

This "lapse into unconsciousness" is not a forgetting of what is learned, but is the correct employment of one aspect of the new framework. The tacit dimension is not isolated from the articulate dimension, as the source of a neurosis is cut off from consciousness in the classical psychoanalytic model; the subsidiary awareness of the framework continues to bear on and work with what stands at the center of our focal awareness: "While focal awareness is necessarily conscious, subsidiary awareness may vary over all degrees of consciousness" (92).

Polanyi concluded his sketch of his alternative understanding of knowledge by returning to the notion of "contact with reality" that forms the core of his understanding of objectivity. Even though the interpretative framework of science may be a set of conceptual tools clearly developed within a human tradition, the whole point of the construction is to "submit to reality" (63):

Yet personal knowledge in science is not made but discovered, and as such it claims to establish contact with reality beyond the clues on which it relies. It commits us, passionately and far beyond our comprehension, to a vision of reality. Of this responsibility we cannot divest ourselves by setting up objective criteria of verifiability—or falsifiability, or testability, or what you will. For we live in it as in the garment of our own skin. . . .

Such is the true sense of objectivity in science, which I illustrated in my first chapter. I called it the discovery of rationality in nature, a name which was meant to say that the kind of order which the discoverer claims to see in nature goes far beyond his understanding; so that his triumph lies precisely in his foreknowledge of a host of yet hidden implications which his discovery will reveal in later days to other eyes. (64)

One cannot directly examine this link with reality because it takes place in the tacit dimension as a result of the skillful integration of any number of subsidiary insights. That is why discovery "commits us . . . far beyond our comprehension." To the skeptic, the commitment to an interpretative framework looks like the acceptance of a figment of the imagination without any guarantee that the construct has a bearing on reality; to Polanyi, the desire to see all the connections between reality and our interpretations of it is a misdirected intellectual passion that runs contrary to the way the mind operates. If the eye were able to visually examine all of its own components, it would be blind to external reality. Only because the retina, rods, cones, nerves, and interpreting structures of the brain function invisibly does the eye open upon the world at large. The same is true of the conceptual frameworks that organize our view of reality and guide our exploration of it. If they were not able to function subsidiarily, they would destroy our capacity to focus on any other dimension of reality.

The Line of Argument in Part Two: The Silent Foundations of Speech

Since the second part of *Personal Knowledge* is dedicated to the exploration of "the tacit component" of knowledge, Polanyi called the opening chapter of this section (Chapter Five, "Articulation") a "digression" (132). If it is a digression from the focus of this section, it is a very important one, as when one digresses from a highway in order to buy the gasoline that makes further journeying possible. Chapter Four dealt with skills in general; Chapter Five concentrates on verbal skills in particular. Polanyi understood "articulation" in the widest possible sense: "Language should be taken from the start to include writing, mathematics, graphs, and maps, diagrams and pictures; in short, all forms of symbolic representation which are used as language in the sense defined by the subsequent description of the linguistic process" (78). "To speak is to *contrive* signs, to *observe* their fitness, and to *interpret* their alternative relations" (82). "All arts are learned by intelligently imitating the way they are practiced by other persons in whom the learner places his confidence. To know a language is an art, carried on by tacit judgments and the practice of unspecifiable skills" (206). This chapter defines what Polanyi meant by tacit and articulate knowledge and shows how the two work together. Polanyi claims that articulation flows from the tacit dimension because while we speak, we silently rely on "the capacity for appraising our own articulation" (91). This essential, potentially fallible capacity to appraise our own speech and writing is not itself articulate. It is an "essentially inarticulable" act, and it draws on our subsidiary awareness in order to determine what one says and does in the articulate dimension of consciousness (70). Polanyi's goal in this chapter, then, is to win the reader's "endorsement of our native powers of making sense of our experience according to our own standards of rationality" (98).

In Polanyi's view, the tacit act of self-appraisal underlying articulation depends on the application of one's own self–set standards (70–71). Personal knowledge is inherently incapable of being fully translated into impersonal forms because it is essentially a tacit *action* of the mind (1) upon some aspect of reality and (2) upon itself (self-appraisal).

The notions of "personal knowledge" and "tacit knowledge" are linked to one another. Knowledge is personal *because* it is tacit or rooted in tacit knowledge. In the following analysis of how some have come to eliminate the scientist from their understanding of science, one might substitute "personal" for "tacit" without changing the meaning of the assertion:

We owe this immense power for self-deception to the operation of the ubiquitous *tacit* coefficient by which alone we can apply any articulate terms to a subject matter described by them. These powers enable us to evoke our conception of a complex ineffable subject matter with which we are familiar, by even the roughest sketch of any of its specifiable features. A scientist can accept, therefore, the most inadequate and misleading formulation of his own scientific principles without ever realizing what is being said, because he automatically supplements it by his *tacit* knowledge of what science really is, and thus makes the formulation ring true. (169; italics mine)

Tacit knowledge is personal knowledge, though not all personal knowledge is tacit. Polanyi's main concern is to show that the tacit dimension has *priority* over the articulate.

In the course of this discussion of the relationship between what one can and cannot say about knowledge, Polanyi indicates that there are at least three levels of meaning of "tacit":

1. The area where the tacit predominates to the extent that articulation is virtually impossible; we may call this the *ineffable domain*.
2. The area where the tacit component is the information conveyed by easily intelligible speech, so that *the tacit is co-extensive with the text of which it carries the meaning*.
3. The area in which the tacit and the formal fall apart, since the speaker

does not know, or quite know, what he is talking about. There are two extremely different cases of this, namely

> a. an ineptitude of speech, owing to which articulation encumbers the tacit work of thought [fumbling, to be *corrected* later by our tacit understanding];

> b. symbolic operations that outrun our understanding and thus anticipate novel modes of thought [pioneering, to be *followed up* later by our tacit understanding].[35]

It is clear from this schema that "tacit knowledge" is not a univocal term. A flexible understanding of what tacit knowledge is allows one to speak somewhat coherently about the unspeakable: "To assert that I have knowledge which is ineffable is not to deny that I can speak of it, but only that I can speak of it adequately, the assertion itself being an appraisal of this inadequacy" (91). Tacit knowledge dwells in the consciousness of the knower, who realizes in the very act of speaking that what is said falls short of what is understood:

> Though I cannot say clearly how I ride a bicycle nor how I recognize my mackintosh (for I don't know it clearly), yet this will not prevent me from saying that I know how to ride a bicycle and how to recognize my mackintosh. For I know that I know perfectly well how to do such things, though I know the particulars of what I know only in an instrumental manner and am focally quite ignorant of them; so that I may say that I know these matters even though I cannot tell clearly, or hardly at all, what it is that I know. (88)

As is the case with most of Polanyi's efforts to demonstrate the reality and meaning of the tacit dimension, it is up to readers to see for themselves that this is so as they evaluate their own use of language. The data that backs up his case lies in the reader's own "sense of inadequate representation" which arises from one's own attempt to be precise and from recognizing "the ultimate failure of this attempt" (91). This insight cannot be forced upon anyone. Some may be so little gifted with the ability to contemplate the operation of their own mind in the act of speaking that they do not experience the peculiar frustration that testifies to the reality of the tacit dimension. Some may be so in command of their own field that they rarely stumble or grope for adequate articulation. Still others may have had such experiences, and may discount them as philosophically insignificant. There is no complete proof

---

35. *PK* 87. The bracketed insertions come from Polanyi's further comments about the domain of sophistication on page 93.

of the proposition that all knowledge is tacit or rooted in tacit knowledge; there is only evidence for those willing and able to see it as such.

Polanyi correlated his analysis of subsidiary and focal awareness with his observations on the relationship between the tacit and the articulate components of knowledge. So long as a subsidiary functions as a pointer to the meaning of a focus, it operates within the tacit dimension (92). Polanyi uses the act of reading as an example of how focal and subsidiary awareness work together. If one pays too much attention to the bearers of the meaning, looking only at the words or even the characters forming the words in isolation from the text that they form, the meaning of the passage disappears from view: "You can destroy meaning wholesale by reducing everything to its uninterpreted particulars" (199). On the other hand, if a reader lacks familiarity with the language used, the subsidiaries never coalesce into a meaningful whole—as a student learning New Testament Greek might fail to recognize a well-known passage from a gospel because the new vocabulary has not yet penetrated to the deeper levels of consciousness.

Because the use of language depends on our tacit consciousness of many subsidiaries, we do not have complete control over our use of language: "For just as, owing to the ultimately tacit character of all our knowledge, we remain ever unable to say all that we know, so also, in view of the tacit character of the meaning, we can never quite know what is implied in what we say" (95). This defect in our articulation is not due to carelessness. It is a function of the way our minds work. Because knowledge and subsequent verbalization depend upon the personal integration of subsidiaries and a concomitant, tacit act of self-appraisal in the act of assertion, it is always the case that *we know more than we can tell* (4). When improvements are made in our ability to speak about an aspect of reality, it changes the nature of our personal knowledge, without ever eliminating the tacit component. Entering into the interpretative framework of a language "is a tacit, irreversible, heuristic feat; it is a transformation of our intellectual life, originating in our own desire for greater clarity and coherence, and yet sustained by the hope of coming by it into closer touch with reality" (106). Polanyi told the story of the modification of the meaning of the term "isotope" in the presence of and against the will of the man who first coined the term. Denotative language must flex under the desire to improve our grasp of reality—the very language that made insight possible is transformed by what is now seen *through* it (111). We may not be able to guarantee the rightness of our words, but the effort to do so as far as we are able is one of the standards that Polanyi sets for himself as an ideal for personal knowledge.

Although Polanyi recognized that language expresses our contact with reality only imperfectly, he did not give up the ideal of truth as the standard by which we are to measure our knowledge. He contrasted his view of the relationship between language, truth, and reality to the view of Wittgenstein and similar linguistic analysts:

> The understatement that language is a set of convenient symbols used according to the conventional rules of a 'language game' originates in the tradition of nominalism, which teaches that general terms are merely names designating certain collections of objects—a doctrine which, in spite of the difficulties admittedly attached to it, is accepted by most writers in England and America, in abhorrence of its metaphysical alternatives. . . . My own view admits this controlling principle by accrediting the speaker's sense of fitness for judging that his words express the reality he seeks to express. Without this, words having an open texture are totally meaningless, and any text written in such words is meaningless. Refusing to make this admission, the nominalist has either to refrain from enquiring how such words can be applied, except arbitrarily, to experience; or else to invoke a set of vague regulative principles—without asking on what authority these rules are to be accepted and how they can be applied, unless arbitrarily, in view of their own vagueness. All these deficiencies are overlooked in an overriding desire to avoid reference to metaphysical notions or at least to cover these up under a cloak of nominalist respectability. (113)

In Polanyi's view, the lack of rules to govern "the speaker's sense of fitness" is a fact about human nature that one must learn to live with. It does not disqualify the speaker from engaging in rational discourse. To those who adopt a critical and objectivist interpretative framework (positivists, empiricists, linguistic analysts), the lack of rules may immediately imply irrationality. The decision to be made is whether to trust or distrust one's ability to grasp aspects of reality in the tacit dimension. If nominalists wish to dwell in suspicion, there is not much that can be said *in their own language* to show them that they are wrong, because "formal operations relying on *one* framework of interpretation cannot demonstrate a proposition to persons who rely on *another* framework" (151). From within Polanyi's conceptual framework, his opponents seem to have abandoned any right to command attention by denying their own capacity to judge the relationship between realities and our understanding of them.

Another strategy for dealing with the vagaries of language is to endorse only what can be formally demonstrated. Polanyi surveys the process of consolidating the solution of a problem in formal terms and points out that the process depends on the tacit powers of intelligence. In the process of developing formal solutions, "the intuitive powers of the investigator are always dominant and decisive" (130). The formal system does not "make sense" without the informal foundation provided by the tacit knowledge of the thinker:

Moreover, a symbolic formalism is itself but an embodiment of our antecedent unformalized powers—an instrument skillfully contrived by our inarticulate selves for the purpose of relying on it as our external guide. The interpretation of primitive terms and axioms is therefore predominantly inarticulate, and so is the process of their expansion and re-interpretation which underlies the progress of mathematics. The alternation between the intuitive and the formal depends on tacit affirmations, both at the beginning and at the end of each chain of formal reasoning. (131)

By its nature, formal reasoning occupies focal awareness, and may obscure the tacit subsidiaries that sustain it. We may be so charmed by figures in the light at center stage that we fail to notice the offstage fixtures that provide the illumination in the first place. For the most part, the practical invisibility of the lighting fixtures is appropriate. Only those theatrical productions which intend to break the standard conventions of the theater call attention to the mechanics of the production. In the normal operations of the mind, when we are more interested in an object than in the mind that contemplates the object, it is very much to our benefit that the supporting mechanisms function virtually unnoticed in the dark background of the tacit dimension. If we focus on the background operations, the object that formerly interested us is cast out of the spotlight into the shadows of tacit awareness.

In Chapter Six, "Intellectual Passions," Polanyi attended to the emotional subsidiaries of knowing. It is a cliché that people hear what they want to hear, but for Polanyi the saying may be applied in a positive sense. In order to focus our attention on what really matters, to spend time and energy assembling the material that will let us hear what reality is saying to us, we must be driven by a desire to understand and we must be sensitive to what happens in the process of investigation. Such feelings are "scientific passions" and "are no mere psychological by-product, but have a logical function which contributes an indispensable element to science" (134–35).

In the actual conduct of science, it may not matter whether the scientists recognize the contributions of their own intellectual passions to their work, so long as they do in fact care enough about what they are doing in order to do it well. Good scientists with an inadequate philosophy of science can still be good scientists; two quite different kinds of skills and intellectual passions are demanded by scientific and philosophical research. The passions necessary for doing science do not stand at the focus of scientific inquiry, but sustain it from within the tacit dimension. Scientists may rely on those specifically scientific subsidiaries without acknowledging that they exist. The reason why it is important to make an issue out of the emotional substratum of science is that the false ideal of dispassionate objectivity harms "the whole system of cultural life" beyond the field of science itself (134). In "The Magic of Marxism" (section eleven of Chapter Seven) Polanyi returns to the question of the cultural ramifications of models of science and shows how "a prophetic idealism spurning all reference to ideals" was derived from a "passion for ruthless objectivity" (227–28).

Polanyi's notion of what constitutes an intellectual passion is related to his reflections on interpretative frameworks. There is a vital circle between what we believe and what we feel. Our intellectual passions reflect our "vision of reality" and at the same time bring it into being. Our "vision of reality" is our ultimate interpretative framework upon which all other conceptual frameworks depend for their orientation:

Our vision of the general nature of things is our guide for the interpretation of all future experience. Such guidance is indispensable. . . .

Our vision of reality, to which our sense of scientific beauty responds, must suggest to us the kind of questions that it should be reasonable and interesting to explore. It should recommend the kind of conceptions and empirical relations that are intrinsically plausible and which should therefore be upheld, even when some evidence seems to contradict them, and tell us also, on the one hand, what empirical connections to reject as specious, even though there is evidence for them—evidence that we may as yet be unable to account for on any other assumptions. In fact, without a scale of interest and plausibility based on a vision of reality, nothing can be discovered that is of value to science; and only our grasp of scientific beauty, responding to the evidence of our senses, can evoke this vision. (135)

Intellectual passions are based on images of what is real. The mind does not see reality except by seeing it through these conceptual constructs and filters; in normal circumstances, one does not notice the frames of reference that are employed to make sense out of the world, because the conceptual frameworks function in subsidiary awareness, just as the eye does not see itself seeing nor the ear hear itself hearing when used to attend to the external world. The fundamental premises on which the mind operates are held tacitly, creating a vision of reality which provides a standpoint for reflection. Polanyi's approach is diametrically opposed to that of the rationalists, which was patterned on the model of algebra and geometry, in which everything is supposed to be derived from a few self-evident propositions. For Polanyi, a tacit vision of reality comes first not only in the exact sciences (165) but even in analytic sciences like mathematics (189, 257).

Our vision of reality—our ultimate interpretative framework—is something larger and less detailed than the theories developed to express it, but without the perceptions and the passions generated by it, we would not know how to go about setting up smaller and more manageable instruments of investigation. Tacit knowledge of our ultimate view of reality provides the foundation for *valuing* the formal operations of the mind. Before we can operate successfully within a formal system, we must be dedicated to it as something worthy of our commitment; otherwise, we will not be willing to spend our time and energy on it. Polanyi emphasized again that the personal appraisal of what counts as fact and which facts are to be counted as significant cannot be reduced to a scientific method—the art of science precedes the development of any mechanical techniques: "Just as the eye sees details that are not there if they fit in with the sense of the picture, or overlooks them if they make no sense, so also very little inherent certainty will suffice to secure the highest scientific value to an alleged fact, if only it fits in with a great scientific generalization, while the most stubborn facts will be set aside if there is no place for them in the established framework of science" (138). The judgment of what is real science and what is counterfeit comes from the tacit vision of reality functioning as the ultimate framework of science.

An interpretative framework is used "by dwelling in it, and this indwelling can be consciously experienced" (195). The conceptual frameworks with which we operate determine facts (47, 240), organize our perceptions (103), suggest where novelties might be discovered (124), prescribe methods (160–61), and establish the grounds of competence within a specialty (318–19). Even though we dwell within these frames of reference, and employ them to reach definite decisions, we are unable to map them completely—"The curious thing is that we have no clear knowledge of what our presuppositions are and when we try to formulate them they appear quite unconvincing" (59). We certainly have tacit knowledge of our premises (162, 165)—they make their presence felt in every decision we make—but they are not wholly under our intellectual control. Polanyi suggests that the most influential ideas in our intellectual lives are *not* "clear and distinct" ideas, but are unclear and intertwined. Like the roots that give life and support to great trees, the most fruitful ideas are hidden in tangled masses deep beneath the surface of consciousness.[36]

The metaphor of "frameworks" in some contexts suggests a fixed position and a rigid structure. But without the ability to shift frameworks, there would be no progress in knowledge. While we rely on our conceptual frameworks to direct our attention and to make evaluation of experience meaningful, we must at the same time be willing to let those frameworks be modified by the passions related to them. Polanyi sketched a threefold role for intellectual passions; these passions are:

1. "selective": determining what is worth paying attention to;
2. "heuristic": connecting "our appreciation of scientific value to a vision of reality, which serves as a guide to inquiry";
3. "persuasive": driving us to defend our commitment to particular interpretative frameworks. (159)

To change our frame of vision is to change ourselves. After a discovery, "my eyes have become different; I have made myself into a person seeing and thinking differently" (143). For Polanyi, there is a natural reluctance to change from one framework to another. So long as a framework of belief satisfies our intellectual passions, we "dwell in" it, using

---

36. I am also thinking here of Douglas Hofstadter's last chapter in *Gödel, Escher, Bach: An Eternal Golden Braid*, "Strange Loops, Or Tangled Hierarchies," 684–719.

it in a subsidiary fashion; when we are compelled by those same passions to convert to a different framework, we "break out" of the old pattern (195–202). But there is a cost involved in making such changes within ourselves. Old habits die hard. New terminology and new methods of operation will have to be practiced until the language and skills defined by the new framework are assimilated as tacit knowledge. The intellectual passions rooted in our vision of reality, the ultimate interpretive framework that upholds our highest ideals of truth, enable us to pay the price of such conversions.

When two interpretative frameworks are in conflict, the resolution of their differences must take place by appeal to the larger visions of reality that uphold them. The ultimate grounds of judgment will be informal, passionate, and personal (189), even though the frameworks themselves may provide formal operations of argument *within* the system they establish. Those who have made the transition from one framework to another constitute a school of thought in which "they think differently, speak a different language, [and] live in a different world" from those who dwell in a competing interpretative framework; so long as the clash of interpretations is unresolved, "at least one of the two schools is excluded to this extent for the time being (whether rightly or wrongly) from the community of science" (151). Because the vision of reality that enables one to choose among conflicting conceptual frameworks is a primarily tacit and essentially personal commitment, the dispute between frameworks almost necessarily descends to *ad hominem* remarks: "In a clash of intellectual passions each side must inevitably attack the opponent's person" (151–52; see also 318–19).

The fact that all significant disagreements are ultimately personal is not a license to abandon whatever formal or quasi-formal arguments there are to be made to demonstrate the inadequacy of the conflicting theories, but it is a comfort to realize why such conflicts "may be tragically inevitable" (159–60, 151–52). There is no guarantee that one will succeed in inducing conversion in another. The risk of appearing "altogether unreasonable" as the argument progresses is part of the price one pays in adopting and defending a fundamental position (viii, 93–94). This is why Polanyi speaks so much about "commitment" in the last chapter of Part Three. Commitment is required even in the most abstract branches of mathematics, for there is no formal system to compel the adoption of the principles upon which the formal systems of mathematics rest (294). Similarly, and to a greater degree, the other sciences appear in this analysis as systems of belief, sustained by the personal and passionate commitments of the scientists themselves (171).

In science and mathematics, new theories are often recommended on the grounds that they are more "beautiful" than others. Although Polanyi recognizes that "a scientific theory . . . is akin to a work of art which calls attention to its own beauty as a token of artistic reality" (133), for him the ultimate beauty of a theory lies in its power to "reveal truth about nature" and not in any "merely formal attractiveness" (149). Polanyi described truth as "the achievement of a contact with reality—a contact destined to reveal itself further by an indefinite range of yet unforseen consequences" (147). This is not a definition that can be used in a formal way to determine what is and is not true, but is a characterization of a fundamental concept in Polanyi's world view. Just as Plato came to the conclusion that justice is what the just person thinks it is, so it may be that truth is what the wise person thinks it is. The recognition of truth is an art that cannot be reduced to a rule: "Nor do I deny, of course, that science is constantly in danger from the incursion of empty speculations, which must be watchfully resisted and cast out; but I hold that the part played by personal knowledge in science makes it impossible to formulate any precise rule by which such speculations can be distinguished from properly conducted empirical investigations" (153). We seize truth gladly when we recognize it, because we desire it passionately, even if we cannot spell out all we know about it or say precisely how it is that it came our way.

Polanyi said that when we have broadened our understanding of science to include the passionate involvement of the knowing person, we will recognize that science is "a vast system of beliefs, deeply rooted in our history and cultivated today by a specially organized part of our society. . . . Science is a system of beliefs to which we are committed" (171). In *Personal Knowledge,* this analysis of science as a fiduciary framework is what makes science resemble religion. For Polanyi, both science and religion are structures of commitment deeply rooted in the intellectual passions of the believer.

In Chapter Seven, "Conviviality," Polanyi explored the social dimension of personal knowledge. The existence of articulate frameworks of discourse allow many to dwell together in the same frame of reference, sharing the same kind of intellectual passions: "The interpersonal coincidence of tacit judgments is primordially continuous with the mute interaction of powerful emotions" (205). Just as one person may undertake a commitment to the pattern of meaning that emerges from the collocation of subsidiary awareness, so society may make the same kind of commitment to a fiduciary framework (245). To dwell in the social framework means to accept as true what one has not verified and perhaps cannot verify for oneself: "The overwhelming proportion of our factual beliefs continue therefore to be held at second hand through trusting others, and in the great majority of cases our trust is placed in the authority of comparatively few people of widely acknowledged standing" (208). The great benefit of this structure of authority and trust is that our vision of reality need not be limited to our own small circle of experience. We rely on others to hold themselves to standards of truth within the sphere of their personal competence in order to ensure that the cultural frame of reference maintains contact with reality: "This system of shared beliefs relies on a chain of overlapping areas, within each of which a few authoritative persons can keep watch over each other's integrity and their sense of what is important" (240). In considering this chain of overlapping authorities, Polanyi accepted a fact which is most often employed in a Marxist critique of social structures—that our social institutions have a vested interest in maintenance of the status quo: "The schools, universities, churches, academies, law courts, newspapers and political parties, are under the protection of the same policemen and soldiers who guard the wealth of landowners and capitalists" (245).

Just as the recognition of personal frames of reference as the source of meaning does not mean that we are bound to remain slaves of the first interpretation that makes sense to us, so acceptance of the role of social frameworks does not mean that they cannot or should not be changed. Polanyi's point is that the process of conversion at both the personal and social level must be driven by free acceptance of ideals that preserve the good that has been derived from admittedly imperfect systems (245). It is our intellectual passions, derived *from* our society and operating within the framework of our personal ideals, that testify *against* our society, showing us that we have fallen short of the mark; it is these passions that enable us to change ourselves and our society; unfortunately, it is these same passions which rend the social fabric if they are not balanced by a realistic appraisal of the limits of our power to obtain what we want both intellectually and socially.

The Line of Argument in Part Three: Recognizing the Personal Foundation of Knowledge

As indicated above, the purpose of the second and third parts of *Personal Knowledge* is to "achieve an acceptable balance of mind" concerning "the inherently personal character of the act by which truth is declared" (70–71). Part Three is entitled, "The Justification of Personal Knowledge." In this section, Polanyi elaborated a model of knowledge that stands between the extremes of objectivism and subjectivism (249). Chapter Eight, "The Logic of Affirmation," presents a reformed "conception of truth" (204) based on the recognition of our commitment to undemonstrated and indemonstrable beliefs "which we have to accept blindly, if we are ever to speak at all" (251). Chapter Eight and Chapter Nine draw on the "series of facts" assembled in the preceding chapters in order to present a coherent view of personal knowledge and to oppose it to objectivist epistemologies. Chapter Ten considers the "wider framework of commitment" (300) as "the only path for approaching the universally valid" (303).

Polanyi opened the discussion in Chapter Eight by exploring the tacit dimension underlying articulation. Because the act of definition is one of the most important acts in establishing a formal system, Polanyi analyzed the process in order to show that it cannot operate without an informal reliance on personally perceived meanings:

Accordingly, in formulating a definition we must rely on watching the way the art of using a word is authentically practiced; or more precisely, watch ourselves applying the term to be defined in ways that *we regard* as authentic. 'Ostensive definitions' are merely a suitable extension of this watching. . . . The formalization of meaning relies therefore *from the start* on the practice of unformalized meaning. It necessarily does so also *in the end,* when we are using the undefined words of the definitions. Finally, the practical interpretation of a definition must rely *all the time* on its undefined understanding by the person relying on it. Definitions only shift the tacit coefficient of meaning; they reduce it but cannot eliminate it. (250)

The tacit dimension precedes articulation, guides its interpretation, and secures its results. Our primary intellectual skills of seeing what things mean and recognizing how concepts coalesce operate beneath the level of formal control.

Polanyi took the word "precision" as a particularly interesting example of our reliance on the tacit coefficient of speech. "Precision or imprecision is a property that can be predicated of *a designation* when it is tested by matching it against something which is *not a designation*, but is the situation on which the designation bears" (251). The act of recognizing that a particular designation aptly describes a situation is a tacit act, and is not logically or grammatically located in the articulation itself:

> It is a tacit performance, and as such lacks the duality which makes the confrontation and the matching of two things—the designation and the designate—logically possible. Therefore, when we say of a descriptive term that it is precise, we declare the result of a test which itself cannot be said to be precise in the same sense. Of course, *the application of the term 'precise'* might once more be said to be precise, or imprecise, when we confront it with the test from which it was derived; but this second confrontation would have to rely once more on a personal appraisal which cannot be said to be precise in the same sense in which a description can be. The precision of a word will ultimately always rely, therefore, on a test which is not precise in the same sense as the word is said to be. (251)

The "tacit performance" of recognizing that terms fit circumstances is an example of performing to self-set standards: "we approve of an act of our own which we have found satisfying while carrying it out" (252). Polanyi's conclusion is that "only a speaker or a listener can mean something *by* a word, and a word *in itself* can mean nothing" (252). A dictionary gives only the most probable range of meanings that a word might take on when it is selected by a tacit act of comprehension, but the list of meanings is incomplete without that act, just as "An unasserted sentence is no better than an unsigned check; just paper and ink without power or meaning" (28).

Even though meaning derives primarily from the domain of personal commitment, the one who speaks does not completely control the meaning of the articulation. In the following passage, Polanyi made a statement of his commitment to the notion of commitment and at the same time admitted that his self-evaluation of his own act of commitment reveals his inability to clarify all that he meant by his credo:

If, then, it is not words that have meaning, but the speaker or listener who means something by them, let me declare accordingly my true position as the author of what I have written so far, as well as of what is still to follow. I must now admit that I did not start the present reconsideration of my beliefs with a clean slate of unbelief. Far from it. I started as a person intellectually fashioned by a particular idiom, acquired through my affiliation to a civilization that prevailed in the places where I had grown up, at this particular period of history. This has been the matrix of all my intellectual efforts. Within it I was to find my problem and seek the terms for its solution. All my amendments to these original terms will remain embedded in the system of my previous beliefs. Worse still, I cannot precisely say what these beliefs are. I can say nothing precisely. The words I have spoken and am yet to speak mean nothing: it is only *I* who mean something *by them*. And, as a rule, I do not focally know what I mean, and though I could explore my meaning up to a point, I believe that my words (descriptive words) must mean more than I shall ever know, if they are to mean anything at all. (252)

The words Polanyi used are a sign of an act of understanding that precedes, accompanies, and transcends the words themselves. Polanyi's belief that "my words . . . must mean more than I shall ever know" may seem unduly pessimistic, but at least the acceptance of limits of formalization is "self-consistent" (252–53). That language alone cannot completely express personal knowledge does not destroy Polanyi's confidence in either language or knowledge, since he convinced himself early in his reflections that "I know more than I can tell." It is only when one assumes the contrary, that only formalized knowledge is knowledge, that a system becomes self-defeating. Polanyi held that his position is "self-justifying, if only it admits its own personal character" (253). Whoever recognizes the tacit act of appraisal upon which speech depends will generate fresh instances of self-appraisal to reflect upon with every affirmation of personal knowledge. To one who stands outside Polanyi's viewpoint, the "self-justifying" character of the affirmation of personal knowledge may appear only self-serving. However, Polanyi did not claim that the self-evidence obtainable in the act of affirmation is self-evident in the classical, rationalistic sense. As personal knowledge, it is evident to the one who adopts the position as a frame of reference for intellectual operations; each act of introspection on the part of the thinker generates fresh evidence from oneself and for oneself about the structure of personal knowledge. The adoption of Polanyi's viewpoint is like the acceptance of a language; *after* accepting "an immensely ramified system of wholly indeterminate uncertainties"

(251) we find that we are able to *use* the system to make sense out of our experience.

Polanyi next moved from consideration of isolated terms of discourse to the act of assertion: "An articulate assertion is composed of two parts: a sentence conveying the content of what is asserted and a tacit act by which this sentence is asserted" (253). The act of assertion is a performance to self-set standards, a tacit, personal act, without which the sentence is incomplete and meaningless (254). In the same way that every part of a fractal pattern bears a resemblance to the pattern as a whole, so every aspect of knowledge shows the same structure of commitment. In Polanyi's view, there is no point at which one may absolve oneself from saying "I believe." The consequence of recognizing this is again an affirmation of personal knowledge: "For having recognized that an 'impersonal allegation' is a contradiction in terms—just as an 'anonymous cheque' would be— we shall no longer try to arrive at any justification of our allegations which would not in its turn be composed of personal allegations of our own" (256).

The purpose of Chapter Eight is to secure "accreditation" for personal knowledge: "To accept the indeterminacy of knowledge requires, on the contrary, that we accredit a person entitled to shape his knowing according to his own judgment, unspecifiably" (264). Polanyi knows that this licensing of belief is offensive to an age raised on objectivist ideals. It may seem like "a futile authorization of my own authority," but "only this manner of adopting the fiduciary mode is consonant with itself: the decision to do so must be admitted to be itself in the nature of a fiduciary act" (256). To the objectivist, this is a vicious circle. To Polanyi, it is a self-justifying assertion of tacit understanding and the subsequent articulation of a standpoint that meets his highest standards of truth-telling. For him, it would be *self-contradictory to secede from the commitment situation as regards the beliefs held within it, but to remain committed to the same beliefs in acknowledging their factual contents as true* (304).

Having assessed the personal coefficient of words and assertions, Polanyi gave his position a third leg to stand on by exploring the realm of inference: "Our intellectual superiority over the animals is almost entirely due to our powers of symbolic operations; it is only by relying on these that we are able to carry out any process of consecutive reasoning" (257). Polanyi adverted to his earlier remarks on the tacit dimension of formal reasoning: "We have seen before that deductive rea-soning may be altogether ineffable and that even the most completely formalized logical operations must include an unformalized tacit coeffi-cient" (257). Tacit knowledge is, of course, also required at the level of understanding each component of a formal system: symbols, axioms, and operations (258).

Polanyi uses mathematics as the paradigm of a formal system of in-ference, and quotes S. C. Kleene's observations on why mathematical operations cannot be completely formalized: "Rules have been stated to formalize the object theory, but now we must understand without rules how those rules work. An intuitive mathematics is necessary even to define the formal mathematics."[37] Polanyi maintained that formal-ization reduces, but can never eliminate, the tacit coefficient of infer-ence (259). After examining the analyses of Gödel and Tarski, which formally demonstrate the limits of formalization, Polanyi concluded: "The act of assent proves once more to be logically akin to the act of discovery: they are both essentially unformalizable, intuitive mental decisions" (261).

Although there is a tacit, subsidiary dimension to formal systems, the whole point of the personal substructures is to allow us to concen-trate on "the assertion of an articulate form" (264). The formal ele-ments of thought are all in the domain of articulation, and at least in principle ought to reflect every step of an argument. Since the neces-sary tacit coefficients of thought cannot be completely articulated, "tac-it knowing cannot be critical. . . . Tacit acts are judged by other stan-dards and are to be regarded accordingly as *a-critical*" (264). Polanyi's post-critical philosophy is not anti-critical; it is an effort to hold both aspects of thought in union in a theory of knowledge, just as they are united, in fact, in any act of knowledge.

Polanyi did not claim that post-critical philosophy is a modern in-novation. He saw himself dwelling within the Augustinian tradition "that all knowledge was a gift of grace, for which we must strive under the guidance of antecedent belief: *nisi credideritis, non intelligitis*" (266). The hallmark of post-critical philosophy is the recognition that belief is "the source of all knowledge. . . . No intelligence, however crit-ical or original, can operate outside of such a fiduciary framework"

---

37. S. C. Kleene, *Introduction to Metamathematics* (New York: D. Van Nostrand, 1952), 62; *PK* 258–59.

(266). Polanyi explicitly denied that his understanding of fiduciary frameworks is self-evident (267). The recognition that knowledge depends on a personal act of commitment is itself a personal act of commitment: "If an ultimate logical level is to be attained and made explicit, this must be a declaration of my personal beliefs. . . . I must conquer my self-doubt, so as to retain a firm hold on this program of self-identification" (267). Although this act of acceptance relies on the tacit dimension, it is an act in which the knower is fully conscious of adopting a standpoint, and therefore is quite different from pre-critical, dogmatic traditions; it is *"a consciously a-critical statement"* or "the deliberate holding of unproven beliefs" (268). He intended his fiduciary program as an antidote for the ills brought on by critical philosophy. "Modern fanaticism is rooted in extreme skepticism which can only be strengthened, not shaken, by further doses of universal doubt" (298).

Polanyi's endorsement of the right to believe whatever one wants to believe is therefore restricted by his insistence that the commitments we make represent the best deployment of all of our intellectual powers, both tacit and articulate. Polanyi's post-critical philosophy does not absolve the knower from striving to meet the highest standards of intellectual achievement. It does declare that the guarantee of sound judgment is in a wisdom that cannot be reduced to a set of rules that could be applied by "a specifiably functioning mindless knower" (264).

In Chapter Eight, the foundation of Polanyi's fiduciary program is derived from the tacit coefficients of language, assertion, and inference. In Chapter Nine, "The Critique of Doubt," Polanyi argued that the alternative stance of objectivism is untenable: "I shall not feel reassured in advocating an attitude of a-critical belief, unless I have first fully met this warning by a critical examination of the principle of doubt" (272).

Polanyi located "the doctrine of doubt" in "the Liberal tradition of philosophic doubt" of Locke, Hume, Kant, Mill, Russell, and a host of nineteenth-century "writers who, with an eye on the natural sciences, declared with complete assurance that they accepted no belief whatever that had not passed the test of unrestricted doubt" (269–71). To Polanyi, it was clear that, despite the rhetoric of doubt, such thinkers operate as much by belief as anyone else, since "proof" is always derived from commitment to a conceptual framework whose "fundamental beliefs are irrefutable as well as unprovable" (271). Because proof follows upon the adoption of a conceptual framework, there is no such thing as antecedent proof that establishes the framework (287–88); we must accept "the brute fact that we can have no proof at all to warrant" the beliefs on which proofs depend (271). Even the apparently presuppositionless advice to doubt everything reflects an act of faith in an interpretative framework because "the admission of doubt proves here to be as clearly an act of belief as does the non-admission of doubt" (294). Polanyi is not embarrassed by the notion of accepting fundamental beliefs without proof, because he accepts this intellectual operation as a normal function of the mind. His philosophy is self-consistent on this score, because it openly acknowledges its own fiduciary roots. It is a difficulty only for those who advocate doubt as the "touchstone of truth" (271).

The undeniable success of reasonable doubt in setting science free from traditional patterns of thought has created a powerful cultural bias in favor of doubt as the hallmark of rationality. The desire to live by objective standards has created an intellectual passion, "a craving rooted in the very depths of our culture" (16):

It remains deeply ingrained in the modern mind—as I find even in my own mind—that though doubt may become nihilistic and imperil thereby all freedom of thought, to refrain from belief is always an act of intellectual probity as compared with the resolve to hold a belief which we could abandon if we decided to do so. To accept a belief by yielding to a voluntary impulse, be it my own or that of others placed in a position of authority, is felt to be a surrender of reason. You cannot teach the necessity for doing this without incurring—even in your own heart—the suspicion of obscurantism. At every step in quest of a post-critical philosophy the warning of a critical age will echo in our minds. (271)

Because the popularity of the principle of doubt derives in large measure from the history of science, Polanyi cast a critical eye on the reading of that history:

There exists, accordingly, no valid heuristic maxim in natural science which would recommend either belief or doubt as a path to discovery. . . . Besides, as there is no rule to tell us at the moment of deciding on the next step in research what is truly bold and what merely reckless, there is none either for distinguishing between doubt which will curb recklessness and thus qualify as true caution, and doubt which cripples boldness and will stand condemned as unimaginative dogmatism. Vesalius is praised as a hero of scientific skepticism for boldly rejecting the traditional doctrine that the dividing wall of the heart was pierced by invisible passages; but Harvey is acclaimed for the very opposite reason, namely for boldly assuming the presence of invisible passages connecting the arteries with the veins. (277)

There is a time to believe and a time to doubt. No formula can tell what is appropriate to particular circumstances. The final judgment is quintessentially personal.

A second paradigm of "reasonable doubt" is drawn from the common law tradition. Here again, Polanyi reads the evidence so as to show that it is belief, not doubt, that is required in the tradition: "The law which orders that a man be presumed innocent until he is found guilty, does not impose an open mind on the court, but tells it on the contrary what to believe at the start: namely that the man is innocent" (278–79). A third area where we are culturally conditioned to favor the principle of doubt concerns religious disputes. "The belief in the efficacy of doubt as a solvent of error was sustained primarily—from Hume to Russell—by skepticism about religious dogma and the dislike of religious bigotry. This has been the dominant passion of critical thought for centuries, in the course of which it has completely transformed man's outlook on the universe."[38] Because Polanyi saw doubt and belief as logically equivalent—doubt is based on the "acceptance of certain beliefs concerning the possibility of proof" (273)—the conflict over religious questions appears as a contest between one kind of faith and another. For Polanyi, "all truth is but the external pole of belief, and to destroy all belief would be to deny all truth" (286). Because adoption of doubt as a philosophic principle is just another fiduciary assumption, Polanyi refused to grant doubt higher standing in the field of reason than other forms of belief: "Since the skeptic does not consider it rational to doubt what he himself believes, the advocacy of 'rational doubt' is merely the skeptic's way of advocating his own beliefs" (297).

As he made clear in Chapter Eight, Polanyi aimed to restore a balance to the Western philosophical tradition by reaffirming the central role of belief in knowledge. He held that "a-critical choices . . . determine the whole being of our minds" (286). We are not wholly incapable of evaluating these a-critical orientations (164), but the principle of philosophical doubt is not the only path out of pre-critical dogma-

38. *PK* 279. Although Polanyi said this is the "main subject" in this chapter, I will defer consideration of his theology until Chapter IV of this study.

tism. One can become conscious of where one stands, spell out some of the implications in partially formalized systems, and decide to affirm, correct, or overthrow some of the a-critical choices with which one began to reason. Yet even in the act of clarifying and correcting initial intellectual positions—the act of making an intellectual commitment—one continues to rely tacitly on personal skills of self-assessment to do so.

Chapter Ten is devoted to the notion of "commitment." Polanyi wanted his readers to pick up the meanings of this term by observing how he used it in various contexts: "The word 'commitment' will be used here in a particular sense which will be established by its usage, the practice of which should also serve to accredit my belief in the existence and justification of commitment" (300). An important quality of commitment is that it is a *choice* made by the knower to take a position on all available data, both tacit and articulate: "A responsible decision is reached, then, in the knowledge that we have overruled by it conceivable alternatives, for reasons that are not fully specifiable" (312). The knower does not have complete control over the tacit dimension of knowledge, and cannot operate with language, assertions, and systems of inference without relying on a personal awareness of meaning, but does have a choice to make about the intellectual positions taken on the basis of such perception. The active-but-impassioned quality of commitment gives Polanyi grounds to "transcend the disjunction between subjective and objective":

On such grounds as these, I think we may distinguish between the personal in us, which actively enters into our commitments, and our subjective states, in which we merely endure our feelings. This distinction establishes the conception of the *personal,* which is neither subjective nor objective. In so far as the personal submits to requirements acknowledged by itself as independent of itself, it is not subjective; but in so far as it is an action guided by individual passions, it is not objective either. (300)

Polanyi's paradigm for commitment is "discovery" because it "is an act in which satisfaction, submission, and universal legislation are indissolubly combined" (301).

One of the standards by which intellectual commitments are judged by Polanyi is that the words in which the position is expressed must correspond to the act of adopting the position:

"I believe that in spite of the hazards involved, I am called upon to search for the truth and state my findings." This sentence, summarizing my fiduciary program, conveys an ultimate belief which I find myself holding. Its assertion must therefore prove consistent with its content by practicing what it authorizes. This is indeed true. For in uttering this sentence I both say that I must commit myself by thought and speech, and do so at the same time. Any enquiry into our ultimate beliefs can be consistent only if it presupposes its own conclusions. It must be intentionally circular. (299)

It is on the basis of his commitment to the concept of commitment that Polanyi portrayed Hume and Russell as victims of the "objectivist dilemma." They were unwilling to admit the necessary role of commitment within their theory of knowledge and at the same time they could not let go of the commitments that they cherish as matters of fact:

But if we regard the beliefs in question non-committally, as a mere state of mind, we cannot speak confidently, without self-contradiction, of the facts to which these beliefs refer. *For it is self-contradictory to secede from the commitment situation as regards the beliefs held within it, but to remain committed to the same beliefs in acknowledging their factual content as true.* It is nonsense to imply that we simultaneously both hold and do not hold the same belief (as implied in our confident reference to the facts) and our denial of the same belief (as implied to our reference to it as a mere state of our mind concerning these facts). (304)

Similarly, Polanyi criticized Kant and his disciples for attempting to evade the notion of commitment by an intellectual sleight-of-hand:

By regulative principles, in the general sense in which the term is employed here, I mean all manner of recommendations to act on a belief while denying, disguising, or otherwise minimizing the fact that we are holding this belief. . . . [Kant's] recommendation to entertain them *as if* they were true is thus seen to be based on the tacit assumption that they are in fact true. By conveying this assumption without asserting it, he avoids any formulation which would require to be upheld as his own personal judgment. (307)

The gambit of proposing commitments without acknowledging that one is doing so looked like hypocrisy to Polanyi.

When we make up our minds, there is a quality of irrevocability to the act of commitment. The personal framework which sets the standards for the knower must be strong enough to bear the weight of commitment, even though we are conscious that the framework or the commitment may need to be revised in the future if evidence develops that the position is untenable. If we attend to the hazardous nature of commitment, we become conscious that the decision is a free choice; if, instead, we attend to the way in which this judgment fits into the structure of our beliefs, the decision seems like a "necessary choice" on the part of the knower (315) that flows from the "utmost exercise of responsibility" (311). Making this kind of commitment does not imply exhaustive knowledge of the reality in question or possession of complete proof. When one undertakes a commitment, it is with the awareness that one is drawing together strands of thought in an integration that another might find unreasonable: "We may firmly believe what we might conceivably doubt; and may hold to be true what might conceivably be false" (312). Polanyi calls this "the decisive issue of the theory of knowledge," because acceptance of commitment as the vehicle of knowledge allows us to make up our minds: "We can wholeheartedly uphold our own convictions, even when we know that we might withhold our assent from them" (312).

Polanyi trusted that the mind *does* make contact with reality even though we do not see all the connections and cannot trace exactly how we know what we know: "We undertake the task of attaining the universal in spite of our admitted infirmity, which should render the task hopeless, because we hope to be visited by powers for which we cannot account in terms of our specifiable capabilities" (324). The objectivist demand to possess explicit awareness of how we know what we know leads to "voluntary mental stupor. Stupor alone can eliminate both belief and error" (314–15).

If those who doubt the validity of tacit knowledge were compelled to adhere to their own standards, they should fall silent: "Strict skepticism should deny itself the possibility of advocating its own doctrine, since its consistent practice would preclude the use of language, the meaning of which is subject to all the notorious pitfalls of inductive reasoning" (315). In his view, the speaking skeptic seems hypocritical; to the skeptic, Polanyi appears gullible. It may be that epithets of contempt or acts of commitment alone can cross the gulf that divides them. The presuppositions of Polanyi's world-view are tacit, personal acts that cannot be analyzed to the skeptic's satisfaction. The purpose of the next chapter is to show that the presuppositions of Newman's world-view place him firmly on Polanyi's side of the dispute about the reasonable conditions of commitment.

III. Comparison of the Epistemologies
Reasoning from Wholes to Wholes

T he purpose of this chapter is to explore the similarities and differences between the epistemologies of Newman and Polanyi. The
thesis of this chapter is that Newman recognized the reality that
Polanyi calls "tacit knowledge" and that Polanyi recognized the reality
that Newman calls "illative sense." While Newman treated the tacit dimension as a matter of fact, Polanyi attempted to develop a theory to
account for this fact.[1] What one man noted in passing, the other
stopped to explore at length. Where Newman focused on the *capacity*
of the mind to regulate itself by means of the illative sense, Polanyi
concentrated on the *product* of this potency in the accumulation of tacit knowledge.

If it is true that there is a substantial intersection between these two
maps of the mind, then the notion of the "illative sense" refers to all the
informal and incompletely specifiable operations of the mind by which
we gain, correct, and employ tacit knowledge. From this standpoint,
Polanyi's reflections appear as a "surprising confirmation" of Newman's view; one would not have predicted from Newman's correspondence with Froude that a scientist would adopt anything like the illative sense as the foundation of a theory of knowledge.

In keeping with the recognition that we know more than we can tell,
there are many more connections between Newman and Polanyi than
this chapter can make explicit. Notions seem to be very much like neurons: they send out connections in every direction and in three dimensions. This analysis of the interconnections between Newman's and

---

1. This claim is patterned on John T. Ford's insight into the nature of Newman's *Essay on
the Development of Doctrine*, which was developed in a course he taught at Catholic University in 1983, entitled "Newman the Theologian."

Polanyi's notions follows only a few of the contact points, and attempts to take them one by one, whereas living ideas, like neurons, constantly sum and re-sum the effects of many impulses wandering through the neural network.

The Tacit, Personal Dimension of the Illative Sense

Reading Newman from a Polanyian perspective, Newman adverted to two quite different kinds of tacit knowledge: that which is only accidentally tacit, because it may be converted into an assertion based on formal reasoning, and that which is irreducibly tacit. Simple assent, being *practically* unconscious, may upon inspection reveal itself as capable of formalization (*GA* 157). In the unreflective state of simple assent, we may remain unconscious of the view from which our assents stem: "Each of us looks at the world in his own way, and does not know that perhaps it is characteristically his own" (*GA* 291).

When confronted with this fact of human experience, it is natural to embark on a conversion project to transform simple assent into complex. "Our inquiries spontaneously fall into scientific sequence, and we think in logic, as we talk in prose, without aiming at doing so. However sure we are of the accuracy of our instinctive conclusions, we as instinctively put them into words, as far as we can" (*GA* 228). There are some notable successes in this effort, as when we move from a hunch to certitude through a long process of finding or creating connections to verify the insight: "It not infrequently happens, that while the keenness of the ratiocinative faculty enables a man to see the ultimate result of a complicated problem in a moment, it takes years for him to embrace it as a truth, and to recognize it as an item in the circle of his knowledge" (*GA* 143). Other fundamental presuppositions resist such illumination. There are some kinds of knowledge that refuse to be cast into formal operations. Just as there are no rules that can replace genius (*GA* 81), so there are no rules that can take the place of real apprehension:

This is the mode in which we ordinarily reason, dealing with things directly, and as they stand, one by one, in the concrete, with an intrinsic and personal power, not a conscious adoption of an artificial instrument or expedient; and it is especially exemplified both in uneducated men, and in men of genius,—in those who know nothing of intellectual aids and rules, and in those who care nothing for them,—in those who are either without or above mental discipline. (*GA* 261)

It is clear that Newman recognizes insight as a skillful performance that integrates many subsidiarily known clues:

[A peasant who can accurately predict the weather] does not proceed step by step, but he feels all at once and together the force of various combined phenomena, though he is not conscious of them. Again, there are physicians who excel in the *diagnosis* of complaints; though it does not follow from this, that they could defend their decision in a particular case against a brother physician who disputed it. They are guided by natural acuteness and varied experience; they have their own idiosyncratic modes of observing, generalizing, and concluding; when questioned, they can but rest on their own authority, or appeal to the future event. (GA 261–62)

Newman discussed similar skills exhibited by lawyers, detectives, other experts, and by all who "read" the character of those with whom they come in contact in their personal affairs.

Polanyi's thesis that we always know more than we can tell seems to map perfectly over Newman's observations on the skill of sound judgment:

What I have been saying of Ratiocination, may be said of Taste, and is confirmed by the obvious analogy between the two. Taste, skill, invention in the fine arts—and so, again, discretion or judgment in conduct—are exerted spontaneously, when once acquired, and could not give a clear account of themselves, or of their mode of proceeding. They do not go by rule, though to a certain point their exercise may be analyzed, and may take the shape of an art or method. (GA 266)

Both authors agree that the mental experiment of translating all assents (commitments) into articulation breaks down in a philosophically significant fashion. If we cannot give a complete account of how we know what we know, we must revise our notions of knowledge and certitude.

Confronted with the fact of tacit knowledge, we face a choice between devaluing our certitudes against the objectivist standard, or else adopting the view that all knowledge is personal knowledge. In the latter model, the illative sense is what holds us to our self-set standards of judgment:

Thus in concrete reasonings we are in great measure thrown back into that condition, from which logic proposed to rescue us. We judge for ourselves, by our own lights, and on our own principles; and our criterion of truth is not so much the manipulation of propositions, as the intellectual and moral character of the person maintaining them, and the ultimate silent effect of his argument or conclusions upon our minds. (GA 240)

Even though words are used to communicate the argument and conclusions, the act of *weighing* the value of the propositions employed is a tacit act. Like Polanyi, Newman saw that the tacit dimension of thought necessarily implies that knowledge remains personal:

Unless I am mistaken, they [certitudes known without formal reasoning] are to be found throughout the range of concrete matter, and that supra-logical judgment, which is the warrant for our certitude about them, is not mere common-sense, but the true healthy action of our ratiocinative powers, an action more subtle and more comprehensive than the mere appreciation of a syllogistic argument. It is often called the "judicium prudentis viri," a standard of certitude which holds good in all concrete matter, not only in those cases of practice and duty, in which we are more familiar with it, but in questions of truth and falsehood generally, or in what are called "speculative" questions, and that, not indeed to the exclusion, but as the supplement of logic. Thus a proof, except in abstract demonstration, has always in it, more or less, an element of the personal, because "prudence" is not a constituent part of our nature, but a personal endowment. (GA 251)

Personal knowledge is ultimately rooted in feelings—hence the appropriateness of the metaphor that this self-reflexive, subsidiary awareness is a sense. Newman did not directly use the (admittedly provocative and contemporary) term "feelings." Instead, he used various forms of the verb, "to feel," in order to distinguish the quality of illation from that of formal argument, as in this passage: "'Rational' is used in contradistinction to argumentative, and means 'resting on implicit reasons,' such as we feel, indeed, but which for some cause or other, because they are too subtle or too circuitous, we cannot put into words so as to satisfy logic" (GA 256). Newman noted that the "personal element" in proof depends on such intellectual passions:

And the language in common use, when concrete conclusions are in question, implies the presence of this personal element in the proof of them. We are considered to feel, rather than to see, its cogency; and we decide, not that the conclusion must be, but that it cannot be otherwise. We say, that we do not see our way to doubt it, that it is impossible to doubt, that we are bound to believe it, that we should be idiots, if we did not believe. (GA 251)

The passionate roots of our convictions cannot be brought wholly into the light of analysis. Even when we are able to dig them out for examination, they cease to function *as* roots so long as they are exhumed from the ground of personal, tacit knowledge that gave them life. When the mind is operating normally, without straining to catch itself in the act of understanding, it is the illative sense that draws upon the roots of knowledge implicitly, without seeing directly how it is that these lines of passion transmit what is necessary for thought and provide stable frameworks for growth.

Newman spoke of the illative sense as an instinctual operation of the mind. Though the term "instinct" may be fraught with difficulties, depending on the model used to interpret this term, Newman's primary concern was to call attention to the fact that the vital functions of our minds have a life of their own that we rely on tacitly: "Reasoning ordinarily shows as a simple act, not as a process, as if there were no medium interposed between antecedent and consequent, and the transition from one to the other were of the nature of an instinct,—that is, the process is altogether unconscious and implicit" (*GA* 260). Because it operates tacitly, the fact of "unconscious and implicit" reason may easily be overlooked in theories of consciousness and knowledge. The subsidiaries of thought work precisely as subsidiaries only when they remain buried beneath the level of focal awareness. Newman noted that in proposing to call such resources "instincts," he did not mean to imply that the correct employment of intelligence is strictly determined by our nature, as might be supposed from the model of instincts employed by naturalists to explain animal behavior:

It is difficult to avoid calling such clear presentiments by the name of instinct; and I think they may be so called, if by instinct be understood, not a natural sense, one and the same in all, and incapable of cultivation, but a perception of facts without assignable media of perceiving. There are those who can tell at once what is conducive or injurious to their welfare, who are their friends, who their enemies, what is to happen to them, and how they are to meet it. Presence of mind, fathoming of motives, talent for repartee, are instances of this gift. (*GA* 263)

Where Polanyi used his distinctions between subsidiary and focal awareness and between tacit and explicit knowledge to call attention to this phenomenon, Newman distinguished between instinct and argument. "It is assent, pure and simple, which is the motive cause of great achievements; it is a confidence, growing out of instincts rather than arguments, stayed upon a vivid apprehension, and animated by a transcendent logic, more concentrated in will and in deed for the very reason that it has not been subjected to any intellectual development."[2] Even though we can integrate new subsidiaries in order to change the pattern of our focal awareness, the new perceptual framework nevertheless exhibits the quality of being given spontaneously to us by an action of the intellect that is as natural as the operation of any of the bodily senses:

We proceed by a sort of instinctive perception, from premiss to conclusion. I call it instinctive, not as if the faculty were one and the same to all men in strength and quality (as we generally conceive of instinct), but because ordinarily, or at least often, it acts by a spontaneous impulse, as prompt and inevitable as the exercise of sense and memory. We perceive external objects, and we remember past events, without knowing how we do so; and in like manner we reason without effort and intention, or any necessary consciousness of the part which the mind takes in passing from antecedent to conclusion. (GA 209)

It seems clear that in his discussion of the illative sense as an instinctive operation, Newman affirmed as a matter of fact that we know more than we can tell about how the mind moves itself to conclusions.

Even though Newman was primarily interested in establishing the tacit dimension of the illative sense as a matter of fact, he provided two substantial sets of observations that help us understand in some measure why we cannot formalize the whole of what we know: first, he held that the things grasped by thought remain fundamentally incommunicable; second, that thought itself is fundamentally nonverbal.

Newman, like Polanyi, believed that apprehension of a reality supplies a *contact* with, but not complete *control* over, that reality. For Newman, a notion about a thing represents only one abstract aspect of a complex fact:

This is true of other inferences besides mathematical. They come to no definite conclusions about matters of fact, except as they are made effectual for their purpose by the living intelligence which uses them. . . . Universals are ever at war with each other; because what is called a universal is only a general; because what is only general does not lead to a necessary conclusion. . . . "Latet dolus in generalibus;" they are arbitrary and fallacious, if we take them for more than broad views and aspects of things, serving as our notes and indications for judging of the particular, but not absolutely touching and determining facts.

---

2. GA 177. Along similar lines, Newman distinguishes between tacit, "mental reasoning" and formal, "verbal reasoning" (GA 212).

> Let units come first, and (so-called) universals second; let universals minister to units, not units be sacrificed to universals. John, Richard, and Robert are individual things, independent, incommunicable. (*GA* 223)

The act of real apprehension does allow us to integrate these partial aspects into a tacit vision of the whole—to develop a *Gestalt* that transforms and unifies our perceptions—but the thing remains something other than our view of it:

> We cannot see through any one of the myriad beings which make up the universe, or give the full catalogue of its belongings. We are accustomed, indeed, and rightly, to speak of the Creator Himself as incomprehensible; and, indeed, He is so by an incommunicable attribute; but in a certain sense each of His creatures is incomprehensible to us also, in the sense that no one has a perfect understanding of them but He. We recognize and appropriate aspects of them, and logic is useful to us in registering these aspects and what they imply; but it does not give us to know even one individual being. (*GA* 226)

We know more than we can tell, then, because the things that we know are not purely rational constructs, but incommunicable realities.

Newman's second observation that helps to explain the tacit dimension shows that thought, like things, eludes articulation. This is a truth that may be confirmed by introspection, but cannot be proven to those who refuse to assent on "reasonings not demonstrative" (*GA* 150). Newman was convinced that it is wrong to assume that "whatever can be thought can be adequately expressed in words" (*GA* 212). Since we cannot inspect others' interior processes, we can only see for ourselves in our own patterns of consciousness that there are indeed "acts of the mind without the intervention of language" (*GA* 220). Newman was conscious of the paradox of attempting to speak about that which language cannot adequately express, and he concedes that examples which confirm his position "are difficult to find, from the very circumstance that the process from first to last is carried on as much without words as with them" (*GA* 254–55). Ironically, some of Newman's most beautiful and arresting rhetoric is devoted to the topic of the inadequacy of language to represent the free flow of thought:

> Science in all its departments has too much simplicity and exactness, from the nature of the case, to be the measure of fact. In its very perfection lies its incompetency to settle particulars and details. As to Logic, its chain of conclusions hangs loose at both ends; both the point from which proof should start, and the

points at which it should arrive, are beyond its reach; it comes short both of first principles and concrete issues. Even its most elaborate exhibitions fail to represent adequately the sum-total of considerations by which an individual mind is determined in its judgment of things; even its most careful combinations made to bear on a conclusion want that steadiness of aim which is necessary for hitting it. As I said when I began, thought is too keen and manifold, its sources are too remote and hidden, its path too personal, delicate, and circuitous, its subject-matter too various and intricate, to admit of the trammels of any language, of whatever subtlety and of whatever compass. (*GA* 227)

It is very appropriate that personal knowledge can only be recognized and accredited by "personal reasoning":

Anyhow, there is a considerable "surplusage," as Locke calls it, of belief over proof, when I determine that I individually must die. But what logic cannot do, my own living personal reasoning, my good sense, which is the healthy condition of such personal reasoning, but which cannot adequately express itself in words, does for me, and I am possessed with the most precise, absolute, masterful certitude of my dying some day or other. (*GA* 227)

It is the illative sense, employing the "more subtle and elastic language of thought" (*GA* 281–82), which tacitly governs such personal reasoning and which secures personal certitude about matters of fact:

Great as are the services of language in enabling us to extend the compass of our inferences, to test their validity, and to communicate them to others, still the mind itself is more versatile and vigorous than any of its works, of which language is one, and it is only under its penetrating and subtle action that the margin disappears, which I have described as intervening between verbal argumentation and conclusions in the concrete. It determines what science cannot determine, the limit of converging probabilities and the reasons sufficient for a proof. It is the ratiocinative mind itself, and no trick of art, however simple in its form and sure in operation, by which we are able to determine, and thereupon to be certain, that a moving body left to itself will never stop, and that no man can live without eating. (*GA* 28-82)

When the mind turns in on itself to discover the principles of its own operation, it paradoxically takes on the character of a thing, and resists analysis: "As we cannot see ourselves, so we cannot well see intellectual motives which are so intimately ours, and which spring up from the very constitution of our minds" (*GA* 264–65). It seems clear that one reason it is appropriate to say we know more than we can tell is that we can think more than we can say.

The essential incommunicability of things and thought creates a situation in which even our words themselves may mean more than we can tell. Articulation gives others clues to our own patterns of thought but does not completely duplicate the vision of reality that is the ultimate silent root of all speaking. Our task is "to avail ourselves of language, as far as it will go, but to aim mainly by means of it to stimulate, in those to whom we address ourselves, a mode of thinking and trains of thought similar to our own, leading them on by their own independent action, not by any syllogistic compulsion" (*GA* 245). Real apprehension, not notional apprehension, is the source of knowledge of reality. Since we may see more than we can say, there is room for development of understanding even while the language of a school is preserved:

Nor is it possible to limit the depth of meaning, which at length he [one who has real apprehension] will attach to words, which to the many are but definitions and ideas.

Here then again, as in the other instances, it seems clear, that methodical processes of inference, useful as they are, as far as they go, are only instruments of the mind, and need . . . that real ratiocination and present imagination which gives them a sense beyond their letter, and which, while acting through them, reaches to conclusions beyond and above them. Such a living *organon* is a personal gift, and not a mere method or calculus. (*GA* 250)

Like Polanyi, Newman recognized that the tacit dimension of the illative sense maintains priority over articulation even in the act of speaking.

Since formal operations cannot govern the full range of assent, we proceed by means of the method of verisimilitude[3] or the cumulation of probabilities: in the modern idiom, if it walks like truth and talks like truth, it probably is truth:

3. Newman used this phrase in his 1871 Preface to the third edition of *US*: "Again: there are two methods of reasoning—*à priori*, and *à posteriori*; from antecedent probabilities or verisimilitudes, and from evidence, of which the method of verisimilitude more naturally belongs to implicit reasoning, and the method of evidence to explicit" (xii). "Faith, viewed in contrast with Reason in these three senses, is implicit in its acts, adopts the method of verisimilitude, and starts from religious first principles. . . . The Author has lately pursued this whole subject at considerable length in his 'Essay in Aid of a Grammar of Assent'" (xvi–xvii). In the *Grammar*, Newman correlates the notions of "inference" and "verisimilitude": "Inference is the conditional acceptance of a proposition, Assent is the unconditional; the object of Assent is a truth, the object of Inference is the truth-like or a verisimilitude. The problem which I have undertaken is that of ascertaining how it comes to pass that a conditional act leads to an unconditional" (209).

It is plain that formal logical sequence is not in fact the method by which we are enabled to become certain of what is concrete; and it is equally plain, from what has been already suggested, what the real and necessary method is. It is the cumulation of probabilities, independent of each other, arising out of the nature and circumstances of the particular case which is under review; probabilities too fine to avail separately, too subtle and circuitous to be convertible into syllogisms, too numerous and various for such conversion, even were they convertible. (GA 230)

Although Newman called this a "method," it is clear that there is very little that is methodical about it, since there are no rules about how many converging probabilities one must discover in order to make the decision that what *seems* like truth *is* truth. When a pioneer of thought is breaking away from the mainstream of opinion, there may be many more lines pointing away from the new position than point toward it. Polanyi's theory of how subsidiaries tacitly bear upon the focus of attention to form *Gestalten* parallels Newman's description of the informal reasoning that leads to certitude. In such acts of personal judgment, the mind is "swayed and determined by a body of proof, which it recognizes only as a body, and not in its constituent parts" (GA 232). When the parts of the proof are brought out of the tacit dimension into focus, they lose the character of subsidiaries and cease to have the power of bearing on the conclusion—the seamless whole falls into pieces and is incapable of being reassembled, because the parts that constitute the whole seem so very different under analysis than they do when functioning as subsidiaries to real apprehension:

If it is difficult to explain how a man knows that he shall die, it is not more difficult for him to satisfy himself how he knows that he was born. His knowledge about himself does not rest on memory, nor on distinct testimony, nor on circumstantial evidence. Can he bring into one focus of proof the reasons which make him so sure? (GA 239)

When a subsidiary is put at the focus of attention, it is normally found to be wanting. It no longer draws strength from the merger with other suggestive patterns of thought, and it is clear under the light of analysis that it does not arrive by itself at the conclusion toward which it tends.

Newman's favorite visual image for the cumulation of probabilities is drawn from Newton's illustration of what he means by a "limit":

I consider, then, that the principle of concrete reasoning is parallel to the method of proof which is the foundation of modern mathematical science, as contained in the celebrated lemma with which Newton opens his "Principia." We know that a regular polygon, inscribed in a circle, its sides being continually diminished, tends to become that circle, as its limit; but it vanishes before it has coincided with the circle, so that its tendency to be the circle, though ever nearer fulfillment, never in fact gets beyond a tendency. (GA 253)

In the same way, converging lines of thought approach the limit of becoming proofs without ever ceasing to be mere probabilities when examined in isolation from the rest of the picture, just as any segment of Newton's polygon will appear as a straight rather than a curved line under sufficient magnification. Newman continued:

In like manner, the conclusion in a real or concrete question is foreseen and predicted rather than actually attained; foreseen in the number and direction of accumulated premises, which all converge to it, and as the result of their combination, approach it more nearly than any assignable difference, yet do not touch it logically (though only not touching it,) on account of the nature of its subject-matter, and the delicate and implicit character of at least part of the reasonings on which it depends. It is by the strength, variety, or multiplicity of premises, which are only probable, not by invincible syllogisms,—by objections overcome, by adverse theories neutralized, by difficulties gradually clearing up, by exceptions proving the rule, by unlooked-for correlations found with received truths, by suspense and delay in the process issuing in triumphant reactions,—by all these ways, and many others, it is that the practiced and experienced mind is able to make a sure divination that a conclusion is inevitable, of which his lines of reasoning do not actually put him in possession. (GA 253–54)

According to the rules of strict logic, it is clear that the two figures are not identical and never can be, given the original definitions of a circle and a regular polygon. From the standpoint of informal reasoning, one may decide that some differences make no difference for all practical purposes. A decision is required in order to cross the gap between what logic supplies and inference suggests, but it is a decision perfectly proportioned to the capacity of the mind to judge that the risks involved are negligible. To use the metaphor of an asymptote, one might say that the converging lines of belief never completely join the axis of reason, but the further one follows the convergence, the smaller the step is from the series of uncertainties to certitude.

For Newman, it is the illative sense that determines whether assent should be granted on the basis of an accumulation of probabilities. Newman characterizes this process as "reasoning from wholes to wholes," all of which are apprehended tacitly and personally:

I say, then, that our most natural mode of reasoning is, not from propositions to propositions, but from things to things, from concrete to concrete, from wholes to wholes. Whether the consequents, at which we arrive from the antecedents with which we start, lead us to assent or only towards assent, those antecedents commonly are not recognized by us as subjects for analysis; nay, often are only indirectly recognized as antecedents at all. Not only is the inference with its process ignored, but the antecedent also. To the mind itself the reasoning is a simple divination or prediction; as it literally is in the instance of enthusiasts, who mistake their own thoughts for inspirations. (GA 260–61)

In formal logic, the rule is that reasoning runs from one clear and distinct idea to another, forming a narrow chain of inference; in informal reasoning, the flow of thought is from one bundle of ideas to another. Each whole that is brought to bear upon another whole may reveal itself under analysis to be the fruit of an illation, so that the project of untangling the lines of thought becomes hopelessly snarled with interconnections. The mind tires of the effort, but every exploration of the phenomenon suggests that the same kind of difficulty of analyzing an integration will be found in every subsequent instance. "The mind is like a double mirror, in which reflections of self within self multiply themselves till they are undistinguishable, and the first reflection contains all the rest" (GA 162). There is no point at which we may say that, at last, we have gotten clear of the obligation to rely on tacit integrations of apprehension. Personal knowledge—"personal certitude" in Newman's terms—depends on the illative sense:

In the extract which I make from it [an argument about literary authorship], we may observe the same steady march of a proof towards a conclusion, which is (as it were) out of sight;—a reckoning, or a reasonable judgment, that the conclusion really is proved, and a personal certitude upon that judgment, joined with a confession that a logical argument could not well be made out for it, and that the various details in which the proof consisted were in no small measure implicit and impalpable. (GA 259)

The act of seeing how "various details" coalesce into good grounds for certitude is very different from spelling out, one by one, how those details support the conclusion. The fact that we cannot say all that we see does not eradicate the fact that we see; the fact that we cannot explain fully how we know does not mean that we do not know. Like Polanyi, Newman holds that we are justified in believing what we cannot prove or fully articulate.

The Illative Dimension of Tacit Knowledge

Just as Newman took note of the tacit and personal dimension of knowledge while pursuing the theme of the illative sense, so Polanyi adverted to the power of illation while concentrating on tacit knowledge. Where the notion of the illative sense highlights the capacity of personal judgment, the notion of tacit knowledge emphasizes the product of using our judgment in a responsible fashion. Newman's metaphor that the power of the mind to come to judgment is a "sense" gives the impression of a singular reality, whereas Polanyi's remarks alternate between singular and plural expressions. The shifts from singular to plural images correspond to the elusive nature of subsidiary and focal awareness, in which many different intellectual inputs (memory, current awareness, hunches, partial proofs, conditional reasoning, testimony, suggestive analogies, etc.) are integrated. An illation often has the quality of an undivided whole even though many component parts subtend the integration. We may ultimately say that tacit knowledge depends on the illative sense.

In assessing how people make contact with external reality, Polanyi implies that "the intuition of rationality in nature [has] to be acknowledged as a justifiable and indeed essential part of scientific theory" (*PK* 15–16). Such "powers for recognizing rationality in nature" (*PK* 13) give birth to the language of science (*PK* 114–15). After an intuitive formation of a vocabulary, there next comes the deployment of rules of operation, which are also managed by means of spontaneous judgment:

Thus both the first active steps undertaken to solve a problem and the final garnering of the solution rely effectively on computations and other symbolic operations, while the more informal act by which the logical gap is crossed lies between these two formal procedures. However, the intuitive powers of the investigator are always dominant and decisive. (*PK* 130)

Where Polanyi speaks of "intuitive powers," Newman would speak of the illative sense as "always dominant and decisive" in the operations of the mind. Just as Newman saw formal reason "hanging loose at both ends," needing to be grasped by the informal reasoning of the illative sense in order to play its proper role in the life of the mind, so Polanyi described the relationship between tacit and formal reason:

Moreover, a symbolic formalism is itself but an embodiment of our antecedent un-formalized powers—an instrument skillfully contrived by our inarticulate selves for the purpose of relying on it as our external guide. The interpretation of primitive terms and axioms is therefore predominantly inarticulate, and so is the process of their expansion and re-interpretation which underlies the progress of mathematics. The alternation between the intuitive and the formal depends on tacit affirmations, both at the beginning and at the end of each chain of formal reasoning.[4]

As was indicated in the first chapter of this essay, the intuitive regulation of "antecedent unformalized powers" of reason is one of the central features of the illative sense.

Polanyi knew well that the notion of intuition is a philosophical can of worms: "I have watched many a university audience listening to my account of intuitive discoveries silently, with sullen distaste" (*PK* 149). The language of "intellectual passions" that he develops to describe the orientating powers of the mind avoids some of the distasteful connotations of intuition; the same is true of Polanyi's reflections on "a sense of intellectual beauty" which gives rise to "an emotional response which can never be dispassionately defined" (*PK* 135). Whether we analyze them from the standpoint of intuition or a taste for beauty, it is the intellectual passions which enable us to "feel our way to success" (*PK* 62):

The unspecifiability of the process by which we thus feel our way forward accounts for the possession by humanity of an immense mental domain, not only of knowledge but of manners, of laws, and of the many different arts which man knows how to use, comply with, enjoy or live by, without specifiably knowing their contents. Each single step in acquiring this domain was due to an effort which went beyond the hitherto assured capacity of some person making it, and by his subsequent realization and maintenance of his success. It relied on an act of groping which originally passed the understanding of its agent and of which he has ever since remained only subsidiarily aware, as part of a complex achievement. (*PK* 62–63)

All of Polanyi's reflections on science as a skillful performance were modelled on this kind of unfolding of the intellectual passions—what Newman might have called the education of the illative sense.

When Polanyi addressed the issue of how we know what we know, he again had no single, pithy term to concentrate attention on the illative dimension of the mind. In his view, knowledge depends on tacit

---

4. *PK* 131. Cf. 258 for another remark on the intuitive foundation of mathematics.

acts of self-appraisal, which in turn are based on "a set of personal criteria of our own which cannot be formally defined" (*PK* 70–71). One of Polanyi's fundamental, indemonstrable beliefs is that "we should accredit in ourselves the capacity for appraising our own articulation" (*PK* 91). In Newman's terms, the capacity for self-appraisal is the illative sense. Polanyi observed that we must rely on this "competent mental efforts overruling arbitrariness" whenever we want to sum up our intellectual position (*PK* 314). Assessing for ourselves when our mental efforts are sufficient to warrant assent is precisely the task of the illative sense.

For Newman, the illative sense depends on views informally adopted, but it also is responsible for affirming or rejecting those fundamental presuppositions of thought. Polanyi similarly held that our intellectual passions are dependent on our "vision of reality," the fundamental interpretative framework that grounds all other conceptual standpoints. Both Newman and Polanyi agreed that the thought which takes a view cannot be adequately expressed in words, even though that thought underlies all of our speaking. For Newman, one's view of things is what establishes the antecedent probability of what will be found to be true. For Polanyi, the patterns (Gestalten) embedded in our interpretative frameworks provide the scale of plausibility that we use to make judgments.

Nothing is more important to the mind than the first principles or fundamental assumptions about reality. All our judgments about what is and what is not flow from our basic convictions. Just as Newman held that the presuppositions of thought are adopted informally by means of the illative sense, so Polanyi portrayed the "self-modifying mental act" as "ultimately an informal act: a transformation of the framework on which we rely in the process of formal reasoning" (*PK* 189). Our critical standards are built upon the foundation of "a-critical choices . . . which determine the whole being of our minds" (*PK* 286), that is, on the foundation of the illative sense. As Newman said, "It is to the living mind that we must look for the means of using correctly principles of whatever kind, facts or doctrines, experiences or testimonies, true or probable, and of discerning what conclusion from these is necessary, suitable, or expedient, when they are taken for granted."[5]

---

5. *GA* 282. The discussion of how the illative sense functions in the selection of first principles continues to the next page as well.

Like Newman, Polanyi recognized that there is a specific emotional quality to the act of assent. For example, "it is by satisfying his intellectual passions that mathematics fascinates the mathematician and compels him to pursue it in his thoughts and give it his assent" (*PK* 188). Polanyi felt that the sense of beauty was intimately connected with the quest for truth, since "no scientific theory is beautiful if it is false and no invention is truly ingenious if it is impracticable" (*PK* 195). For Newman, the illative sense is that which upholds our personal standards of excellence. Polanyi attributed the same function to *"the tacit faculty* which accounts in the last resort for all the increase in knowledge achieved by articulation, and the nature of the urge to exercise it" (*PK* 100; italics mine). In Newman's epistemology, the tacit faculty underlying all our judgments is the illative sense.

Both Newman and Polanyi judged that speech depends on a wordless center of awareness. The illative sense may be understood as what Polanyi called "tacit coefficient of speech" supplied by our "powers of inarticulate judgment" (*PK* 86–87). Newman's notion of the illative sense implies the integration of all of the "powers of inarticulate judgment" that are at our disposal. Polanyi also calls the cumulation of these various intellectual inputs a "sense of fitness for judging that his words express the reality he seeks to express" (*PK* 113). Newman saw the illative sense as the deepest ground of all other rational judgments. Similarly, Polanyi affirmed the need to rely on one's own sense of of fitness: "To accept the indeterminacy of knowledge requires, on the contrary, that we accredit a person entitled to shape his knowing according to his own judgment, unspecifiably" (*PK* 264). Just as Newman saw the illative sense as the source of sound judgment about how and when we may assent, so Polanyi placed "personal judgment"[6] at the heart of his epistemology:

While the logic of assent merely showed that assent is an a-critical act, 'commitment' was introduced from the start as a framework in which assent can be re-

---

6. "Personal judgment" is an expression which occurs frequently in *PK*: 18–19, 20, 31, 79–80, 105–6, 119, 259, 307, 312, 367. For the most part, one may substitute Newman's phrase "the illative sense" in these passages without altering Polanyi's meaning, e.g.: "I have given evidence before of the emotional upheaval which accompanies the mental reorganization necessary for crossing the logical gap that separates a problem from its solution. I have pointed out that the depth of this upheaval corresponds to the force of personal judgment [the illative sense] required to supplement the inadequate clues on which a decision is being based" (*PK* 367).

sponsible, as distinct from merely egocentric or random. The center of tacit assent was elevated to the seat of responsible judgment. It was granted thereby the faculty of exercising discretion, subject to the obligations accepted and fulfilled by itself with universal intent. A responsible decision is reached, then, in the knowledge that we have overruled by it conceivable alternatives, for reasons that are not fully specifiable. (*PK* 312)

If the integration of these two positions is correct, one may say that "the center of tacit assent" is the illative sense.

In the following summary of Polanyi's reflections on the knowledge of thought and of things, his assertion of a personal component of thought has the same character as Newman's notion of an illative sense:

To this extent, then, whether thought operates indwellingly within a universe of its own creation, or interprets and controls nature as given to it from outside, the same paradoxical structure prevails through the articulate systems so far surveyed. There is present a personal component, inarticulate and passionate, which declares our standards of values, drives us to fulfil them and judges our performance by these self-set standards. (*PK* 195)

Newman's understanding of the illative sense shares all of the characteristics listed by Polanyi in the passage just quoted.

personal component	*illative sense*
is inarticulate	is nonverbal (217) and supralogical (251)
is passionate	is an instinct or inspiration (280)
declares standards of values	chooses its own authority (279)
drives us to fulfill them	binds us to believe (251)
judges by self-set standards	is a rule to itself (283)

The two conceptual maps, though not identical, cover the same intellectual territory in similar fashion.

Newman's method of verisimilitude may not appear very methodical in the modern world, since it proceeds by informal rather than formal reasoning. It is on the basis of the illative sense that one sums up all of the lines of thought at one's disposal and decides that the accumulated evidence is close enough to the truth to be taken as true. In Polanyi's view, the ability to integrate disparate subsidiaries is one of the most important skills required by science:

The perturbations of the planetary motions that were observed during 60 years preceding the discovery of Neptune, and which could not be explained by the mutual interaction of the planets, were rightly set aside at the time as anomalies by most astronomers, in the hope that something might eventually turn up to account for them without impairing—or at least not essentially impairing—Newtonian gravitation. Speaking more generally, we may say that there are always some conceivable scruples which scientists customarily set aside in the process of verifying an exact theory. Such acts of personal judgment form an essential part of science. (PK 20)

As Newman said, one may assent on grounds that are not demonstrative. The scientist exercises personal judgment in deciding that it is right to ignore certain strands of evidence in order to pull others together: "The wise neglect of such evidence prevents scientific laboratories from being plunged forever into a turmoil of incoherent and futile efforts to verify false allegations" (PK 138). Even mathematicians, unencumbered by the requirement that their speculations have any bearing on physical reality at all, must rely on the skill of deciding for themselves what evidence they will accept as persuasive. Because Gödel showed that the ambition to prove everything in mathematics is fruitless, even this most rigorous form of reason now appears as a fiduciary framework:

The inarticulate coefficient by which we understand and assent to mathematics is an active principle of this kind; it is a passion for intellectual beauty. It is on account of its intellectual beauty, which his own passion proclaims as revealing a universal truth, that the mathematician feels compelled to accept mathematics as true, even though he is today deprived of the belief in its logical necessity and doomed to admit forever the conceivable possibility that its whole fabric may suddenly collapse by revealing a decisive self-contradiction. And it is the same urge to see sense and make sense that supports his tacit bridging of the logical gaps internal to every formal proof. (PK 189)

The Cartesian model of strict proof descending from self-evident principles does not work for science in general or mathematics in particular: "The alternative to this, which I am seeking to establish here is to restore to us once more the power for the deliberate holding of unproven beliefs" (PK 268). The illative sense is just such a power to believe what we cannot prove.

Other Intersections

The aim of this study is to show the convergence of Newman and Polanyi's fundamental insights into the tacit and personal dimension of human judgment rather than to develop a complete harmonization of their terminology. Some of the similarities between the two positions are less surprising than others, given that both authors wrote in English in England. A complete catalogue of all points of contact would be more exhausting than illuminating. If the first two sections of this chapter have not persuaded the reader that the two positions share the same fundamental insights, then it is doubtful that inspection of subsidiary similarities in this section will make the case. If, however, the reader grants the thesis that the two positions are remarkably alike, one may acknowledge that Newman is a post-critical philosopher, even though his ideas are not identical in all respects to Polanyi's.

There are three further areas of relatively common ground that will be briefly considered in this section: (1) the conscience of the intellect; (2) fundamental epistemic options; (3) illative integration of subsidiaries.

1. The Conscience of the Intellect

At first glance, Newman and Polanyi appear to hold quite different views of conscience. In his *Letter to the Duke of Norfolk*, Newman took a theological standpoint and spoke of conscience as the "voice of God" and not "a creation of man" (*DN* 128). While upholding this view "from above" that conscience is God's work within human nature, Newman nevertheless clearly saw how conscience appears "from below" as a human act. Notice in his subsequent discussion how strong his affirmation is of conscience as a "constituent element of the mind" and "a law of the mind":

When Anglicans, Wesleyans, the various Presbyterian sects in Scotland, and other denominations among us, speak of conscience, they mean what we mean, the voice of God in the nature and heart of man, as distinct from the voice of Revelation. They speak of a principle planted within us, before we have had any training, though such training and experience is necessary for its strength, growth, and due formation. They consider it a constituent element of the mind, as our perception of other ideas may be, as our powers of reasoning, as our sense of order and the beautiful, and our other intellectual endowments. They consider it, as Catholics consider it, to be the internal witness of both the existence and the law of God. . . . They would not allow, any more than we do, that it could be resolved into any combination of principles in our nature, more elementary than itself; nay, though it may be called, and is, a law of the mind, they would not grant that it was nothing more; I mean, that it was not a dictate, nor conveyed the notion of responsibility, of duty, of a threat and a promise, with a vividness which discriminated it from all other constituents of our nature.[7]

Newman's complaint is against reductionist accounts of conscience, not against the observation of the role that it may play in a philosophical account of the operations of the mind.

"Conscience," as such, is not a term that Polanyi uses frequently in *Personal Knowledge;* the word does not appear in the index of that book. The correlative terms in his framework would be values, ideals, intellectual passions, and self-set standards. He does use the word in one very illuminating context:

It is the act of commitment in its full structure that saves personal knowledge from being merely subjective. Intellectual commitment is a responsible decision, in submission to the compelling claims of what in good conscience I conceive to be true. It is an act of hope, striving to fulfill an obligation within a personal situation for which I am not responsible and which therefore determines my calling. This hope and this obligation are expressed in the universal intent of personal knowledge. (*PK* 65)

In no case does Polanyi claim that conscience is not an indicator of a Divine Judge; that issue, for the most part, simply falls outside the scope of Polanyi's focus in this book. In the *University Sermons,* Newman gave another definition of conscience which fits very well with Polanyi's nontheological approach to the concept:

Conscience is the essential principle and sanction of Religion in the mind. Conscience implies a relation between the soul and something exterior, and that, moreover, superior to itself; a relation to an excellence which it does not possess, and to a tribunal over which it has no power. And since the more closely this inward monitor is respected and followed, the clearer, the more exalted, and the more varied its dictates become, and the standard of excellence is ever outstripping, while it guides, our obedience, a moral conviction is thus at length obtained of the unapproachable nature as well as the supreme authority of that, whatever it is, which is the object of the mind's contemplation. (*US* 18–19)

7. *DN* 128. We will see in Chapter IV how Newman uses his presumption about the nature of conscience to back an affirmation of the existence of God.

There seems to be ample room within this definition for Polanyi's description of the "act of hope" in which we make a personal commitment to the ideal of truth and strive to remain open to (in Newman's words) "whatever it is . . . which is the object of the mind's contemplation." Although Polanyi's highest standards are "self-set," in the sense of being personally endorsed, they clearly have the hallmarks of placing us before "something exterior"—Polanyi's notion of "reality," which functions like the tribunal in the passage above, to which the mind submits and over which the mind ultimately has no power.

It seems that "conscience" appears most frequently in Polanyi's earlier collections of essays, *Science, Faith and Society* (1946)[8] and *The Logic of Liberty* (1951).[9] Polanyi notes the important role of conscience in the development of a discovery:

He breaks the law as it is, in the name of the law as he believes it ought to be. He has an intensely personal vision of something which in his view henceforth everyone must recognize. . . . Therefore, his most personal acts of intuition and conscience link him firmly to the universal system and the canons of science. (*LL* 40)

Polanyi clearly sees conscience as constitutive of the scientific endeavor: "To guess the solution to a problem offered by nature—as demanded of the scientist—requires the exercise of intuitive faculties controlled by an intellectual conscience" (*LL* 43–44). *The Logic of Liberty* concludes, "It remains in the last resort for each of us in his own conscience to balance the perils of complacency against those of recklessness" (*LL* 200). In the 1963 introduction to *Science, Faith and Society*, Polanyi explicitly connects his reflections on conscience with the notion of commitment developed in *Personal Knowledge*:

From beginning to end he himself is the ultimate judge in deciding on each consecutive step of his enquiry. He has to arbitrate all the time between his own passionate intuition and his own critical restraint of it. The reach of these ultimate decisions is wide: the great scientific controversies show the range of basic questions which may remain in doubt after all sides of an issue have been examined. The scientist must decide such issues, left open by opposing arguments, in the light of his own scientific conscience. My book *Personal Knowledge*

8. An informal survey of *SFS* shows references to "conscience" on pages 15, 39, 40, 41–42, 45–46, 56–57, 66–67, 80–84.
9. An informal survey of *LL* shows references to "conscience" on pages 4, 40, 43–44, 200.

(1958) attempts to buttress this final commitment against the charge of subjectivity. (*SFS* 15)

The special character of personal knowledge—the fusion of the objective and subjective poles of knowledge—is therefore a matter of good conscience. In this collection, Polanyi speaks of "scientific conscience" as the key to making contact with reality:

> We see higher interests conflicting with lower interests. That must involve questions of conviction and of faithfulness to an ideal; it makes the scientist's judgment a matter of conscience. . . .
>
> Scientific conscience cannot be satisfied by the fulfillment of any rules, since all rules are subject to its own interpretation. . . .
>
> The scientist's task is not to observe any allegedly correct procedure but to get the right results. He has to establish contact, by whatever means, with the hidden reality of which he is predicating. His conscience must therefore give its ultimate assent always from a sense of having established that contact. And he will accept therefore the duty of committing himself on the strength of evidence which can, admittedly, never be complete; and trust that such a gamble, when based on the dictates of his scientific conscience, is in fact his competent function and his proper chance of making his contribution to science. (*SFS* 39–40)

It seems fair to say that for Polanyi, scientific certitude is a special form of moral certitude; without the guidance of the intellectual, scientific conscience, science could not stay in touch with a universe that defies complete formalization. He calls this "a moral element in the foundations of science" (*SFS* 41).

The next essay in the collection is entitled "Authority and Conscience." It further develops the theme that scientific knowing depends upon the personal integrity of the investigator:

> We have seen that the propositions embodied in natural science are not derived by any definite rule from the data of experience. They are first arrived at by a form of guessing based on premises which are by no means inescapable and cannot even be clearly defined; after which they are verified by a process of observational hardening which always leaves play to the scientist's *personal judgment*. In every judgment of scientific validity there thus remains implied the supposition that we accept the premises of science and that the scientist's conscience can be relied upon. (*SFS* 41; italics mine)

In this passage, the phrase "personal judgment" functions as an exact parallel to Newman's notion of the illative sense. It is always the reflective self-awareness of the mind that tells us (tacitly and informally) when it is appropriate to close questions and when to leave them open for further exploration.

Newman seemed reluctant to make a similar identification between illative sense and conscience. In the *Letter to the Duke of Norfolk,* Newman seemed to reject the identification explicitly:

> 1. I am using the word "conscience" in the high sense in which I have already explained it; not as a fancy or an opinion, but as a dutiful obedience to what claims to be a divine voice, speaking within us.
>
> 2. . . . conscience is not a judgment upon any speculative truth, any abstract doctrine, but bears immediately on conduct, on something to be done or not done. "Conscience," says St. Thomas, "is the practical judgment or dictate of reason, by which we judge what *hic et nunc* is to be done as being good, or to be avoided as evil." (*DN* 134)

In the section of the *Grammar* entitled "The Nature of the Illative Sense," Newman used Aristotle's idea of *phronesis* as the model of sound personal judgment (*GA* 276–81). Even though Newman did not go as far as Polanyi in speaking of an intellectual or scientific "conscience," there can be no question that he saw the same need for conscientious adherence to principles that cannot be fully articulated or formalized:

> Fourthly, in no class of concrete reasonings, whether in experimental science, historical research, or theology, is there any ultimate test of truth and error in our inferences besides the trustworthiness of the Illative Sense that gives them its sanction; just as there is no sufficient test of poetical excellence, heroic action, or gentleman-like conduct, other than the particular mental sense, be it genius, taste, sense of propriety, or the moral sense, to which those subject-matters are severally committed. Our duty in each of these is to strengthen and perfect the special faculty which is its living rule, and in every case as it comes to do our best. And such also is our duty and our necessity, as regards the Illative Sense. (*GA* 281)

If the *action* of judgment is the good of the intellect, and if the scope of conscience governs all human actions—if assent itself is an action that requires the engagement of the will—then it seems reasonable to call the Illative Sense the conscience of the intellect. Forming a judgment is an action which falls under Newman's definition of "something to be done or not done," even though the scope of the action may be confined to the domain of the mind:

Assent is an act of the mind, congenial to its nature; and it, as other acts, may be made both when it ought to be made, and when it ought not. It is a free act, a personal act for which the doer is responsible, and the actual mistakes in making it, be they ever so numerous or serious, have no force whatever to prohibit the act itself. (*GA* 189)

This formula for knowing—"a free act, a personal act for which the doer is responsible"—sounds very much like something Polanyi might have written in *Personal Knowledge*.

Later in the *Grammar*, Newman somewhat reluctantly took the position that all certitude is moral certitude:

This certitude and this evidence are often called moral; a word which I avoid, as having a very vague meaning; but using it here for once, I observe that moral evidence and moral certitude are all that we can attain, not only in the case of ethical and spiritual subjects, such as religion, but of terrestrial and cosmical questions also. (*GA* 252)

It is very important to bear in mind that for both Newman and Polanyi—and contrary to the implications of "moral certitude" in ordinary language—there is no higher form of certitude than this. In the *Idea of a University*, Newman had shown how well he was aware of the vulnerability of "moral certitude" when the object in question is "ethical and spiritual subjects" rather than "terrestrial and cosmical questions":

The physical nature lies before us, patent to the sight, ready to the touch, appealing to the senses in so unequivocal a way that the science which is founded upon it is as real to us as the fact of our personal existence. But the phenomena, which are the basis of morals and Religion, have nothing of this luminous evidence. Instead of being obtruded upon our notice, so that we cannot possibly overlook them, they are the dictates either of Conscience or of Faith. They are faint shadows and tracings, certain indeed, but delicate, fragile, and almost evanescent, which the mind recognizes at one time, not at another,—discerns when it is calm, loses when it is in agitation. . . . How easily can we be talked out of our clearest views of duty! how does this or that moral precept crumble into nothing when we rudely handle it! how does the fear of sin pass off from us, as quickly as the glow of modesty dies away from the countenance! and then we say, "It is all superstition." (*Idea* 387)

We may have a deep longing for an impersonal knowledge that would not depend upon the vagaries of human conscience, but that kind of

beatific vision is not granted us in this lifetime. When we follow Newman's program of "going by facts," we recognize that all knowing is the
fruit of skillful actions taken under the guidance of conscience. Newman recognized that science and the Christian faith both depend upon
the quality of our character:

> To be dispassionate and cautious, to be fair in discussion, to give each phenom-
> enon which nature successively presents its due weight, candidly to admit those
> which militate against our own theory, to be willing to be ignorant for a time, to
> submit to difficulties, and patiently and meekly proceed, waiting for farther light,
> is a temper (whether difficult or not at this day) little known to the heathen
> world; yet it is the only temper in which we can hope to become interpreters of
> nature, and it is the very temper which Christianity sets forth as the perfection of
> our moral character. (US 9–10)

From Polanyi's point of view, it is our intellectual passions that move us
to maintain the qualities of character required by serious investigation.

There is clearly a vital circle between the operations of the intellect
and those of the conscience. If we search the mind, we find the will at
work; search the will, we find the mind at work. Without the intellectual passions and the conscience of the intellect, the mind loses touch
with reality; without the light of the intellect, the will cannot operate.
Affirming the circumincession of intelligence and conscience may seem
to pose a problem of infinite regress, but, like Zeno's paradoxes, the difficulty is only due to abstraction from a living process (or a collection of
living processes) in which the co-dependence of these two functions is
a given.

In the last analysis, the phrase "illative sense" refers to the impressions produced on consciousness by the actions of the mind evaluating
itself. It is not a "thing," not a separate "faculty," but an abstraction
calling attention to a quality of thought thinking about itself. It is the
aspect of mental operations which determines when we must make or
refuse to make the act of assent. Insofar as it evaluates proposed actions, it seems to be a special dimension of conscience; but insofar as it
settles questions of truth, it seems to be a function of intellect.

2. Fundamental Epistemic Options

Conscience may be recognized as the voice of God from the theological standpoint, but being conscientious in seeking, identifying and
obeying the dictates of conscience is a human skill which requires edu-

cation and personal development. The human experience of the development of conscience, particularly the conscience of the intellect, suggests that everything hinges on the fundamental options made by the person. These presumptions establish the grounds of what one personally understands to be the good, the true, and the beautiful. The adoption of first principles is a tacit, a-critical, illative, and inescapably personal action that makes all the difference in our vision of reality and in all of our subsequent commitments. Polanyi would certainly agree with Newman's description of the vital circle created by the act of presumption:

I am what I am, or I am nothing. I cannot think, reflect, or judge about my being, without starting from the very point which I aim at concluding. My ideas are all assumptions, and I am ever moving in a circle. I cannot avoid being sufficient for myself, for I cannot make myself anything else, and to change me is to destroy me. (GA 272–73)

Where Polanyi speaks of self-set standards, Newman describes an act of self-creation:

Nor is this progress mechanical, nor is it of necessity; it is committed to the personal efforts of each individual of the species; each of us has the prerogative of completing his inchoate and rudimental nature, and of developing his own perfection out of the living elements with which his mind began to be. It is his gift to be the creator of his own sufficiency; and to be emphatically self-made. This is the law of his being, which he cannot escape; and whatever is involved in that law he is bound, or rather he is carried on, to fulfill. (GA 274)

In consequence of the structure of human nature, each person is bound to become "his own law, his own teacher, and his own judge in those special cases of duty which are personal to him" (GA 278).

One of the key acts in the formation of the self-made mind is that of "taking a view." It seemed to Newman to be such an essential ingredient to the health of the intellect that he considered even inadequate views better than no view at all:

When the intellect has once been properly trained and formed to have a connected view or grasp of things, it will display its powers with more or less effect according to its particular quality and capacity of the individual. . . . In all it will be a faculty of entering with comparative ease into any subject of thought, and of taking up with aptitude any science or profession. All this it will be and will do in a measure, even when the mental formation be made after a model but partially true; for, as far as effectiveness goes, even false views of things have more influence and inspire more respect than no views at all. Men who fancy they see what is not are more energetic, and make their way better, than those who see nothing; and so the undoubting infidel, the fanatic, the heresiarch, are able to do much, while the hereditary Christian, who has never realized the truths which he holds, is unable to do anything. (*Idea* xliii–xliv)

The formation of a view is primarily a tacit act motivated by the intellectual passion for understanding:

This method is so natural to us, as I have said, as to be almost spontaneous; and we are impatient when we cannot exercise it, and in consequence we do not always wait to have the means of exercising it aright, but we often put up with insufficient or absurd views or interpretations of what we meet with, rather than have none at all. . . . Though it is no easy matter to view things correctly, nevertheless the busy mind will ever be viewing. We cannot do without a view, and we put up with an illusion, when we cannot get a truth. (*Idea* 56–57)

Newman's definition of knowledge is linked to the idea of taking a view: "When I speak of Knowledge, I mean something intellectual, something which grasps what it perceives through the senses; something which takes a view of things; which sees more than the senses convey; which reasons upon what it sees, and while it sees; which invests it with an idea" (*Idea* 85). The positive contribution of the mind to the act of knowing is one of the elements of Newman's epistemology which separates him from the empiricists; for them, it would be anathema to grasp "more than the senses convey." For Newman, the refusal to interpret the senses through ideas is tantamount to a rejection of knowledge itself.

Polanyi similarly emphasized the decisive intervention of presumptions in the act of knowing. In a section entitled "Implicit Beliefs," he noted, "Our formally declared beliefs can be held to be true in the last resort only because of our logically anterior acceptance of a particular set of terms, from which all our references to reality are constructed" (*PK* 287). In the following section, he described three stratagems employed to defend the system of implicit beliefs:

1. meeting objections one by one from a circular position;
2. letting the system expand itself to cover unforeseen difficulties;
3. neglecting counterexamples which would germinate alternatives. (*PK* 288–92)

Although such defenses may defeat the development of knowledge, they also contribute to the reliability of the interiorized position: "The axiomatized system is therefore circular: our anterior acceptance of mathematics lends authority to its axioms, from which we then deduce in turn all mathematical demonstrations" (*PK* 289). Even when confronted with the power of the mind to deceive itself through its own epistemic options, we cannot decide not to form such interpretative frameworks—the mind itself demands that we make fiduciary acts: "Once more, the admission of doubt proves here to be as clearly an act of belief as does the non-admission of doubt" (*PK* 294). Newman made precisely the same observation that unbelief is an act of faith: "Unbelief, indeed, considers itself especially rational, or critical of evidence; but it criticizes the evidence of Religion, only because it does not like it, and really goes on presumptions and prejudices as much as Faith does, only presumptions of an opposite nature" (*US* 230).

Lastly, very much like Newman, Polanyi also endorses the idea that even false assumptions can lead to valuable results:

The practice of science is usually sound, even when it is conducted in the name of false principles. It is even possible that valuable research *must* be based on absurd assumptions. Consider the recent exploration of various parts of the brain by electrodes of microscopic size, which showed the nervous system operating as a machine. This splendid inquiry would be hampered by keeping in mind the fact, that the assumption of the whole nervous system operating as a machine is nonsensical.[10]

It seems clear that both authors have the same outlook on the role of assumptions in knowing.

Since the adoption of these positions is tacit, there is unavoidable risk in the act of commitment to a view of reality: "Personal knowledge is an intellectual commitment, and as such inherently hazardous" (*PK* viii). Newman recognized the same reality in his *University Sermons:*

We are so constituted, that if we insist upon being as sure as is conceivable, in every step of our course, we must be content to creep along the ground, and can never soar. If we are intended for great ends, we are called to great hazards; and, whereas we are given absolute certainty in nothing, we must in all things choose between doubt and inactivity, and the conviction that we are under the eye of

10. Michael Polanyi, "Science and Religion: Separate Dimension or Common Ground?" *Philosophy Today* 7 (1963): 10–11.

One who, for whatever reason, exercises us with the less evidence when He might give us the greater. (*US* 215)

There are no risk-free intellectual commitments: "We must assume something to prove anything, and can gain nothing without a venture" (*US* 214–15).

One can appreciate why many search for formal methods or impersonal mechanisms that would take the place of personal commitment. In the abstract, the theory of intellectual commitment describes both the progress of science and the development of pseudosciences. Accepting the positive contribution that the mind makes may seem to reduce science to the level of the imaginary and the fictitious. But in Newman's view and in Polanyi's, it is clear that the imagination—the power to view and to interpret—is the vehicle of contact with reality. Ian Ker argues that "the whole theory of real assent demands that there should be notional concepts so vividly realized as to become facts in the imagination, that is to say, images."[11] Unfortunately, the imagination is also the source of fiction, self-delusion, and loss of contact with reality. To those who follow Kant, the positive contribution of the mind to the act of knowing seems always to stand in the way of knowing the thing-in-itself. For Polanyi and Newman, the constructs of intelligence no more obstruct insight than the structures of the eye inhibit seeing. When the supporting presumptions are functioning in a healthy fashion, they sink into the tacit dimension and do not prevent the mind from making contact with reality. In fact, the constructs are the tools or probes that the mind skillfully employs to *make* contact possible.

Newman's notion of "real apprehension" is not the same as an empiricist's theory of perception, although sense perception gives Newman some easy examples of what he means about the recognition of things—"The sun shines" and "The prospect is charming" are propositions based upon real apprehension (*GA* 38–39). As will become clear in Chapter IV, real apprehension can grasp realities that are not given by the senses but are affirmed by the judgment of the mind. In such self-modifying and synthetic acts, real apprehension appears as an accomplishment of the mind, not just a passive association drawn from impressions.

11. Ian Ker, "Recent Critics of Newman's *Grammar of Assent*," *Religious Studies* 13 (1977): 71.

Perhaps the ancient image of the eyes producing light is true to the nature of the mind. We *do* shine the light of the intellect on things. *We* teach animals to speak and invent languages for subatomic particles to tell us what they are. As in the difficulty posed in the preceding section about the impossibility of conscience and intellect depending on each other, so here: the fear that the constructs of the mind are obstacles to knowledge comes from the act of pulling subsidiaries out of the tacit dimension and placing them at the focus of inquiry. A pianist cannot pay too much attention to the individual movements of the fingers; an athlete must not think too much about the components of the sport; epistemologists should not focus too much on the particular structures that subserve knowing. The power of the mind to create views or interpretations subserves our contact with reality; it may on occasion generate false views and misinterpretations, but we recognize this very fact because the very same power that we are tempted to distrust supplies us with grounds to criticize itself. Newman describes the process in terms that fit well with the experimental method in science:

Error may flourish for a time, but Truth will prevail in the end. The only effect of error ultimately is to promote Truth. Theories, speculations, hypotheses, are started; perhaps they are to die, still not before they have suggested ideas better than themselves. These better ideas are taken up in turn by other men, and, if they do not yet lead to truth, nevertheless they lead to what is still nearer to truth than themselves; and thus knowledge on the whole makes progress. The errors of some minds in scientific investigation are more fruitful than the truths of others. A Science seems making no progress, but to abound in failures, yet imperceptibly all the time it is advancing, and it is of course a gain to truth to have learned what is not true, if nothing more. (*Idea* 360)

Both Newman and Polanyi realized that in the process of advocating one's own fundamental beliefs, one leaves the arena of proof and enters the field of persuasion: "When men understand each other's meaning, they see, for the most part, that controversy is either superfluous or hopeless" (*US* 201). Because knowing is ultimately a free moral action, "it is as absurd to argue men, as to torture them, into believing" (*US* 63).

3. The Illative Integration of Subsidiaries

As was pointed out above (104–7), there is a very striking resemblance between Newman's notion of the "cumulation of probabilities," accomplished by the illative sense, and Polanyi's understanding of the tacit integration of subsidiaries. In the *Apologia,* Newman outlined how the convergence of logically incomplete arguments contributes to the judgment by the intellectual conscience that one must give full assent to an unproved proposition (see above, page 8). His first point was that the certitude proper to religion comes from "an *assemblage* of concurring and converging possibilities" (*Apo* 29–30). The illative sense "determines what science cannot determine, the limit of converging probabilities and the reasons sufficient for a proof" (*GA* 282).

Ian Ker brought together three key images used by Newman to illustrate how inadequate arguments bound together by an illative assessment take on a strength that no one of them possesses alone. Intellectual integrations resemble a weight-bearing framework, a cable, or a bundle of twigs:

The "proof of Religion," [Newman] wrote in a letter in 1861, using a striking analogy, "I liken . . . to the mechanism of some triumph of skill . . . where all display is carefully avoided, and the weight is ingeniously thrown in a variety of directions, upon supports which are distinct from, or independent of each other" [*LD* xix, 460]. Or, as he later explained by an even more compelling analogy, "The best illustration . . . is that of a *cable* which is made up of a number of separate threads, each feeble, yet together as sufficient as an iron rod," which represents "mathematical or strict demonstration" [*LD* xxi, 146] The cable will certainly break if enough threads give way, but if the threads hold, then the cable is as strong as any metal bar. For, to use yet another image, a cumulation of probabilities is like a "bundle of sticks, each of which . . . you could snap in two, if taken separately from the rest" [*LD* xxiv, 146].[12]

Other grammars of assent dictate that reasoning should begin with clear and distinct ideas and then create chains of argument from the simple elements; in such formal systems, the argument is never any stronger than the weakest link in the chain. As we saw above (101), Newman begins with ideas that cannot be completely expressed in words and supposes that even those trains of thought which stop short of the goal nevertheless make a definite contribution to the final act of judgment through a "cumulation of probabilities." When the pieces of

12. Ian Ker, *The Achievement of John Henry Newman* (Notre Dame: University of Notre Dame Press, 1990), 50–51.

the intellectual framework are assembled, or the strands of thought woven into a cable, or the branches of probability gathered into a bundle, one can no longer see each component separately and cannot directly inspect its contribution to the function of the whole, but the whole draws strength from—and gives strength to—each part.

The parallel in Polanyi's epistemology is the tacit integration of subsidiaries. Polanyi associates subsidiary and focal awareness with the difference between parts and wholes. In an integrated perception of a whole, we are only "subsidiarily aware of its parts" (*PK* 57–58). Gestalt psychologists have shown how the perception of parts changes radically when examined in isolation from the whole. This phenomenon provides one of the prime analogues for personal knowledge: "All these curious properties and implications of personal knowledge go back to what I have previously described as its logical unspecifiability; that is to the disorganizing effect caused by switching our attention to the parts of a whole" (*PK* 63). Although he lacked any consistent terminology to point to the difference between subsidiary and focal awareness, Newman was very much aware of the need to see parts in right relationship to larger wholes:

All that exists, as contemplated by the human mind, forms one large system or complex fact, and this of course resolves itself into an indefinite number of particular facts, which, as being portions of a whole, have countless relations of every kind, one towards another. Knowledge is the apprehension of these facts, whether in themselves, or in their mutual positions and bearings. And, as all taken together form one integral subject for contemplation, so there are no natural or real limits between part and part; one is ever running into another; all, as viewed by the mind, are combined together, and possess a correlative character one with another. (*Idea* 33–34)

Like Polanyi, Newman asserts that meaning is derived from part/whole (or subsidiary/focal) relationships:

That only is true enlargement of mind which is the power of viewing many things at once as one whole, of referring them severally to their true place in the universal system, of understanding their respective values, and determining their mutual dependence. Thus is that form of Universal Knowledge, of which I have on a former occasion spoken, set up in the individual intellect, and constitutes its perfection. Possessed of this real illumination, the mind never views any part of the extended subject-matter of Knowledge without recollecting that it is but a part, or without the associations which spring from this recollection. It makes every thing in some sort lead to everything else; it would communicate the image of the whole to every separate portion, till that whole becomes in imagination like a spirit, every where pervading and penetrating its component parts, and giving them one definite meaning. (*Idea* 103)

The mature mind is the one that is capable of correctly relating subsidiaries to the focus that binds them together. Newman describes this aspect of the mind in terms of "centers of thought, around which our knowledge grows and is located" (*Idea* 378).

For Polanyi, all constructs of the intellect have this quality of drawing meaning *from* the subsidiaries *to* the focus which integrates them. We use "the sign or symbol" by an act of "personal commitment" to its meaning (*PK* 61). To dredge up the subsidiaries of an integration and bring them into focal awareness destroys their function and dis-integrates the meaning they had formerly supported (*PK* 63).

Polanyi's treatment of the "from-to" structure of all meaning and knowledge clearly goes beyond the special case that interested Newman, namely assent based on the cumulation of probabilities. It seems likely, however, that Polanyi would have acknowledged the close correspondence between his position and Newman's. Inspired by Gestalt psychology, Polanyi defined perception as "a comprehension of clues in terms of a whole" (*PK* 97). Like Newman, Polanyi sees knowledge as going far beyond the passive impressions brought to the mind by the senses: "A discovery of objective truth . . . while using the experience of our senses as clues, transcends this experience by embracing the vision of a reality beyond the impressions of our senses" (*PK* 5–6). For Newman, a real apprehension based on the cumulation of probabilities transcends the meaning of any element of the integration. Where Newman talks about "probabilities" that are formally incomplete arguments, Polanyi refers to "clues" that are integrated by "the force of personal judgment required to supplement the inadequate clues on which a decision is being based" (*PK* 367). In Newman's terms, the illative sense is what draws together the individually inadequate probabilities and prompts the mind to assent to what has not been fully apprehended or proven.

When confronted with complex data, there are often competing illative integrations that compete with each other for the focal attention of the mind. Just as some visual images can be interpreted in two radically different ways, so conflicting interpretations can be placed on the data of experience:

> Now, Revelation presents to us a perfectly different aspect of the universe from that presented by the Sciences. The two informations are like the distinct subjects represented by the lines of the same drawing, which, accordingly as they are read on their concave or convex side, exhibit to us now a group of trees with branches and leaves, and now human faces hid amid the leaves, or some majestic figures standing out from the branches. (*Idea* 301)

Gestalt psychologists have shown how completely one interpretation *(Gestalt)* blocks the other. When the mind reads the picture as trees, all of the evidence that points toward faces disappears, and vice-versa.

Newman also uses the example of recognizing faces to illustrate the process of implicit reasoning. When we strain to decide whether we recognize someone or try to sum up all of the elements of implicit reason, the mind is "unequal to complete analysis of the motives which carry it on to a particular conclusion, and is swayed and determined by a body of proof, which it recognizes only as a body, and not in its constituent parts" (*GA* 233). Looking at the parts in isolation from the whole destroys their meanings as subsidiaries and dissolves the force which the "body of proof" provides when treated as a whole. The power of the mind to gain knowledge comes not so much from analysis as from synthesis: "I say, then, that our most natural mode of reasoning is, not from propositions to propositions, but from things to things, from concrete to concrete, from wholes to wholes" (*GA* 260–61). Clearly, in his own way, Newman anticipated Polanyi's observations on subsidiary awareness and tacit knowledge when he observes that "those antecedents commonly are not recognized by us as subjects for analysis" (*GA* 260–61).

Just as Newman affirms the necessity of "reasoning from wholes to wholes," so Polanyi speaks of the integrations that give us access to "knowledge of comprehensive entities."[13] Broadly speaking, the mind has two great powers: to take things apart and to put them back together again. One way to understand an automobile is to reduce it to its approximately ten thousand component parts; another way is to enter it and use it as a whole. The two modes of its existence and the corre-

13. Michael Polanyi, "Science and Religion: Separate Dimension or Common Ground?" *Philosophy Today* 7 (1963): 11.

sponding modes of knowing it are quite distinct, and neither is complete without the other. There is a time for analysis and a time for synthesis. Of the two powers, it is synthetic reason which guides the process of the disintegration and reintegration of particulars. Without the vision that comes from the illative integration of subsidiaries, there can be no intelligent estimate of the value or meaning of the disassembled parts.

Science as a Model of Certitude

In contemporary language, "science" could be simply defined as "what scientists do." Our everyday notion of scientists may summon up images of white coats, test tubes, laboratory conditions, careful controls, mathematical precision, and unimpassioned objectivity. As a culture, Americans are generally not conscious of the other meanings of "science" stemming from its long history in philosophical debate about *epistēmē* and *scientia* as "knowledge through causes."[14] Science originally meant any body of knowledge based on first principles and carried on through formal operations. Philosophy and theology were ranked as sciences more rigorous and definite than the fields that we now think of as truly scientific, such as physics and chemistry:

Going back to the medieval precursors of modern science, one finds that they consistently associated the Latin term *scientia* with causal knowledge. *Scientia est cognitio per causas.* It was precisely on this basis that they differentiated *scientia* from other forms of knowledge: science was concerned with causes, whereas other types of knowing were not. To have scientific knowledge was to know perfectly, *scire simpliciter,* to know that something is so because it could not be otherwise and this, in turn, because of the causes that make it be as it is. Thus, the early understanding of science—from which the modern notion grew—was that it must be concerned with a search for causes. And the explanations for which science was ultimately searching, from its beginnings among the Greeks to the seventeenth century, were causal explanations.[15]

The medieval understanding, in turn, derives from Aristotle:

The superior kind of knowing that he [Aristotle] calls science *(epistēmē)* can only be achieved by one who can successfully identify the cause *(aitia)* that makes a

---

14. William Wallace, *Causality and Scientific Explanation,* 2 volumes (Ann Arbor: University of Michigan, 1972–74), vol. 1:6, 11.
15. Wallace, *Causality,* vol. 1:6.

fact *(pragma)* be what it is: he must know the cause from which the fact results, as the cause of that fact and no other, and accordingly the fact cannot be otherwise. Causes thus function for Aristotle as reasons or explanatory factors that make scientific knowing possible. . . . To proceed scientifically, for Aristotle, is essentially a matter of putting questions to nature, and his detailed analysis centers around the way in which such questions may be asked.[16]

Prior to the nineteenth century, "natural philosophy" meant the systematic study of the material world, while "science" generally meant knowledge that could be formally demonstrated. So, for example, "Hobbes was especially enamored of geometry, extolling it as 'the only science that it hath pleased God hitherto to bestow on mankind.'"[17] Locke held that "natural philosophy" (the study of nature) "is not capable of being made a science."[18] How this last sentence grates on the modern ear! Our standards of linguistic taste and epistemology have changed so that our age is much more inclined to say that no philosophy may be thought of as a science, while natural philosophy, the study of nature, is the only science there is.

When the term "scientist" was coined in the 1830s, it was in part the result of wanting to distinguish the philosophers of nature from the other branches of philosophy:

Science . . . loses all traces of unity. A curious illustration of this result may be observed in the want of any name by which we can designate the students of the knowledge of the material world collectively. We are informed that this difficulty was felt very oppressively by the members of the British Association for the Advancement of Science, at their meetings . . . in the last three summers. . . . *Philosophers* was felt to be too wide and lofty a term . . . ; *savans* [sic] was rather assuming . . . ; some ingenious gentleman proposed that, by analogy with *artist,* they might form *scientist,* and added that there could be no scruple in making free with this termination when we have such terms as *sciolist, economist,* and *atheist*—but this was generally not palatable.[19]

By 1840, William Whewell—whom Peter Medawar calls "the greatest ever nomenclator"[20] —was willing to adopt the term: "We need very much a name to describe a cultivator of science in general. I should in-

16. Wallace, *Causality*, vol. 1:11.

17. Wallace, *Causality*, vol. 2:18.

18. Wallace, *Causality*, vol. 2:27.

19. *Quarterly Review* 51 (1834): 59, quoted in the *OED* (second edition, 1989) as the earliest known instance of the use of the word "scientist."

20. Peter Medawar, *The Limits of Science* (Oxford: Oxford University Press, 1984), 9.

cline to call him a Scientist."[21] By the end of the nineteenth century, "science" had lost its Aristotelian and medieval sense and was almost wholly identified with the study of the natural world.

Newman's use of the word "science" alternated between the pre-modern and modern senses of the word. The modern world might be slow to call mathematics or logic a science, because we tend not to call mathematicians and logicians scientists. Carl Sagan, for example, asserted that "mathematics is as much a 'humanity' as poetry."[22] For Newman (who was an Aristotelian at heart), mathematics provided his dominant model of science.[23] He spoke of the logic as "a science or scientific art" (GA 215). Even in less rigorous conduct of thought, Newman felt that "our inquiries spontaneously fall into scientific sequence, and we think in logic, as we talk in prose, without aiming at doing so" (GA 228). In keeping with the pre-modern nomenclature, he spoke of all of the disciplines as sciences: "All sciences, except the science of Religion, have their certainty in themselves; as far as they are sciences, they consist of necessary conclusions from undeniable premises, or of phenomena manipulated into general truths by an irresistible deduction" (DN 132).

It is on the basis of this pre-modern model that Newman called theology a science. When the intellect is true to its own nature in examining the articles of faith, "it is ever active, inquisitive, penetrating; it examines doctrine and doctrine; it compares, contrasts, and forms them into a science; that science is theology. Now theological science, being thus the exercise of the intellect upon the *credenda* of revelation, is, though not directly devotional, at once natural, excellent, and necessary."[24] While acknowledging that there is *a* role for this science of theology, the whole thrust of the *Grammar* is to show that this kind of rigorous, formal approach to the faith is too narrow a foundation for religious certitude. The "scientific knowledge and argumentative proof" provided by theology is secondary to the simple, direct, and intuitive form which provides the real "basis of personal Christianity" (GA 91). "Personal Christianity" depends on personal knowledge, which can

21. William Whewell, *Philosophy of the Inductive Sciences* 1 (1840): 113, quoted in *OED*.

22. Carl Sagan, *The Dragons of Eden: Speculations on the Evolutions of Human Intelligence* (New York: Ballantine Books, 1977), 82.

23. GA 211–12, 215, 228, 240, 251–52, 268–69, 275, 279, 280–82, 285, 319–21.

24. GA 127; cf. also 62, 91, 109, 194–95.

never be completely translated into formal operations: "That is why science has so little of a religious tendency; deductions have no power of persuasion" (*GA* 89). Formal reasoning may dominate the head, but the heart moves for other reasons.

There are two premises drawn from science as a model of certitude which are corrosive to faith. Although they may not be logically consistent with each other, they seem to coexist in modern culture.

1. Only science is certain, because scientists prove everything.

2. Science is never certain, because scientists keep changing their minds.

Scientists manage to have both an air of infallibility and the humble posture of those who professes systematic incertitude. If those who are seen as *knowers* cannot be certain, then it seems to follow that no other human discipline could possess certitude equal to or greater than that of science. Polanyi describes the paradox that the authority of science has been increased by the anti-authoritarian rhetoric of the modern age:

> In medieval times you could shatter an opinion on the grounds that it was contrary to religion, but today you can do so by showing that it is contrary to science. The reason is obviously that the authority of religion has been impaired by the principle of doubt, while that of science has been further increased by it.[25]

The widespread acceptance of science as a model of certitude is evident in the quest to bring other disciplines up to the standards of the hard sciences:

> Some students of man will stop at nothing in their desperate endeavor to appear scientific. Some psychologists have turned away from the study of consciousness in order to become truly scientific. Economists are incessantly worried by doubts whether economics is really a science. The usual consolation in such heart-searchings is to concede that one's study—be it economics or psychology, history, politics, or beer-brewing—is still a young science. It is implied that when it gets older it will become a fully-fledged science in the manner of physics, which is acknowledged as the only quite exact science, a science that is strictly verifiable.[26]

---

25. Michael Polanyi, "Science and Conscience," *Religion in Life* 23 (1953): 51.
26. Polanyi, "Science and Conscience," 52.

When physics is taken to be the model of knowledge—provisional results obtained from precise laboratory methods—the act of faith proper to Christianity as well as to other religious and philosophical wisdom traditions suffers by comparison.

Although Newman most often spoke of science on the Aristotelian model of a body of knowledge based on a set of principles, he also at times used "science" to designate "that circle of knowledge which is the boast of the present age" (GA 185). He recognized that a scientific method is valuable because a methodical analysis allows two different minds to enter into the same view of things, operating jointly on the basis of reason rather than authority. Most importantly for the purposes of this study, he made the claim that the kind of certitude found in Christian faith is very much like the certitude found in the study of the natural world: "The Catholic Church then, though not universally acknowledged, may without inconsistency claim to teach the primary truths of religion, just as modern science, though but partially received, claims to teach the great principles and laws which are the foundation of secular knowledge" (GA 195–96). At first glance, a personal Christianity based on the operations of the illative sense may appear inferior to the hard-headed, experimental certitudes of modern science. This impression dissolves when we recognize that scientists are equally dependent on the illative sense: "The motions of the heavenly bodies are almost mathematical in their precision; but there is a multitude of matters, to which mathematical science is applied, which are in their nature intricate and obscure, and require that reasoning by rule should be completed by the living mind" (GA 222–23). It seems clear that in Newman's view, there is no science dealing with realities (physical, mathematical, moral, or religious) which can function without the support of the illative sense, which guides "the more subtle and elastic language of thought" (GA 281).

Because the illative sense is involved in the modern sciences, one can learn from them how it functions in other disciplines. Newman consciously modelled the method of verisimilitude on Newton's notion of an approach to a limit: "In coming to its conclusion, it proceeds always in the same way, by a method of reasoning, which, as I have observed above, is the elementary principle of that mathematical calculus of modern times, which has so wonderfully extended the limits of abstract science" (GA 281). Like Polanyi, Newman suggested the paradox that science is not thoroughly scientific because the intervention of the illative sense cannot be completely governed by formal logic:

> Great as are the services of language in enabling us to extend the compass of our inferences, to test their validity, and to communicate them to others, still the mind itself is more versatile and vigorous than any of its works, of which language is one, and it is only under its penetrating and subtle action that the margin disappears, which I have described as intervening between verbal argumentation and conclusions in the concrete. It determines what science cannot determine, the limit of converging probabilities and the reasons sufficient for a proof. It is the ratiocinative mind itself, and no trick of art, however simple in its form and sure in operation, by which we are able to determine, and thereupon to be certain, that a moving body left to itself will never stop, and that no man can live without eating. (GA 281–82)

In the last analysis, religious certitude is just as weak and just as strong as modern scientific certitude, because both are built upon the same foundation of the illative sense; recall the discussion above (see page 119) of Newman's assertion that "moral evidence and moral certitude are all that we can attain, not only in the case of ethical and spiritual subjects, such as religion, but of terrestrial and cosmical questions also" (GA 252). As hard as it may be for modern consciousness to accept, the one who has faith in the principles of Christianity and the one who has faith in the principles of modern science are very much in the same boat of personal certitude—because all certitude is, at root, moral certitude.

The Positive Role of Doubt

Those who would object to classifying religion and modern science as similar intellectual activities have good reason to do so. Newman sought a stable foundation for unchanging Christian dogma, but modern science seems to flourish by abandoning any kind of dogmatic stability. William Wallace wryly observed, "Truth is difficult enough to attain; certainty is an idol before which only the pure mathematician is now willing to torture himself."[27] Newman did not live to see the development of modern models of incertitude in science, and so cannot be held accountable for not foreseeing what no one else anticipated. In assessing Newman's argument with Froude about the possibility of us-

27. Wallace, *Causality*, vol. 2: 325.

ing doubt as a tool of research, one may grant that in the natural sciences, real progress has been made by calling into question things which formerly were taken for granted. In the light of contemporary judgments about the provisional nature of scientific research, the history of science may be read as a process in which the growth of understanding comes at the expense of earlier dogmatisms. Unlike the theorists of the nineteenth century, we affirm the reality of the developments without attempting to predict how much more progress may be made in any area of inquiry. Wallace shows that breakthroughs like Harvey's successful explanation of blood circulation and Newton's work in motion and optics "open up the possibility of continued advance in scientific knowledge at the level of proximate causes, while not requiring their followers to embrace a total systematic explanation that would pretend to say the last word with regard to the ultimate causes of all phenomena."[28] In Chapter IV, we will grapple again with the question of how the science of theology can learn from the natural sciences to accept its provisional nature without thereby dissolving the structure of commitment that is necessary for the religious (and scientific) imagination. In his last, unsent letter to Froude, Newman asserted his belief that there is room for such growth of understanding within the certitudes of faith: "What then you say of mechanical science, I say emphatically of theology, viz. that it 'makes progress by being always alive to its own fundamental uncertainties.'"[29]

Polanyi's epistemology is of great value in pursuing the resolution of this question on at least two grounds. He *did* have the good fortune to witness many of the scientific developments in this century, and he had a long and successful career as a natural scientist before turning his attention to the humanities. Wallace's survey of the history of science shows that while personal familiarity with science does not necessarily produce good philosophies of science, neither does a good philosophy necessarily produce good science. Different skills are required for each discipline. Nevertheless, Polanyi's success as a natural scientist ought to give his opinion some weight when attempting to evaluate his philosophy of science. At the very least, it will no longer be possible to suppose, as Harper did, that all scientists have the same attitude toward the role of commitment in science. Harper judged that, because

28. Wallace, *Causality*, vol. 1: 193.
29. Harper, *Newman and Froude*, 207; LD XXIX, 118.

Newman's argument "so completely ignored the laws of evidence," it would necessarily be repulsive to scientists: "Froude could not allow, nor could other scientists, that there was any duty to believe anything, unless, indeed, it was proved by the most rigorous of tests."[30] In a nicely ironic turn of events, the "laws of evidence" upon which Harper rested his case have, in Polanyi's investigation, become a function of the tacit integration of subsidiaries and can no longer be treated as an impersonal court of appeals divorced from scientists' own illative commitments.

Post-critical thinking does not abandon the undeniable benefits of critical reflection. The goal is an integration of informal and formal reasoning. Carl Sagan speaks of the need to call on both powers of the mind: "The search for patterns without critical analysis, and rigid skepticism without a search for patterns, are the antipodes of incomplete science. The effective pursuit of knowledge requires both functions."[31] The illative sense is not the enemy of critical awareness, nor is tacit knowledge an obstacle to articulation. Affirmation of the informal dimensions of thought is not denial of the formal dimensions, but reflects an effort to restore a balance that may have been lost due to an understandable enthusiasm for the "scientific method." Much of Polanyi's value to theology lies in his opposition to false dichotomies between faith and reason. Polanyi explicitly interpreted his epistemology as an ally of the Christian synthesis of faith and reason: "I believe indeed that this kind of effort, if pursued systematically, may eventually restore the balance between belief and reason on lines essentially similar to those marked out by Augustine at the dawn of Christian rationalism."[32]

While Newman would clearly agree with Polanyi that science and religion resemble each other when considered as acts of commitment, he also noted the difference in method between the two. In reading the following passage, notice how Newman, operating in an Aristotelian framework, denied that physics is as "scientific" as theology!

The argumentative method of Theology is that of a strict science, such as Geometry, or deductive; the method of Physics, at least on starting, is that of an empirical pursuit, or inductive. This peculiarity on either side arises from the nature

---

30. Harper, *Newman and Froude*, 77–78.

31. Sagan, *Dragons*, 192.

32. Michael Polanyi, "Faith and Reason," *The Journal of Religion* 41 (1961): 239.

of the case. In Physics a vast and omnigenous mass of information lies before the inquirer, all in a confused litter, and needing arrangement and analysis. In Theology such varied phenomena are wanting, and Revelation presents itself instead. What is known in Christianity is just that which is revealed, and nothing more; certain truths, communicated directly from above, are committed to the keeping of the faithful, and to the very last nothing can really be added to those truths. From the time of the Apostles to the end of the world no strictly new truth can be added to the theological information which the Apostles were inspired to deliver. It is possible of course to make numberless deductions from the original doctrines; but, as the conclusion is ever in its premisses, such deductions are not, strictly speaking, an addition; and, though experience may variously guide and modify those deductions, still, on the whole, Theology retains the severe character of a science, advancing syllogistically from premisses to conclusion. (*Idea* 331–32)

Here Newman and Polanyi part company. As we shall see in the next chapter, Polanyi does not have the same notion of revelation that characterizes Newman's theology.

IV. Some Theological Implications of Post-Critical Consciousness

Since the purpose of this chapter is to trace the implications of the epistemology that Newman and Polanyi have in common, the focus will tend to swing back and forth between theological and epistemic issues. The purpose of this chapter is to sketch *a* view, not *the only* view or all possible views, of post-critical theologies. Before considering the details of Newman's theological position, I will consider the general features of the view that develops from awareness of illative sense and tacit knowledge. The failures of the critical, impersonal experiments in epistemology do not automatically determine what post-critical views should replace them. Just as there are two non-Euclidean geometries and several post-critical models of mathematics, so there are many theologies having very little in common besides the rejection of the epistemic standards set by an inadequate view of science. Both Newman and Polanyi recognize that the development of ideas cannot be determined in advance by a formal system of logic, and therefore conflicting interpretative frameworks must be accepted as a necessary part of the exploration of post-critical territory. Only after a new standpoint is reached by the informal and tacit processes of the illative sense can a clear path be marked out by formalization. In the interim, the maps of the pioneers of the post-critical era will often disagree in many respects. They share the common view that the project of critical reason has failed to meet its own standards, but may take divergent paths from there in search of a new and more satisfying vision of reality.

One cannot deduce theology from epistemology any more than one can deduce omelettes from eggs. Even if the decision has been made that this particular egg will not be allowed to develop as a chicken, it may be fried, poached, scrambled, souftéed, or dried and powdered; it may be mixed with other ingredients to produce pancakes, waffles, bread, pasta, soup, or any number of other dishes. The post-critical mentality provides a rich range of materials for reflection, but does not automatically dictate how they are to be assembled in the final products of thought. The critical mentality said, "Give me my starting-points, and I will deduce the universe." Newman and Polanyi said in effect, "Choose your standpoint, and see what develops in dialogue with reality." Newman did not think that the initial view had to be clear, distinct, and self-evident. Even mistaken assumptions could initiate a learning process: "Certainly, I have always contended that obedience even to an erring conscience was the way to gain light, and that it mattered not where a man began, so that he began on what came to hand, and in faith; and that any thing might become a divine method of Truth; that to the pure all things are pure, and have a self-correcting virtue and a power of germinating" (*Apo* 162).

It is not easy for a fundamental theologian to stop picking away at the foundations of thought, or for the systematic theologian to accept an unsystematic framework, or for the dogmatic theologian to be non-dogmatic about the grounds of certitude. Well-meaning believers, addicted to the drug of rationalism, may become like the Pharisees in John's gospel, who are blinded to Jesus by their conviction that they already possess the truth (John 9.39–40). In epistemology, the drive to see can blind us. The mind resists admitting its own limitations. Newman and Polanyi decided to cherish the limited insight available to us, even though it may fall short of our passion for understanding. Polanyi believed that a frank admission of the mind's shortcomings would not bar the path to insight: "We undertake the task of attaining the universal in spite of our admitted infirmity, which should render the task hopeless, because we hope to be visited by powers for which we cannot account in terms of our specifiable capabilities" (*PK* 324). In the act of admitting its limits, the mind opens itself to what lies beyond its own powers of comprehension.

The epistemologies of Newman and Polanyi assure us that it is right to commit ourselves to views of reality, even when we do not see clearly all that our commitment may entail. Newman wished to clear the mind of inadequate grammars of assent so that the power of belief may be freely exercised. Like Polanyi, Newman saw that we could not do otherwise than to satisfy our intellectual passions by performing to self-set standards with universal intent: "He knows what has satisfied and satisfies himself; if it satisfies him, it is likely to satisfy others; if, as he believes and is sure, it is true, it will approve itself to others also, for there is but one truth" (GA 300). For Newman, religious truth is personal knowledge: "Any one who honestly attempts to set down his view of the Evidences of Religion . . . brings together his reasons, and relies on them, because they are his own, and this is his primary evidence" (GA 301).

Like Newman, Polanyi holds that there is no knowledge outside the structure of personal commitment. In his determination to renew the respectability of the act of commitment, Polanyi would surely endorse Newman's description of the necessity of using the illative sense to interpret reality: "If I have done no more than view the notorious facts of the case in the medium of my primary mental experiences, under the aspects which they spontaneously present to me, and with the aid of my best illative sense, I only do on one side of the question what those who think differently do on the other" (GA 318). We have no ground to stand on other than that created by our own personal judgments about reality. Polanyi's self-consistent declaration of this truth is a model of personal knowledge: "Throughout this book I am affirming my own beliefs, and more particularly so when I insist, as I do here, that such personal affirmations and choices are inescapable, and, when I argue, as I shall do, that this is all that can be required of me" (PK 209). We always approach reality through our own personal view of reality—we can never use anyone else's mind to think for ourselves—and yet reality is able to challenge the assumptions we have brought to bear on it. Polanyi adopted St. Augustine's dictum about the priority of faith over understanding as an apt description of his own approach: "nisi credideritis non intellig[e]tis" (PK 267). We can only revise our misbegotten beliefs by believing something different, but we can never operate outside of a fiduciary framework.

Polanyi was not trained as a theologian. He had a history of crossing from one discipline to another: while he was serving as a medical doctor, he wrote the articles that formed the basis of his Ph.D. in physical chemistry; while working as a physical chemist, he did groundbreaking research in economics; while assigned to a department of economics and social studies, he turned to the deep philosophical questions that underpin social structures; his studies in philosophy then led him to make various remarks on theological issues.[1] In each movement of thought, Polanyi wanted to be taken seriously, even though he may have lacked the academic background and credentials of others who had remained within the boundaries of chemistry, economics, social studies, philosophy, or theology. Because Polanyi was very reserved about his religious commitments, it is sometimes difficult to determine exactly where he stood on theological issues. There are ambiguities in his writings which allow strong theistic interpretations (Gelwick, Scott, Torrance, Apczynski, Dulles, and others) as well as atheistic interpretations (Grene, Prosch, Wetherick, Weightman, and others). Because of Polanyi's lack of formal training in theology and because of his independence from any particular Christian tradition, it may be somewhat unfair to expect precision and clarity from him in his reflection on religious issues. The key point that I would like to make in this brief sketch is that although the epistemologies of Newman and Polanyi converge, their theologies diverge. They would agree that we must use the mind, weak as it is, to make contact with reality; it seems they would disagree about the nature and extent of human contact with divine realities.

In affirming Newman's view of the real apprehension of and assent to the dogmas of God, Trinity, and revelation, I argue that one may have an epistemology like Polanyi's (as Newman did) but not share his theology, just as non-Euclidean geometries have four postulates in common with each other and with Euclid but differ in the fifth.[2] The

---

1. Bill Scott, "At the Wheel of the World," in *From Polanyi to the 21st Century: Proceedings of a Centennial Conference,* edited by Richard Gelwick (Biddeford, Me: The Polanyi Society, 1997), 341–64.

2. Euclid's first four postulates deal with the nature of a straight line, extensions of straight lines, the nature of a circle, and the equality of all right angles. The fifth postulate treats of parallel lines and says that two parallel lines lying in the same plane and extended to infinity in either direction never intersect. Given these five postulates, all other theorems in Euclidean geometry can be derived by formal methods. In the eithteenth and nineteenth centuries, mathematicians tried to show that the fifth postulate could be formally derived from the first four: "The early investigations with Euclid's Fifth tried to assuage the doubts of its validity by attempting to derive it logically from the other axioms, which seemed to be self-evident. It would then become a theorem and its status would be assured. These attempts failed, and for good reason—we now know that it cannot be so derived. This was established by 1868" (Philip J. Davis and Reuben Hersh, *The Mathematical Experience,* introduction by Gian-Carlo Rota [Boston: Houghton Mifflin, 1981], 219). At least two different non-Euclidean geometries can be generated by adopting a different fifth postulate, Lobachevskian and Riemannian; surprisingly, the latter proved more serviceable than Euclidean geometry in interpreting Einstein's theory of relativity.

theologies of Newman and Polanyi do not flow from their epistemology in a hypothetico-deductive fashion any more than the fifth postulate of Euclid flows from the first four. The theological implications of epistemology derive from additional *assumptions* about the nature of divine reality and the possibility and content of divine revelation. Newman's *Essay on Development of Doctrine* and his *Apologia* detail the process by which he came to adopt the dogmas of Catholicism as his frame of reference, while Polanyi identified most closely with Paul Tillich and "a progressive Protestant theology" (*PK* 283n1). Although the two men made different theological assumptions, each would acknowledge the other's right and obligation to do so in order to enter into dialogue with reality and with each other.

The goal of this chapter is to show how Newman and Polanyi construct dissimilar theologies using similar epistemic tools. Newman devoted the fifth and the tenth chapters of his *Grammar* to persuasive illustrations of how his epistemology and theology interact with each other. Chapter Five, "Apprehension and Assent in the Matter of Religion," has three parts:

1. Belief in One God
2. Belief in the Holy Trinity
3. Belief in Dogmatic Theology

The tenth and final chapter of the book, "Inference and Assent in the matter of Religion," has two parts:

1. Natural Religion
2. Revealed Religion

In comparing and contrasting the theologies of Newman and Polanyi in these five areas, I will take up only those aspects that most clearly relate to the topic of illative sense and tacit knowledge. The final section will consider some of Polanyi's observations on God as the ultimate comprehensive entity—the ultimate meaning of the universe.

Belief in One God

Newman's first words in Chapter Five present his understanding of dogma and distinguish between religion and theology:

We are now able to determine what a dogma of faith is, and what it is to believe it. A dogma is a proposition; it stands for a notion or a thing; and to believe it is to give the assent of the mind to it, as it stands for the one or the other. To give a real assent to it is an act of religion; to give a notional, is a theological act. It is discerned, rested in, and appropriated as a reality, by the religious imagination; it is held as a truth, by the theological intellect. (*GA* 93)

Accepting a dogma as true does not automatically create the necessary impression on the religious imagination. In his preceding chapter, as an example of "the change of Notional Assent into Real" (*GA* 76), Newman indicated that we must cultivate a personal awareness of the realities of faith:

To the devout and spiritual, the Divine Word speaks of things, not merely of notions. . . . The purpose, then, of meditation is to realize them; to make the facts which they relate stand out before our mind as objects, such as may be appropriated by a faith as living as the imagination which apprehends them. (*GA* 79)

Newman was convinced that theology is about realities that can settle questions, just as the realities of science and mathematics inspire, resist, and correct our notions of them. Newman called the belief in one God "a natural truth, the foundation of all religion" (*GA* 94). We are not trapped within the small circle of our ideas about God, but make contact with a living reality:

Can I attain to any more vivid assent to the Being of a God, than that which is given merely to notions of the intellect? Can I enter with a *personal knowledge* into the circle of truths which make up that great thought? Can I rise to what I have called an imaginative apprehension of it? Can I believe as if I saw? Since such a high assent requires a present experience or memory of the fact, at first sight it would seem as if the answer must be in the negative; for how can I assent as if I saw, unless I have seen? but no one in this life can see God. Yet I conceive a real assent is possible, and I proceed to show how. (*GA* 95–96; italics mine)

The realities of religion are hidden from the senses. To perceive them, they "must be set before the mind in propositions. The formula, which embodies a dogma for the theologian, readily suggests an object for the worshipper" (*GA* 109).

To give real assent there must be real apprehension. For Newman, the primary way to grasp the reality of God is through conscience: "This being taken for granted, I shall attempt to show that in this special feeling, which follows on the commission of what we call right or wrong, lie the materials for the real apprehension of a Divine Sovereign Judge" (*GA* 97–98). The transformation of "this special feeling" into a source of real apprehension depends upon the conviction that we are being addressed interiorly by a reality that is not of our own making: "If, as is the case, we feel responsibility, are ashamed, are frightened, at transgressing the voice of conscience, this implies that there is One to whom we are responsible, before whom we are ashamed, whose claims on us we fear" (*GA* 101). If one is willing to construe the experience of conscience as Newman does, then the image of God becomes a guide to the interpretation of all of one's experiences in life:

[A religious imagination] has a living hold on truths which are really to be found in the world, though they are not upon the surface. It is able to pronounce by anticipation, what it takes a long argument to prove—that good is the rule, and evil the exception. It is able to assume that, uniform as are the laws of nature, they are consistent with a particular Providence. *It interprets what it sees around it by this previous inward teaching, as the true key of that maze of vast complicated disorder;* and thus it gains a more and more consistent and luminous vision of God from the most unpromising materials. Thus conscience is a connecting principle between the creature and his Creator; and the firmest hold of theological truths is gained by habits of personal religion. When men begin all their works with the thought of God, acting for His sake, and to fulfil His will, when they ask His blessing on themselves and their life, pray to Him for the objects they desire, and see Him in the event, whether it be according to their prayers or not, they will find everything that happens tend to confirm them in the truths about Him which live in their imagination, varied and unearthly as those truths may be. (*GA* 106–7; italics mine)

Obtaining "living hold" on these non-self-evident truths is clearly an act of the illative sense, which endorses the assumption that our inner feelings reflect the presence of a divine reality and which constructs "the luminous vision of God" from converging lines of thought and experience. If we take the view that there is a God who is speaking to us from within, further evidence will accumulate under "the guise . . . of coincidences, which are indications, to the illative sense of those who believe in a Moral Governor, of His immediate Presence, especially to those who in addition hold with them the strong antecedent probability that, in His mercy, He will thus supernaturally present Himself to our apprehension" (*GA* 333)

Those who are determined not to grant Newman his presuppositions about the nature of conscience will have no difficulty dismantling his view. It is the *assumption* that God speaks in our conscience which enables the believer to assemble the religious frame of reference "from the most unpromising materials." The modern mind wants *proof,* not assumptions—the kind of proof that scientists have at their disposal: bomb blasts, power production, synthesis of new materials, space flight, and medical miracles, to name just a few. "Show me, and then I will believe," says the hard-headed modern. "Believe, and then you will see," replies Newman. He was not interested in knocking heads with those who adopt an unreasonably strict notion of "proof" as their standard of knowledge; he wished to show how the meaning of experience is transformed when one adopts the view that there is a God. His goal was "not . . . to set forth the arguments which issue in the belief of these doctrines, but to investigate what it is to believe in them, what the mind does, what it contemplates, when it makes an act of faith" (GA 93–94). Nevertheless, Newman believed that the use of the illative sense in contemplating reality creates a force for conviction that goes beyond logic-chopping:

To feel the true force of an argument like this, we must not confine ourselves to abstractions, and merely compare notion with notion, but we must contemplate the God of our conscience as a Living Being, as one Object and Reality, *under* the aspect of this or that attribute. We must patiently rest in the thought of the Eternal, Omnipresent, and All-knowing, rather than of Eternity, Omnipresence, and Omniscience; and we must not hurry on and force a series of deductions, which, if they are to be realized, must distil like dew into our minds, and form themselves spontaneously there, by a calm contemplation and gradual understanding of their premisses. (GA 249)

The necessary processes of assimilation are tacit. Although we give ourselves over to this process, and rely on it implicitly, it is not under our control in the same way that the operations of focal, articulate, and formal knowledge are.

Newman considered that reality is a text capable of being read in many different ways. Truth is in the eye of the beholder: "According to the subtlety and versatility of their gift, are men able to read what comes before them justly, variously, and fruitfully" (GA 265–66). One person may look at the universe, and read there the message that there is no God: "This is the first lesson we gain from human affairs. What strikes the mind so forcibly and so painfully is, His absence (if I may so speak) from His own world" (GA 309). Without denying the data which may be read as evidence that there is no God, Newman brought a different "power of looking at things" to bear on the same text, and found evidence there that "His hand is not shortened, but that our iniquities have divided between us and our God" (GA 310).

Newman acknowledged that not everyone is willing to read the texts of personal experience as he does, but he pointed out that there are no truths "which are not disputed by some schools of philosophy or some bodies of men" (GA 109–10). Just as there are people who suffer from color blindness or tone deafness, there may be some who "are deficient either in the religious sense or in their memory of early years" and who therefore "never had at all what those around them without hesitation profess, in their own case, to have received from nature" (GA 110–11). Newman suggests that for those who have eyes to see and ears to hear, the evidence of God in the universe is sufficient.

As we saw above (114ff.) Polanyi would have agreed with Newman on the epistemic principle that knowledge depends upon the sound operation of conscience; however, Polanyi claimed that it makes no sense to speak of God as a matter of fact:

Religion, considered as an act of worship, is an indwelling rather than an affirmation. God cannot be observed, any more than truth or beauty can be observed. He exists in the sense that He is to be worshipped and obeyed, but not otherwise; not as a fact—any more than truth, beauty or justice exist as facts. All these, like God, are things which can be apprehended only in serving them. The words 'God exists' are not, therefore, a statement of fact, such as 'snow is white,' but an accreditive statement, such as '"snow is white" is true,' and this determines the kind of doubt to which the statement 'God exists' can be subjected. (PK 279–80)

Since there is no observation of God, religion is to be aligned "with the great intellectual systems, such as mathematics, fiction, and the fine arts, which are validated by becoming happy dwelling places of the human mind" (PK 280). Polanyi thought that "the degree of our personal participation varies greatly within our various acts of knowing," depending on the relationship between "relatively objective facts" and the "supervening personal fact" (PK 36). For him, religion calls forth the highest degree of personal participation *because* "our personal participation is in general greater in a validation than in a verification. . . . Both *verification* and *validation* are everywhere an acknowledgment of a commitment: they claim the presence of something real and external to the speaker" (*PK* 202). Although science and theology resemble each other as acts of commitment, when Polanyi applied the notion of validation to Christianity, he seems to have distinguished science from religion because there is no thing "real and external" to the act of religious validation: "As a framework expressing its acceptance of itself as a dwelling place of the passionate search for God, religious worship can say nothing that is true or false" (*PK* 281). For Polanyi, unlike the Catholic tradition which embraces both worship and reflection, there is no framework outside of worship within which one can meaningfully assert the existence of God.

It seems ironic that Polanyi used religious imagery to depict a self-revealing universe, but denied that same kind of power to a self-revealing God:

One may say, indeed, quite generally, that a theory which we acclaim as rational in itself is thereby accredited with *prophetic powers.* . . . In this wholly indeterminate scope of its true implications lies the deepest sense in which objectivity is attributed to a scientific theory. . . . It inspires us, on the contrary, with the hope of overcoming the appalling disabilities of our bodily existence, even to the point of conceiving a rational idea of the universe which can *authoritatively speak for itself.* (*PK* 5; italics mine)

Polanyi had some excellent observations on the nature of "the worshipper's striving towards God" (*PK* 281); unlike Newman, he seems to have lacked any conviction that God might be striving to make contact with us.

Avery Dulles cautions against pushing this reading of Polanyi too far: "Although Polanyi can be misunderstood as denying the objective intent of religious language, his aim was rather to call attention to the evocative character of such language. Since it remains to a great extent tacit, religious knowledge relies heavily on symbol and metaphor. It does not deliver a clear concept of God, whom Polanyi often describes as a paradoxical 'coincidence of opposites.'"[3] There are at least some texts in Polanyi that contribute to this "misunderstanding":

None of these beliefs [the Fall, Redemption and "ultimate victory through Christ"] makes any literal sense. They can be destroyed as easily as the actuality of Polonius' death upon the stage, should anyone attempt to defend its reality in the world of facts. Both are works of the imagination, accepted by us as mean-

3. Avery Dulles, "Faith, Church and God: Insights from Michael Polanyi," *Theological Studies* 45 (1984), 548. The quotation from Polanyi is from *Meaning*, 129.

ingful integrations of quite incompatible clues that move us deeply and help us to pull the scattered droplets of our lives together into a single sea of sublime meaning. (*Meaning* 157)

The contents may continue to seem completely implausible to us, while yet we see in the creation stories, the miraculous-birth stories, the Crucifixion and Resurrection stories a meaning expressing the whole significance of life and the universe in genuine and universal feeling terms. Then we can say: It does not matter. If not this story exactly, then *something like this* is somehow true—in fact, is somehow the highest truth about all things. (*Meaning* 159)

If, as Dulles contends, Polanyi did not mean to deny "the objective intent of religious language," then he seems to have expressed himself very poorly in these and similar passages in *Personal Knowledge;* he is far more vigorous in denying the power of religious language than in affirming it. Nevertheless, there are other passages in Polanyi which seem to grant the objectivity of God—see the section on "Comprehensive Entities" below (176). Polanyi seemed willing to grant the reality of God but to deny the power of language to declare much, if anything, about the nature of that reality.

Belief in the Holy Trinity

Newman's concern in discussing the doctrine of the Trinity is to show how we may apprehend the reality of the tri-personal God in spite of the fact that "this doctrine, thus drawn out, is of a notional character" (*GA* 112). The pathway to real apprehension of the Trinity is to focus on each aspect of the mystery and to recognize that the language used to express it is addressed to the imagination:

No human words indeed are worthy of the Supreme Being, none are adequate; but we have no other words to use but human, and those in question are among the simplest and most intelligible that are to be found in language. . . . There are then no terms in the foregoing exposition which do not admit of a plain sense, and they are used in that sense; and, moreover, that sense is what I have called real, for the words in their ordinary use stand for things. The words, Father, Son, Spirit, He, One, and the rest, are not abstract terms, but concrete, and adapted to excite images. (*GA* 113)

We do not apprehend the totality of this reality directly: "Our image of Him never is one, but broken in numberless partial aspects, independent of each other" (*GA* 116).

For Newman, the proposition that the Trinity is a *mystery* is not a dogma but an insight derived from experiencing our inability to imagine how all of the partial aspects presented by dogma can be reconciled:

If an educated man, to whom it is presented, does not perceive that mysteriousness at once, that is a sure token that he does not rightly apprehend the propositions which contain the doctrine. Hence it follows that the thesis "the doctrine of the Holy Trinity in Unity is mysterious" is indirectly an article of faith. But such an article, being a reflection made upon a revealed truth in an inference, expresses a notion, not a thing. It does not relate to the direct apprehension of the object, but to a judgment of our reason upon the object. (GA 114)

There are, then, two quite different modes of apprehending the Trinity: "That systematized whole is the object of notional assent, and its propositions, one by one, are the objects of real [assent]" (GA 119).

Polanyi did not address the theology of the Trinity directly. His remarks on the instrumentality of concepts might be used to illuminate Newman's view of the creed:

A small set of consistently used symbols which, owing to their peculiar manageability, enable us to think about their subject matter more swiftly in terms of its symbolic representation, can be used to carry information to other people if they can use this representation as we do. This can happen only if speakers and listeners have heard the terms used in similar circumstances, and have derived from these experiences the same relation between the symbols and the recurrent features (or functions) which they represent. Both speakers and listeners must also have found the symbols in question manageable, as otherwise they could not have acquired any fluency in their use. (PK 204–5)

Newman's goal in considering the language of the creed is to show that each aspect of belief in the Trinity is "manageable" when considered in isolation from the other aspects. In order to dwell in the interpretative framework established by the dogma of the Trinity, one must *use* the propositions as personal instruments of understanding:

Like the tool, the sign or symbol can be conceived as such only in the eyes of a person who *relies on them* to achieve or to signify something. *This reliance is a personal commitment which is involved in all acts of intelligence by which we integrate some things subsidiarily to the center of our focal attention.* Every act of personal assimilation by which we make a thing form an extension of ourselves through our subsidiary awareness of it, is a commitment of ourselves; a manner of disposing of ourselves. (PK 61)

The act of assimilation of the Trinitarian framework is a skillful performance that underlies the use of dogmatic language. To be a member of the community means more than repeating the words of the creed; it also means adopting the "essentially inarticulable" presuppositions of the Christian language:

When we accept a certain set of pre-suppositions and use them as our interpretative framework, we may be said to dwell in them as we do in our own body. Their uncritical acceptance for the time being consists in a process of assimilation by which we identify ourselves with them. They are not asserted and cannot be asserted, for assertion can be made only *within* a framework with which we have identified ourselves for the time being; as they are themselves our ultimate framework, they are essentially inarticulable. (*PK* 59)

In order to experience real apprehension of the manifold aspects of the Trinity, one must cease to look at the propositions which express the dogma and instead *rely* on them a-critically. Only then do the clues fall into place as a whole beyond the reach of articulation and grant us the quasi-real apprehension (realization) of the mystery.

As suggested in Chapter III (125), Polanyi's reflections on the structure of perception support and enrich Newman's understanding of the development of real apprehension. Polanyi saw the effect of "heuristic passion" as driving us to transform ourselves and therefore to make an effort to transform the patterns of our perception. Such a conversion is accomplished informally, by the illative sense, because formal operations can take place only within an established frame of reference. Even though the new framework contains language at its focus, the act of *understanding* the bearing of that language on reality is a tacit act:

Maps, graphs, books, formulae, etc., offer wonderful opportunities for reorganizing our knowledge from ever new points of view. And this reorganization is itself, as a rule, a tacit performance, similar to that by which we gain intellectual control over our surroundings at the pre-verbal level, and akin therefore to the process of creative reorganization by which new discoveries are made. . . . The pondering and reconsideration of various subject matters in terms of symbols designating them . . . is now seen to be a tacit, a-critical process. (*SM* 24)

The words which communicate the doctrine of the Trinity are only the focal point of a personal integration of tacit subsidiaries. They provide a kind of conceptual map for believers to follow in exploring their experience of God. Each part of the Trinitarian system must be handled carefully with a silent awareness of its bearing on the whole. As New-man observed, we can take up only one part of the whole at a time: "Creeds and dogmas live in the one idea which they are designed to ex-press, and which alone is substantive; and are necessary, because the human mind cannot reflect upon it except piecemeal, cannot use it in its oneness and entireness, or without resolving it into a series of as-pects and relations."[4] No one proposition is sufficient to communicate the whole of Christianity from one person to another, just as no one proposition is sufficient to communicate the whole of mathematics or the whole of physics. A multitude of views must be coordinated by a vi-sion that makes sense of the disparate elements:

> If Christianity is a fact, and impresses an idea of itself on our minds and is a subject matter of exercises of the reason, that idea will in course of time expand into a multitude of ideas, and aspects of ideas, connected and harmonious with one another, and in themselves determinate and immutable, as is the objective fact itself which is thus represented. It is a characteristic of our minds, that they cannot take an object in, which is submitted to them simply and integrally. We conceive by means of a definition or description; whole objects do not create in the intellect whole ideas, but are, to use a mathematical phrase, thrown into a series, into a number of statements, strengthening, interpreting, correcting each other, and with more or less exactness approximating, as they accumulate, to a perfect image. There is no other way of learning or teaching. We cannot teach except by aspects or views, which are not identical with the thing itself which we are teaching. (*Dev* 41)

Holding the faith, then, is a matter of keeping the parts and the whole in a delicate and dynamic balance.

Newman probably would have agreed that adoption of the Trini-tarian *Gestalt* is a self-modifying mental act that has some of the char-acteristics of a discovery. If the dogma does not change one's way of seeing things, then it is clear that the person has not reached the real apprehension and real assent that Newman understood as the heart of religious faith. One of the most important tacit skills to be absorbed from the believing community is knowing when and how language fails to serve the religious experience. There is a time to speak and a time to be silent. Recognition of the real limits of religious language must be acquired by personal experience of them—as is true, Polanyi says, of the language of *any* interpretative framework:

---

4. *Dev* 39, quoting *US* xv, sections 20–23 (pp. 329–32 in the third edition of *US*).

To assert that I have knowledge which is ineffable is not to deny that I can speak of it, but only that I can speak of it adequately, the assertion itself being an appraisal of this inadequacy. . . . Such reflections must of course appeal ultimately to the very sense of inadequacy which they intend to justify. They do not try to eliminate, but only to evoke more vividly our sense of inadequate representation, by persevering in the direction of greater precision and reflecting on the ultimate failure of this attempt. (*PK* 91)

The language of the Trinity creates a framework for the specific religious experience of becoming tongue-tied in the presence of understanding that goes beyond the words that brought it about. In such moments, the believer compares an interior vision with the language available and recognizes personally how far speech falls short of what faith has revealed. Nevertheless, without the articulate structure of dogma, there would be no common vision shared by the community of faith. As we shall see in the next section, Polanyi may move too quickly to limit the scope of religious affirmations, declaring them inadequate before relying on them to find out just what kind of peculiar inadequacy they have.

Belief in Dogmatic Theology

At first glance, the title of this section is ambiguous. One might read it as "what dogmatic theology says about belief," or as "the role of belief in the conduct of dogmatic theology" or as "acceptance of dogmatic theology as a valid discipline." The last reading seems closest to Newman's original intent. Newman usually made a firm distinction between "religion" as a series of real assents based upon apprehension of concrete truths and "theology" as notional assent grounded in intellectual operations on ideas. In his view, certitude is the property of religion, because through religious assent "we have a direct and conscious knowledge of our Maker, His attributes, His providences, acts, works, and will, from nature, and revelation," while theology, being notional and abstract, does not let us "advance beyond probabilities or to attain more than an opinion" (*GA* 193–94). In the final section of Chapter Five, "dogmatic theology" appears as an exception to Newman's normal distinction between religion and theology. In Newman's first sketch of the role of the Church in teaching faith, he spoke as if the scope of faith were limited to concrete propositions: "Its declarations are categorical, brief, clear, elementary, of the first importance, expressive of the concrete, the objects of real apprehension, and the basis and rule of devotion" (*GA* 125). History shows, however, that the Church has not limited itself to proposing such "objects of real apprehension," but has defined certain notions as well in order to subserve the primary propositions about divine realities. Misunderstandings must be ruled out if there is to be revelation, and this leads to the dogmatic and *notional* development of doctrine:

I cannot deny that a large and ever-increasing collection of propositions, abstract notions, not concrete truths, become, by the successive definitions of Councils, a portion of the *credenda,* and have an imperative claim upon the faith of every Catholic; and this being the case, it will be asked me how I am borne out by facts in enlarging, as I have done, on the simplicity and directness, on the tangible reality, of the Church's dogmatic teaching. . . . She makes it imperative on every one, priest and layman, to profess as revealed truth all the canons of the Councils, and innumerable decisions of the Popes, propositions so various, so notional, that but few can know them, and fewer can understand them. (*GA* 125–26)

The behavior of the Church disrupts Newman's neat distinction between real and notional propositions and between religion and theology: it asks for religious assent to theological speculation.

Newman accepted the dogmatic imposition of speculation as intrinsic to the proclamation of the realities of faith:

Now theological science, being thus the exercise of the intellect upon the *credenda* of revelation, is, though not directly devotional, at once natural, excellent, and necessary. It is natural, because the intellect is one of our highest faculties; excellent, because it is our duty to use our faculties to the full; necessary, because unless we apply our intellect to revealed truth rightly, others will exercise their minds upon it wrongly. Accordingly, the Catholic intellect makes a survey and a catalogue of the doctrines contained in the *depositum* of revelation, as committed to the Church's keeping; it locates, adjusts, defines them each, and brings them together into a whole. (*GA* 127)

It is the illative sense that bears primary responsibility for this process of assembling partial views "into a whole." It is personal judgment that passes from notional to real apprehension, and back again, silently assessing the weight of relationships and maintaining contact with living realities that escape our partializing intellectual views of them. The Catholic intellect operates illatively, both in the life of the individual and in corporate life: "It is the Church's use of History in which the Catholic believes; and she uses other informants also, Scripture, Tradition, the ecclesiastical sense, or *phronema*, and a subtle ratiocinative power, which in its origin is a divine gift" (*DN* 177). The illative sense brings both the individual and the Church to a reflex awareness that a question can or cannot be answered.

Although the Church relies on the illative sense to come to judgment about itself, the personal judgment of its members is not identical in all cases and is not necessarily infallible. A crucial ingredient in the Catholic intellect is the willingness to restructure one's own thought according to the "one rule of faith" (*GA* 129). Newman believed that revelation puts us in touch with realities that exceed the grasp of our notions; we must therefore be ready to modify our notions as new aspects of those realities present themselves to view. The articulate dimension of the faith resembles Polanyi's account of scientific theories, which, because they make contact with a hidden reality, can be expected to provide new disclosures beyond those recognized at first. So, too, Newman saw that "in the act of believing it at all, we forthwith commit ourselves by anticipation to believe truths which at present we do not believe, because they have never come before us;—we limit henceforth the range of our private judgment in prospect by the conditions, whatever they are, of that dogma" (*GA* 130). The "range of our private judgment"—the range of our illative sense—is limited by our commitment to the illative judgment of the Church. Newman's description of how we "commit ourselves by anticipation to believe truths which at present we do not believe" dovetails with Polanyi's understanding of commitment to realities that will continue to make new disclosures to us: "Such knowing is indeed *objective* in the sense of establishing contact with a hidden reality; a contact that is defined as the condition for anticipating an indeterminate range of yet unknown (and perhaps yet inconceivable) true implications" (*PK* vii–viii). Surrendering to the teaching authority of the Church therefore includes not just a commitment to what has already been voiced, but openness to future decisions of the Church.

In Chapter Seven of the *Grammar*, "Certitude," Newman clarified the notion of infallibility. Newman did not suppose that we must be infallible in order to be certain:

First, as to fallibility and infallibility. It is very common, doubtless, especially in religious controversy, to confuse infallibility with certitude, and to argue that, since we have not the one, we have not the other, for that no one can claim to be certain on any point, who is not infallible about all; but the two words stand for things quite distinct from each other. . . . A certitude is directed to this or that particular proposition; it is not a faculty or gift, but a disposition of mind relatively to a definite case which is before me. Infallibility, on the contrary, is just that which certitude is not; it *is* a faculty or gift, and relates, not to some one truth in particular, but to all possible propositions in a given subject-matter. (*GA* 183)

Newman made it very clear that being honest about the weaknesses and limitations of the human intellect does not undercut his assurance that the Church cannot err in formulating the propositions that are required for the transmission of the faith: "We may be certain of the infallibility of the Church, while we admit that in many things we are not, and cannot be, certain at all. . . . I can believe then in the infallible Church without my own personal infallibility" (*GA* 184, 185). In the *Grammar*, Newman did not directly address the question of how the Church as a whole can be infallible; Newman's remarks in the *Grammar* aimed only to show the clear distinction between the notions of certitude and infallibility. In his *Letter to the Duke of Norfolk*, Newman argued that the root of infallibility is not to be found in "fallible man" but in "a supernatural infallible guidance" (*DN* 185). Newman did not think that people can come to agreement on "religious and moral perceptions" without God's help: "We need the interposition of a Power, greater than human teaching and human argument, to make our beliefs true and our minds one" (*GA* 293).

Religious assent to dogmatic speculation hinges on acceptance of the infallibility of the Church, which Newman considered "the fundamental dogma of the Catholic religion" (*GA* 131). Newman was not concerned in Chapter Five with *why* one might be persuaded that the Church should be believed in the full scope of its teaching, both real and notional—that is the issue in the final section of the *Grammar*. The issue here is how to preserve the power of real assent even when it leads us into the brambles of speculation. The propositions which elicit, focus, and sustain faith are not the faith itself, for the act of commitment which uses the articulate structure of dogma is primarily a tacit reality.

Although Newman accepted the fact that the Church has the right to define notions as well as to propose realities, the "system" of belief can never be completely systematized:

Now a religion is not a proposition, but a system; it is a rite, a creed, a philosophy, a rule of duty, all at once; and to accept a religion is neither a simple assent to it nor a complex, neither a conviction nor a prejudice, neither a notional assent nor a real, not a mere act of profession, nor of credence, nor of opinion, nor of speculation, but it is a collection of all these various kinds of assents, at once and together, some of one description, some of another.[5]

Because the Church is a complex and living reality, it is impossible to predict in advance the shape that this system of belief can or will take. This does not mean that there is no value in such systematization as is possible—though the heart has its own reasons, the mind hungers for the proper intellectual development of faith. When "the real intrinsic connection of part with part" is spelled out in a systematic fashion, "it must be constructed on definite principles and laws, the knowledge of which will enlarge our capacity of reasoning about it in particulars" (GA 210). Newman concludes that formalization of the faith provides "scientific methods" for grasping the faith that are more comprehensive than personal insight.

The gift of spelling out the inner connection of one part of a tacit integration with the other parts cannot be produced on demand. Polanyi emphasized that we do not know how much we can know until breakthroughs grant us a new interpretative framework:

Even a small map multiplies a thousandfold the original input of information; and add to this that, actually, the number of meaningful and interesting questions one could study by means of such a map is much greater and not wholly foreseeable. Much less can we control in advance the myriads of arrangements in which nouns, adjectives, verbs and adverbs can be meaningfully combined to form new affirmations or questions, thus developing, as we shall see, the meaning of the words themselves ever further in these new contexts. Verbal speculation may therefore reveal an inexhaustible fund of true knowledge and new substantial problems, just as it may also produce pieces of mere sophistry. (PK 94–95)

---

5. GA 196–97. Polanyi would have agreed with Newman's view of the complex structure of religion: "Religion, we can see, is a sprawling work of the imagination involving rites, ceremonies, doctrines, myths, and something called 'worship.' It is a form of 'acceptance' much more complex, therefore, than any of the other forms we have been attending to" (Meaning 152).

Systematic theology provides some notional maps of religious realities. In Newman's view, some of these maps may be imposed by the authority of the Church (Trinitarian speculation, grace, Christology) while others remain in the domain of nondogmatic systematization (the Jesuit/Dominican controversy over grace, speculations about the divine and human consciousness of Christ, Newman's own theories on the development of doctrine, etc.).

Embracing the dogmatic theology of the Church should not close us to the interaction with sacred realities that may transform our view in the future. It takes skill to know how to integrate all of the aspects of the world of faith—to know when to submit to the legitimate authority of the Church as the vehicle of revelation and when to resist mistaken assertions of authority. Because the scope of the faith has not been and cannot be completely mapped out systematically, we must develop our illative sense to judge how to apply the rule of faith to our lives. For Newman, the first step is to use others' judgment as a guide until we learn how to think for ourselves:

Instead of trusting logical science, we must trust persons, namely, those who by long acquaintance with their subject have a right to judge. And if we wish ourselves to share in their convictions and the grounds of them, we must follow their history, and learn as they have learned. We must take up their particular subject as they took it up, beginning at the beginning, give ourselves to it, depend on practice and experience more than on reasoning, and thus gain that mental insight into truth, whatever its subject-matter may be, which our masters have gained before us. By following this course, we may make ourselves of their number, and then we rightly lean upon ourselves, directing ourselves by our own moral or intellectual judgment, not by our skill in argumentation. (GA 268–69)

In Newman's view of religion, there is a time for everything: a time for dogmatism, a time for speculation, a time to believe, and a time to doubt. The art of thinking with the Church depends on knowing when it is appropriate to submit and when it is not.

Polanyi's discussion of the art of science might be used to show how the skill of thinking with the Church can be communicated from person to person, even though it cannot be completely formalized.

The exact sciences are a set of formulae which have a bearing on experience. We have seen that in accrediting this bearing, we must rely to varying degrees on our power of personal knowing. . . . Science is operated by the skill of the scientist and it is through the exercise of his skill that he shapes his scientific knowledge. . . . *The aim of a skillful performance is achieved by the observance of a set of rules which are not known as such to the person following them.* (PK 49)

We might extract three principles for theology from this passage:

1. Systematic theology provides a set of formulae which have a bearing on Christian experience.
2. Entering systematic theology depends in varying degrees upon the skill of personal knowing.
3. The goal of theological integration may be achieved by observing rules embedded in the tradition which are not known as such by the person following them.

Keeping a balance between notional constructs and the religious experience which they are to illuminate is unquestionably a "skillful performance" directed by tacit knowledge. The theologian must have a "feel" for how the concepts of theology interact with the affirmations of religion, just as the scientist and mathematician must know how to *use* articulation to subserve the realities they contemplate:

To rely on a theory for understanding nature is to interiorize it. For we are attending from the theory to things seen in its light, and are aware of the theory, while thus using it, in terms of the spectacle that it serves to explain. This is why mathematical theory can be learned only by practicing its application: its true knowledge lies in our ability to use it. (*TD* 17)

Dogmatic theology imposes theories for understanding the data of faith. The skill of thinking with the Church—dwelling within its interpretative framework—is very much a matter of keeping one's balance. Just as Polanyi saw that the ability to *use* a theory is the highest evidence that one has truly come to dwell in the interpretative framework it provides, so Newman recognized that entering into the faith was more than a matter of remembering the propositions that express it. The believer needs to know how to keep all the separate assertions in balance: "We must have a whole doctrine stated by a whole Church. The Catholic Truth in question is made up of a number of separate propositions, each of which, if maintained to the exclusion of the rest, is a heresy" (*Dev* 11). So, for example, the faith teaches us that God is the author of our salvation. If we press this truth too far, it becomes the heresy of quietism, which obliterates the fact that God invites us to co-operate freely with his gift of grace. The fact that we must work with God in our own salvation can likewise be pressed too far and become the heresy of Pelagianism.

Jesus did not give his disciples a list of propositions to be mem-orized—he gave himself to them in an enduring relationship that com-pletely transformed their vision of reality. The most valuable knowl-edge they possessed could not be put into words because it was a matter of personal apprehension of a divine Person. A list of dogmati-cally correct propositions about Jesus can never replace that core expe-rience. As with any act of knowledge, the disciples undoubtedly saw more in Jesus than they could ever say. If so, then the most important element of Christian tradition is the "ineffable process of thought" (*Dev* 11) communicated tacitly from Jesus to His disciples: "We must con-clude that the transmission of knowledge from one generation to the other must be predominantly tacit" (*TD* 60–61). If all knowledge is tac-it or rooted in tacit knowledge—and if, as Newman taught, Christian faith is real knowledge—then we must say that all revelation is tacit or rooted in tacit knowledge.

Polanyi had no difficulty in affirming the importance of "submitting to the authority of a personal example as a carrier of tradition" (*PK* 53) in the conduct of science and society (*PK* 55, 124, 206, 208). Unfortu-nately, his presuppositions about religious language seem to have pre-vented him from extending this model of knowledge to Christian belief. For him, "the ritual of worship is expressly designed to induce and sus-tain [a] state of anguish, surrender and hope" (*PK* 198). There seems to be no room in Polanyi's view for anything like dogmatic theology. Where Newman believed that one may find joy and freedom in the cer-titudes revealed in Christianity, Polanyi believed dogmatic convictions would destroy faith. In his view, "a sense of its own imperfection is es-sential to . . . faith" (*PK* 280).

This is where Newman and Polanyi most clearly part company. As will be seen in the section on revealed religion, Newman held that the necessary incompleteness of religious belief is no bar to the special re-pose associated with certitude. Polanyi did not suppose that there may be an authoritative transmission of tacit knowledge in Christianity be-cause he apparently did not think it possible for God to make Himself known to us. It may be that his view of religious knowledge was biased by using mysticism as the model of divine knowledge. Polanyi held that the mystic "strives for absolute ignorance of particulars which grants union with him who is beyond all being and all knowledge" (*Meaning* 128). While "absolute ignorance of particulars" may be a valid gift given to some as an intrinsic part of being swallowed up in the love of God, it is not clear that this is meant to be the typical condition of Christians, who have been commissioned to "make disciples of all nations" (Mt 28:19). Polanyi never claimed to be speaking from personal religious or mystical experience. In this case, he seems to have been operating on theories derived from secondhand sources. Operating at best only on the fringe of Christianity, Polanyi seems to have taken one element from the tradition—the notion that God is always greater than any of our ideas of God—and emphasized it to the detriment of those elements of tradition which emphasize that God has made himself known to us through the Person and the Spirit of Jesus.

Natural Religion

The tenth and final chapter of the *Grammar*, "Inference and Assent in the Matter of Religion," addresses the evidence in favor of natural and revealed religion (*GA* 300). The section "Natural Religion" reprises the theme of belief in God from Chapter Five, that the data of conscience may be interpreted as signs of the existence of God. Like Polanyi, Newman recognizes the sovereignty of personal knowledge, because the operations of "our own mind" provide "the rule by which we test, interpret, and correct what is presented to us for belief, whether by the universal testimony of mankind, or by the history of society and of the world" (*GA* 303). The illative sense may incline the mind "to give an interpretation to the course of things"—to read the text of nature—so as to disclose the presence of God in the world, "leading the great majority of men to recognize the Hand of unseen power, directing in mercy or in judgment the physical and moral system" (*GA* 312–13). As with any question of proof, the conclusion depends upon the "personal first principles and judgments" which are employed to gather data and construct arguments. Newman did not care to follow such arguments in detail. His commitment to informal apologetics is especially evident when he says that if "an illogical exercise of reason" brings someone knowledge of God, then "if logic finds fault with it, so much the worse for logic" (GA 313). For Newman, apprehension of facts matters more than adherence to the formalisms of reason narrowly defined. The key to natural religion is "the sense of sin; it recognizes the disease, but cannot find, it does but look out for the remedy" (GA 375). If we let conscience speak, it will point us Godward.

Although Polanyi was unwilling to go as far as Newman in accepting the reality of God as a matter of fact, he seemed to read the universe as pointing beyond itself to some higher reality. In seeking to learn something new, "we hope to be visited by powers for which we cannot account in terms of our specifiable capabilities" (PK 324). Polanyi calls this act of hope "a clue to God" and associates it with the upward dynamism of evolution in the last chapter of *Personal Knowledge*.[6] Polanyi was unwilling to say "God exists," but he seems to have been equally unwilling to say that God is only a figment of our imagination:

[Man] is strong, noble and wonderful so long as he fears the voices of this firmament; but he dissolves their power over himself and his own powers gained through obeying them, if he turns back and examines what he respects in a detached manner. Then law is no more than what the courts will decide, art but an emollient of nerves, morality but a convention, tradition but an inertia, God but a psychological necessity. (PK 380)

The very last words of *Personal Knowledge* once again suggest an implicit belief in a divinity as the ultimate foundation of all meaning in the universe:

We may envisage then a cosmic field which called forth all these centers by offering them a short-lived, limited, hazardous opportunity for making some progress of their own towards an unthinkable consummation. And that is also, I believe, how a Christian is placed when worshipping God. (PK 405)

Polanyi certainly seems to have come close to the door of religious belief, even if he himself did not go beyond its threshold. Polanyi understood that, for believers, God appears to be the ultimate *Gestalt* which makes sense out of everything else; the whole universe then appears "not focally, but as part of a cosmos, as features of God" (PK 197–98). In *Science, Faith and Society*, Polanyi had developed a similar view that

6. PK 324. The final section of the last chapter is called "First Causes and Ultimate Ends" (PK 402–5).

the correct reading of human experience leads one to the affirmation of the existence and action of a divine being:

Such an interpretation of society would seem to call for an extension in the direction towards God. If the intellectual and moral tasks of society rest in the last resort on the free consciences of every generation, and these are continually making essentially new additions to our spiritual heritage, we may well assume that they are in continuous communication with the same source which first gave men their society-forming knowledge of abiding things. How near that source is to God I shall not try to conjecture. But I would express my belief that modern man will eventually return to God through the clarification of his cultural and social purposes. Knowledge of reality and the acceptance of obligations which guide our consciences, once firmly realized, will reveal to us God in man and society. (SFS 83–84)

As will be seen in the next section, Polanyi probably would have preferred to see such revelation take place along the lines of the progressive discovery of the laws of nature rather than through a specific historical channel.

Revealed Religion

All of Newman's reflections on apprehension, assent, inference, and certitude come to a head in the declaration that Christianity is "absolutely certain knowledge":

But the very idea of Christianity in its profession and history, is something more than this; it is a "Revelatio revelata;" it is a definite message from God to man distinctly conveyed by His chosen instruments, and to be received as such a message; and therefore to be positively acknowledged, embraced, and maintained as true, on the ground of its being divine, not as true on intrinsic grounds, not as probably true, or partially true, but as absolutely certain knowledge, certain in a sense in which nothing else can be certain, because it comes from Him who neither can deceive nor be deceived. (GA 302)

In the act of faith, the illative sense judges that God-given standards must be applied to all subsequent judgments: we "must receive it all, as we find it, if we accept it at all" on the basis of "valid testimonials of its right to demand our homage" (GA 302). The last section of the Grammar explores some of the "valid testimonials" that persuade one to adopt the standards of revelation.

Newman's goal was clearly persuasion rather than proof in the strict sense of that term. The "absolutely certain knowledge" given by Christianity may be affirmed by the judgment of the believer, but cannot be imposed by argument on one who chooses to view reality differently. Newman approaches natural theology as "a matter of private judgment" that goes beyond the scope of "demonstration" (GA 318–19). Newman's objective in this section is an informal apologetics. He intended "to prove Christianity in the same informal way in which I can prove for certain that I have been born into this world, and that I shall die out of it" (GA 319). The method used was the "accumulation of various probabilities," no one of which independently could "satisfy the severe requisitions" of formal logic.[7] In this passage, Newman's statement of his theological presupposition is short—"the providence and intention of God"—while his description of the need to appeal from his own illative sense to that of his reader is long:

Here then at once is one momentous doctrine or principle, which enters into my own reasoning, and which another ignores, viz. the providence and intention of God; and of course there are other principles, explicit or implicit, which are in like circumstances. It is not wonderful then, that, while I can prove Christianity divine to my own satisfaction, I shall not be able to force it upon any one else. Multitudes indeed I ought to succeed in persuading of its truth without any force at all, because they and I start from the same principles, and what is a proof to me is a proof to them; but if any one starts from any other principles but ours, I have not the power to change his principles, or the conclusion which he draws from them, any more than I can make a crooked man straight. Whether his mind will ever grow straight, whether I can do anything towards its becoming straight, whether he is not responsible, responsible to his Maker, for being mentally crooked, is another matter; still the fact remains, that, in any inquiry about things in the concrete, men differ from each other, not so much in the soundness of their reasoning as in the principles which govern its exercise, that those principles are of a personal character, that where there is no common measure of minds, there is no common measure of arguments, and that the validity of a proof is determined, not by any scientific test, but by the illative sense. (GA 321)

It is clear from this long description of our freedom to choose our view of reason and reality that Newman expects epistemic and not theological objections to his position. In an earlier chapter, Newman pointed out the danger of trying to turn a matter for personal judgment into a system of inferences. The real, personal reasons that persuade some-

---

7. GA 320. See the discussion in Chapter III above, page 125.

one to believe in "the divine origin of the Church, . . . the being of God, and the immortality of the soul" are "recondite and impalpable," while efforts to formulate arguments in support of faith "will sometimes only confuse his apprehension of sacred objects, and subtracts from his devotion quite as much as it adds to his knowledge" (*GA* 264–65). Although there is sufficient apprehension of the realities involved to make an act of certitude—"I know that I know Christianity is from God"—there is nothing like the grasp of clear and distinct ideas necessary for a formal proof, because the foundation of this particular certitude is an illative integration of subsidiaries. The focus of this tacit integration is a concrete reality, God-revealing-God, not just a single idea or proposition. Any number of notions may flow from contact with that single and ultimate Reality.

Although Polanyi did not share Newman's view of revelation, he would undoubtedly have sympathized with Newman's decision to attempt persuasion rather than proof. Polanyi understood the limits of formal logic very well:

I do not assume that I can force my view on my opponents by argument. Though I accept truth as existing independently of my knowledge of it, and as accessible to all men, I admit my inability to compel anyone to see it. Though I believe that others love truth as I do, I can see no way to force their assent to this view. (*SFS* 81)

Accepting the limits of proof does not mean that Polanyi abandoned all restraints on belief. One guard against unreasonable speculation is the collective conscience of the scientific community:

Men might say: "If there is no demonstrable truth, I shall call true whatever I like, for example whatever is to my advantage to assert." Or: "If you admit that your belief of truth is ultimately based on your personal judgment, then I, the State, am entitled to replace your judgment by my own and determine what you shall believe to be true." This, however, is not a correct reference to my position. Though I deny that truth is demonstrable, I assert that it is knowable, and I have said how. My position could be accused of leading to such general license only if this condition could be shown to follow from a general assertion by everyone of the truth as he knows it in the light of his own conscience. But I cannot admit the possibility of such a result since the coherence of all men's consciences in the grounds of the same universal tradition is an integral part of my position. (*SFS* 82)

Newman likewise relied on the coherence of conscience as reflected in "the primary teachings of nature in the human race."[8] Both Newman and Polanyi agree with St. Augustine: "Securus judicat orbis terrarum."[9]

Newman held that from the experience of God speaking from within the person there arises an expectation of a corresponding objective revelation from without. "Some minds will feel it to be so powerful, as to recognize in it almost a proof, without direct evidence, of the divinity of a religion claiming to be the true, supposing its history and doctrine are free from positive objection, and there be no rival religion with plausible claims of its own" (GA 328–29). In Newman's view, of course, there is no such rival. "There is only one Religion in the world which tends to fulfill the aspirations, needs, and foreshadowings of natural faith and devotion. . . . It alone has a definite message addressed to all mankind. . . . Christianity . . . is in its idea an announcement, a preaching; it is the depository of truths beyond human discovery, momentous, practical, maintained one and the same in substance in every age from its first, and addressed to all mankind" (GA 333–34). From the close fit between what conscience expects and Christianity provides, Newman suggested that "either Christianity is from God, or revelation has not yet been given to us" (GA 334). For Newman, this is a simple act of recognition—like recognizing a friend's face—in which he saw that what the Church offers is what his heart desired. For him, it was a personally self-evident truth that "some authority there must be if there is a revelation given, and other authority there is none but she. A revelation is not given, if there be no authority to decide what is given" (Dev 65). For Newman, the recognition that revelation implies a living interpretative authority led him "by a stern logical necessity to accept the whole" (Dev 69). He knew that not everyone will view the facts as he did nor feel this "stern logical necessity" leading to acceptance of the

8. GA 324. Newman suggested the nature of these teachings by outlining a "system of opinion" that he believed is "simply false" (GA 323–44).

9. Literally, "The whole world judges justly"; the sense of the epigram is that we can rely on what the whole body of believers believe to be true. Newman concludes his reflections on this Augustinian proverb by saying that "the deliberate judgment, in which the whole Church at length rests and acquiesces, is an infallible prescription and final sentence against such portions of it as protest and secede" (Apo 98). Newman and Polanyi respect different circles of judgment, of course; Newman looked to the judgment of the whole Church while Polanyi relies on the distributed, but very effective authority of the scientific community.

authority of the Church, but his goal is to show what it was that persuaded him to adopt this position.

Newman rounded out the *Grammar* with a reading of the history of Judaism and Christianity in order to show how these two religions "profess to be the organ of a formal revelation . . . directed to the benefit of the whole human race" (*GA* 341). To try to evaluate his view that "no other religion but these two" (*GA* 341) makes such a claim would take us far afield into the realm of comparative religions. Even if we restricted the scope of inquiry to the history of Judaism and Christianity, it might be hard to reconstruct Newman's view that "there never was a time when that revelation was not,—a revelation continuous and systematic, with distinct representatives and an orderly succession" (*GA* 335). Twentieth-century historical consciousness would probably be more comfortable with a quantum-probabilistic model of revelation in which the development of doctrine is seen to be relatively discontinuous and unsystematic. Contemplating the progression from candles to gas burners to electric light, Polanyi highlighted the complete displacement of one system by another: "Each new improved form of illumination simply displaces its predecessor. Instead of the development of a single principle, we see a series of logically disconnected attempts to serve a steady purpose" (*LL* 75). In the same way, the "steady purpose" of the self-revealing God may inspire quantum leaps from one *Gestalt* to another. Such "logically disconnected" developments may be seen to derive from illation rather than from formal reasoning.

The Problem of the Papacy

For Polanyi, one of the beauties of modern science is its ability to operate through a loose system of distributed authority. He explored "polycentricity" in economics as a model of distributed discipline in science. Each scientist stands at the center of his or her own field and has the ability to criticize other scientists working in nearby fields. Such a system of "self-co-ordination . . . will succeed over a wide range of polycentricity in which central direction is completely impracticable" (*LL* 183–84). The reality of distributed centers of authority prevents science from developing itself scientifically; for Polanyi, "to 'plan' science is to suppress it" (*LL* 198–99). Nevertheless, progress in science is real and quite reliable, even if it proceeds unsystematically through personal acts of discovery. Criticism of new *Gestalten* is intrinsic to the progression, even if criticism alone is sterile: "Unfettered intuitive speculation would lead to extravagant wishful conclusions; while rigorous fulfillment of any set of critical rules would completely paralyze discovery" (*SFS* 41). Once again, some (illative) sense of balance is required to know how to keep a fruitful balance between the constructive and destructive powers of reason.

Polanyi used his polycentric model of science to criticize the centralized authority of Roman Catholicism:

The realms of science, of law, and of Protestant religion which I have taken as examples of modern cultural communities are each subject to control by their own body of opinion. Scientific opinion, legal theory, Protestant theology are all formed by the consensus of independent individuals, rooted in a common tradition. In law and religion, it is true, there prevails a measure of official doctrinal compulsion from a center, which is almost entirely absent from science. The difference is marked; yet in spite of such compulsion as legal and religious life are subjected to, the conscience of the judge and of the minister bears an important responsibility in acting as its own interpreter of the law or of the Christian faith. Thus the life of science, the law, and the Protestant Church all three stand in contrast to the constitution, say, of the Catholic Church which denies to the believer's conscience the right to interpret the Christian dogma and reserves the final decision in such matters to his confessor. There is here the profound difference between two types of authority; one laying down general presuppositions, the other imposing *conclusions*. We may call the first a General, the latter a Specific Authority. (*SFS* 57)

In Polanyi's view, the "Specific Authority" of Rome stifles the possibility of polycentric creativity because it "makes all important reinterpretations and innovations by pronouncements from the center."[10] If science were structured like the Roman Catholic Church, "all progress would stop. No recruit with any love of science would join any institution governed by such decisions" (*SFS* 53). Although Polanyi did not make the comparison explicit, it is clear that he saw the Roman church making the same error as the Russian state, attempting to dictate progress through ideology. Polanyi's alternative ideal is "a society of explorers":

10. *SFS* 59. "The theological authority of the Medieval Church was severe and specific to a degree which seems intolerable today" (*SFS* 75).

Any tradition fostering the progress of thought must have this intention: to teach its current ideas as stages leading on to unknown truths which, when discovered, might dissent from the very teachings which engendered them. Such a tradition assures the independence of its followers by transmitting the conviction that thought has intrinsic powers, to be evoked in men's minds by intimations of hidden truths. It respects the individual for being capable of such a response: for being able to see a problem not visible to others, and to explore it on his own responsibility. Such are the metaphysical grounds of intellectual life in such a society. I call this a society of explorers. (*TD* 82–83)

It is easy to see how the polycentric model of personal exploration corresponds to a Protestant mentality. Each believer or group of believers acts as a center of personal judgment and operates under the careful but nonauthoritarian inspection of neighboring Christians, just as each scientist or group of scientists takes responsibility for their own judgments under the eye of other scientists:

Each will rely on standards which he believes to be obligatory both for himself and the other. Every time either of them makes an assertion as to what is true and valuable in science, he relies blindly on a whole system of collateral facts and values accepted by science. And he relies also on it that his partner relies on the same system. Indeed, the bond of mutual trust thus formed between the two is but one link in the vast network of confidence between thousands of scientists of different specialties, through which—and through which alone—a consensus of science is established which may be said to accept certain facts and values as scientifically valid. . . . Though each may dissent (as I am myself dissenting) from some of the accepted standards of science, such heterodoxies must remain fragmentary if science is to survive as a *coherent system of superior knowledge, upheld by people mutually recognizing each other as scientists, and acknowledged by modern society as its guide.* (PK 375)

The success of noncentralized science then becomes a powerful apologetic for the progress of Christianity under the distributed authority of Protestant polycentrism. Christianity may be seen as a "coherent system . . . upheld by people mutually recognizing each other" as Christians. In this view, the General Authority of responsible judgment by individual Christians replaces the Specific Authority of Roman institutions.

Newman's *Apologia* clearly reveals a different mentality. Although the Roman church possesses a center which can (somehow) think for itself and render judgment on behalf of all, it need not be the totalitarian monster Polanyi feared. Polanyi seems to have looked at the Roman Catholic Church from without and from afar, with rather unsympathetic eyes, concentrating only on those aspects which make it most dissimilar from the fields that he knew and loved personally. Newman read the text of Church history quite differently. He denied the idea that "authority has so acted upon the reason of individuals, that they can have no opinion of their own" because "it is individuals, and not the Holy See, that have taken the initiative, and given the lead to the Catholic mind, in theological inquiry" (*Apo* 203). In a short sketch of the development of doctrine, Newman showed that "individual reason was paramount" (*Apo* 203). Commitment to the Church did not block personal insight. "There never was a time when the intellect of the educated class was more active, or rather more restless, than in the middle ages" (*Apo* 205). Although the Church has, in principle, the right to inspect any propositions which touch on her mission to spread the good news, not all thought can or does travel to Rome first for approval. In that sense, Newman would have agreed with Polanyi about the absurdity of centralizing all the operations of theology:

Many a man has ideas, which he hopes are true, and useful for his day, but he is not confident about them, and wishes to have them discussed. He is willing, or rather would be thankful, to give them up, if they can be proved to be erroneous or dangerous, and by means of controversy he obtains his end. He is answered, and he yields; or on the contrary he finds that he is considered safe. He would not dare to do this, if he knew an authority, which was supreme and final, was watching every word he said, and made signs of assent or dissent to each sentence, as he uttered it. Then indeed he would be fighting, as the Persian soldiers, under the lash, and the freedom of his intellect might truly be said to be beaten out of him. But this has not been so . . . —by reason of the very power of the Popes they have commonly been slow and moderate in their use of it. (*Apo* 205)

Some might well argue whether the exercise of authority has been as "slow and moderate" as Newman claimed, but even the unwise exercise of ecclesial authority can perhaps provide grist for the mill of theological reflection and nourishment for a new age of understanding and freedom. Although the reality of Roman Catholicism cannot be modelled with complete accuracy by the pure polycentric diagram, in which no one node has final authority over another, it would be equally inaccurate to suppose that there is no distribution of authority outside the ecclesiastical center. The power of the Church to make up its mind depends on a large, loose network of reflection and judgment in which there is ample scope for personal knowledge.

In his *Essay on the Development of Doctrine,* Newman advances the idea that "from the nature of the human mind, time is necessary for the full comprehension and perfection of great ideas; and . . . the highest and most wonderful truths, though communicated to the world once for all by inspired teachers, could not be comprehended all at once by the recipients, but, as being received and transmitted by minds not inspired and through media which were human, have required only the longer time and deeper thought for their full elucidation. This may be called the *Theory of Development of Doctrine*" (*Dev* 21–22). Newman would probably have agreed with Polanyi that it would be a mistake to select one understanding of the Church and freeze it for all time as *the* right way to be Christian—theological developments cannot be planned in advance any more than scientific discoveries can be planned. "The development then of an idea is not like an investigation worked out on paper, in which each successive advance is a pure evolution from a foregoing, but it is carried on through and by means of communities of men and their leaders and guides; and it employs their minds as its instruments, and depends upon them, while it uses them" (*Dev* 29). Newman's main goal in the *Essay on Development* was to establish the fact of development in doctrine, not to bring the process of development to an end (as perhaps Hegel attempted to do) but to affirm the process of development as legitimate, intelligible, and necessary. He compares the faith to a river that grows deeper and more powerful as it flows further from its source. At each stage of its development, the river "changes . . . in order to remain the same. In a higher world it is otherwise, but here below to live is to change, and to be perfect is to have changed often" (*Dev* 30). The Church has changed often, but, to the eye of a believer, it has done so only to be true to its role in God's plan of salvation.

At the end of the nineteenth century, some scientists thought that they were coming to the end of science, and that soon all knowledge would be neatly packaged, leaving only the relatively trivial task of improving precision as the work of future scientists. The history of science in the last hundred years has shown how wrong that judgment was and has given us a healthy lesson in humility before the mysteries of nature. When one becomes well acquainted with the history of the development of doctrine, it seems clear that it would be foolish to suppose that the process has come to an end. Without giving up the conviction that the Church is an instrument of revelation, one may nevertheless suppose that there is still room for growth in understanding. For Newman, the infallibility of the Church does "lessen the task of personal inquiry" just as Scripture limits the freedom of speculation, but the task remains (*Dev* 60–61). The illative sense of the believer is transformed by both the tacit and the articulate dimensions of revelation, but is not destroyed by adoption of the interpretative framework of the Church. Seeds are planted in the mind of the believer that slowly bear fruit through the process of reflection. At first, "a body of thought is gradually formed without his recognizing what is going on within him," but in time "he is led to regard as consequences, and to trace to principles, what hitherto he has discerned by a moral perception, and adopted on sympathy; and logic is brought in to arrange and inculcate what no science was employed in gaining" (*Dev* 138). Where the "spontaneous process which goes on within the mind itself" (*Dev* 139) will lead the Church cannot and need not be predicted in advance. Newman trusted that God's providence would always supply both for the individual and for the community.

Besides the *de facto* evidence that the Church has always been a developing reality, there is also the abstract question of whether Polanyi's totalitarian model of a Specific Authority correctly describes the relationships between mind and mind in the Roman Catholic communion. In his *Letter to the Duke of Norfolk*, Newman takes a strong stand against the idea of a "despotic aggressive Papacy, in which freedom of thought and action is utterly extinguished" (*DN* 200). It is true that Roman Catholics conceive of the papacy as having supreme authority to declare the *data* of faith, but this leaves ample scope for both personal and collective centers of reflection and insight. The Pope claims "the *supreme direction* of Catholics in respect to all duty" but "'supreme' is not 'minute,' nor does 'direction' mean supervision or 'management'" (*DN* 113).

The data of faith are not like those of science, which may be duplicated at will in any suitably equipped laboratory. The Church guards a message given in history. The life and words of Jesus may not be replayed at will by any noncommitted stranger under rigorous laboratory conditions. To become acquainted with Jesus, one must accept testimony from those who know him. Besides narrating the life, death and resurrection of Jesus, the Church also mandates adoption of its own dogmatic, interpretative framework, which gives definite meanings to the historical data:

Our Divine Master might have communicated to us heavenly truths without telling us that they came from Him, as it is commonly thought He has done in the case of heathen nations; but He willed the Gospel to be a revelation acknowledged and authenticated, to be public, fixed, and permanent; and accordingly, as Catholics hold, He framed a Society of men to be its home, its instrument, and its guarantee. The rulers of that Association are the legal trustees, so to say, of the sacred truths which He spoke to the Apostles by word of mouth. As He was leaving them, He gave them their great commission, and bade them "teach" their converts over all the earth, "to observe all things whatever He had commanded them;" and then He added, "Lo, I am with you always, even to the end of the world." (*DN* 184)

Laying down the rules of grammar and spelling does not determine what people will say. The rigidity of the ASCII table and the rules of the operating systems of computers do not determine the use that will be made of the system; the definiteness of the rules and regulations makes it possible for other software packages to run on the system. Similarly, the power which the Church possesses to declare what is "public, fixed, and permanent" creates a matrix for indwelling thought that breaks out into new interpretative frameworks without destroying the data and interpretation that nourished the new insights. The Copernican and Ptolemaic systems of understanding planetary motion are bound together by the data that they attempted to interpret; the heliocentric system is judged superior because it does a better job of explaining the motion of the planets in the night sky than the geocentric system. The Copernican revolution did not abolish the data set, but gave it a radically different interpretation from the preceding forms of science which had collected the data. Definition of dogmas, like astronomic observation, fixes points for reflection, but there are no self-interpreting definitions: "None but the *Schola Theologorum* is competent to determine the force of Papal and Synodal utterances, and the exact interpretation of them is a work of time" (*DN* 76). Proposed interpretations of the teaching of the Church must preserve the data of revelation, just as the Copernican revolution preserved the data of observation.

Newman's notion of the *Schola Theologorum* in many respects re-sembles Polanyi's notion of the General Authority of a "Society of Explorers." Newman clearly wants to give reason as much scope as possible because it has its own proper nature:

No one can go straight up a mountain; no sailing vessel makes for its port without tacking. . . . If we invite reason to take its place in our schools, we must let reason have fair and full play. If we reason, we must submit to the conditions of reason. We cannot use it by halves; we must use it as proceeding from Him who has also given us Revelation; and to be ever interrupting its processes, and diverting its attention by objections brought from a higher knowledge, is parallel to a landsman's dismay at the changes in the course of a vessel on which he has deliberately embarked, and argues surely some distrust either in the powers of Reason on the one hand, or the certainty of Revealed Truth on the other. . . . Let us eschew secular history, and science, and philosophy for good and all, if we are not allowed to be sure that Revelation is so true that the altercations and perplexities of human opinion cannot really or eventually injure its authority. That is no intellectual triumph of any truth of Religion, which has not been preceded by a full statement of what can be said against it; . . . Great minds need elbow-room, not indeed in the domain of faith, but of thought. And so indeed do lesser minds, and all minds. (*Idea* 357–58)

Although theology must have wide latitude, in order to be true to the nature of thought, it must also cling to that peculiar center which is a function of the definiteness of revelation. Newman is quite certain that the adoption of the empirical model of theology is untrue to the nature of a revealed religion.

That empirical method which has done such wonderful things in physics and other human sciences, has sustained a most emphatic and eloquent reversal in its usurped territory,—has come to no one conclusion,—has illumined no definite view,—has brought its glasses to no focus. . . . What can be more sacred than Theology? What can be more noble than the Baconian method? But the two do not correspond; they are mismatched. The age has mistaken lock and key. It has broken the key in a lock which does not belong to it; it has ruined the wards by a key which will never fit into them. Let us hope that its present disgust and despair at the result are the preliminaries of a generous and great repentance. (*Idea* 336–37)

Polanyi and his disciples undoubtedly would reject the pessimism expressed in this passage about the alleged failure of the Protestant model of polycentric authority to come to "one conclusion," a "definite view" or a single "focus." They would probably approach the same data with a different *Gestalt,* celebrating the openness and the freedom of their methods in theology. In the last analysis, we have come to one of those turning points where the conceptual maps of Newman and Polanyi cease to support each other. The choice of which fork to follow from this point is very much a matter of personal judgment and theological taste.

Visionary Theology

Despite the divergence over the proper role of authority in theology, the convergence of the epistemologies of Newman and Polanyi suggests that there may be a renovation of a patristic method in theology. Both of them draw substantial inspiration from the visionary movement that led to the integration of Christian thought. Newman absorbed himself in the study of the Fathers and found that for them, too, informal reasoning was the ground of faith: "They held that men were not obliged to wait for logical proof before believing; on the contrary, that the majority were to believe first on presumptions and let the intellectual proof come as their reward" (*Dev* 238). Polanyi did not study the Fathers as thoroughly as Newman did, but he sensed that they had much to teach us about the right orientation toward reality:

Since an art cannot be precisely defined, it can be transmitted only by examples of the practice which embodies it. He who would learn from a master by watching him must trust his example. He must recognize as authoritative the art which he wishes to learn and those of whom he would learn it. Unless he presumes that the substance and method of science are fundamentally sound, he will never develop a sense of scientific value and acquire the skill of scientific enquiry. This is the way of acquiring knowledge, which the Christian Church Fathers described as *fides quaerens intellectum,* "to believe in order to know." (*SFS* 15)

Without giving up the benefits brought about by later developments in the power of critical reasoning, Newman nevertheless sought to locate such developments in a broader framework of compassionate understanding and gentle wisdom. "Arguments will come to be considered as suggestions and guides rather than logical proofs; and developments as the slow, spontaneous, ethical growth, not the scientific and compulsory results, of existing opinions" (*Dev* 242). Both theology and science undercut themselves when they attempt to live in "pure reason." In a post-critical age, we recognize that the instruments of reason must be held in the hand of a visionary wisdom that knows tacitly and intuitively when to press for clarity and when to stand in awe of what goes beyond us.

The pressing question for our age is not so much whether theology is a science as whether science is a theology. The success of Newman's integration of awareness of the freedom of the illative sense with the demands of revelation suggests that even in an age of scientific revolutions we may still hold fast to a living center of truth that will not cease to invite and require our allegiance.

Polanyi's Hierarchy of Comprehensive Entities

Insofar as Polanyi tried his hand at theology, there were three major themes that interested him: (1) analysis of the structure of worship as an integration of subsidiaries; (2) recognition of the underlying similarity of the acts of commitment that uphold both science and religion; and (3) affirmation of the meaningfulness of the concept of God as the goal of all evolutionary striving. The first two themes have been touched on toward the end of Chapter III above (125, 130). Polanyi develops the third theme at length in Part Four of *Personal Knowledge* in the section entitled "Knowing and Being." A later article gives a concise view of his understanding of the hierarchy of being:

> The knowing of comprehensive entities thus establishes a series of ascending levels of existence. The relationship I have just outlined obtains throughout between succeeding levels of this hierarchy. The existence of a higher principle is always rooted in the inferior levels governed by less comprehensive principles. Within this lower medium and by virtue of it, the higher principle can operate widely but not unconditionally, its range being restricted and its every action tainted by the very medium on which it has to rely for exercising its powers.[11]

The various disciplines of human knowing respond to the various levels of existence. From a foundation in physics and chemistry, one ascends to knowing machines, living things, human beings, and, ultimately, perhaps, something supernatural:

> I have mentioned divinity and the possibility of knowing God. These subjects lie outside my argument. But my conception of knowing opens the way to them.

11. Polanyi, "Faith and Reason," 246.

Knowing as a dynamic force of comprehension uncovers at each step a new hidden meaning. It reveals a universe of comprehensive entities which represent the meaning of their largely unspecifiable particulars. A universe constructed as an ascending hierarchy of meaning and excellence is very different from the picture of a chance collocation of atoms to which the examination of the universe by explicit modes of inference leads us. The vision of such a hierarchy inevitably sweeps on to envisage the meaning of the universe as a whole. Thus natural knowing expands continuously into knowledge of the supernatural.[12]

The higher the level of being engaged in the act of knowing, the greater the degree of commitment involved on the part of the knower (PK 363). If the hierarchy is pursued to its highest level, one takes on the posture of worship:

So far as we know, the tiny fragments of the universe embodied in man are the only centers of thought and responsibility in the visible world. If that be so, the appearance of the human mind has been so far the ultimate stage in the awakening of the world; and all that has gone before, the strivings of the myriad centers that have taken the risks of living and believing, seem to have all been pursuing, along rival lines, the aim now achieved by us up to this point. They are all akin to us. For all these centers—those which led up to our existence and the far more numerous others which produced different lines of which many are extinct—may be seen engaged in the same endeavor towards ultimate liberation. We may envisage then a cosmic field which called forth all these centers by offering them a short-lived, limited, hazardous opportunity for making some progress of their own towards an unthinkable consummation. And that is also, I believe, how a Christian is placed when worshipping God. (PK 405)

Polanyi's strongest affirmations about God occur in contexts like this.

It is important to note that the relationships between higher and lower levels are not deterministic. Polanyi sees each level of being (and the corresponding knowledge about that level) as having its own integrity which remains intact even when it is organized or controlled by a higher level of being. So, for example, he considers how machines take advantage of opportunities created by the lower levels of physics and chemistry without violating any physical or chemical laws:

You may ask, how is it possible for a mechanism which obeys the laws of physics and chemistry to be determined also by another principle, not accountable by physics and chemistry. The answer is that the physical sciences expressly leave open certain conditions of a system, that are usually described as its

12. Polanyi, "Faith and Reason," 246.

boundary conditions, and that the operational principles of a mechanism take effect by controlling these boundary conditions. As a result, physical and chemical laws *are made to serve* the physiological mechanism of living beings.[13]

This is a very suggestive analogue for the relationship between epistemology and theology. Just as machines build on physics and chemistry without being determined by them, so theology, perhaps, can build upon epistemology in a nondeterministic fashion. Just as the failure of machines comes from the resistance of lower levels to complete control, so, too, some failures in theology may come from attempting to push reason past its proper limits.

Newman does not pursue a view like Polanyi's of an ascending series of comprehensive entities. In the delicate relationship between the power of faith and the power of reason, however, he does seem to describe something like the control of the resources of the lower level of reason by the higher level of faith:

Reason analyzes the grounds and motives of action: a reason is an analysis, but is not the motive itself. As, then, Conscience is a simple element in our nature, yet its operations admit of being surveyed and scrutinized by Reason; so may Faith be cognizable, and its acts be justified, by Reason, without therefore being, in matter of fact, dependent upon it; . . . That art is the sovereign awarder of praise and blame, and constitutes a court of appeal in matters of taste; as then the critic ascertains what he cannot himself create, so Reason may put its sanction upon the acts of Faith, without in consequence being the source from which Faith springs. (*US* 183–84)

Newman holds strongly that "Faith is a process of the Reason" (*US* 217–18) that is not reducible to merely rational principles—just as a machine is a construction *of* physical and/or chemical components that is not explicable solely *in* physical or chemical terms. The special field of epistemology is not necessary for the act of faith to be reasonable:

Here, then, are two processes, distinct from each other,—the original process of reasoning, and next, the process of investigating our reasonings. All men reason, for to reason is nothing more than to gain truth from former truth, without the intervention of sense, to which brutes are limited; but all men do not reflect upon their own reasonings, much less reflect truly and accurately, so as to do justice to their own meaning; but only in proportion to their abilities and attainments.

13. Polanyi, "Science and Religion," 10.

In other words, all men have a reason, but not all men can give a reason. We may denote, then, these two exercises of mind as reasoning and arguing, or as conscious and unconscious reasoning, or as Implicit Reason and Explicit Reason. And to the latter belong the words, science, method, development, analysis, criticism, proof, system, principles, rules, laws, and others of a like nature. (*US* 258–59)

Having a blueprint of a machine may be helpful in its construction and repair, but it is not intrinsic to the existence or functioning of the machine. Similarly, one need not have any explicit epistemology to feel and act upon what one believes to be true:

> Clearness in argument certainly is not indispensable to reasoning well. Accuracy in stating doctrines and principles is not essential to feeling and acting upon them. The exercise of analysis is not necessary to the integrity of the process analyzed. The process of reasoning is complete in itself, and independent. The analysis is but an account of it; it does not make the conclusion correct; it does not make the inference rational. It does not cause a given individual to reason better. It does but give him a sustained consciousness, for good or for evil, that he is reasoning. (*US* 259)

Good materials do not necessarily make for good machines; good design and construction both must also contribute their part. A good philosophy of science may not make a person a good scientist. A satisfying account of how we know what we know may not bring us to the knowledge of God. Nevertheless, Newman and Polanyi, each in his own way, hoped that clarifying the nature of reason would increase our openness to faith. Polanyi saw "intense, absorbing, devoted labor" as preparation "for receiving a truth from sources over which [one] has no control."[14] Newman similarly perceived reason as waiting to be placed in the service of something beyond itself: "Reason can but ascertain the profound difficulties of our condition, it cannot remove them; it has no work, it makes no beginning, it does but continually fall back, till it is content to be a little child, and to follow where Faith guides it" (*US* 351). It is fundamental to all theology that faith seeks understanding; it is characteristic of the epistemologies of Newman and Polanyi to recognize that understanding also seeks faith.

14. Polanyi, "Faith and Reason," 247.

Conclusion: Breaking into Dogma

These final remarks differ dramatically in tone and content from the preceding chapters. Those chapters focus on the intersections and divergences of the thought of Newman and Polanyi. The purpose of these reflections, in Newman's terms, is to "take a view" of Christianity; in Polanyi's terms, my goal is to explore briefly the interpretative framework that makes sense of my own personal commitments. Although my view is personal, I hope it is not hopelessly isolated; I recommend this way of seeing reality to all inquirers, and I imagine that they can make the same personal commitments that I have, even though we come from different backgrounds. As Newman did in the concluding chapter of the *Grammar,* I would like to explore a vision of Christianity in an easy and informal manner. I am aware, sometimes even painfully aware, that I am brushing past dense thickets of scholarly argument, but I believe that it is important to give a consciously a-critical account of the life of faith.

For Polanyi, the progress of science takes place by a process of dwelling in the scientific tradition and then, by a process of personal discovery, breaking out of the old framework and establishing a new way of imagining and interpreting reality. While I recognize that scientific discovery is an excellent model for many aspects of the act of faith, especially the personal recognition of the love of God made manifest in Christ, I find the analogy of "breaking out" of the framework of the Christian tradition incompatible with the conviction that Jesus is "the way and the truth and the life" (Jn 14:6). For me, the progress of Christian thought takes place by dwelling in the tradition and breaking *into* the heart of what we really take to be true. I believe that there is no limit to the depths of understanding that may be achieved by a succession of such personal discoveries about Christianity, and yet, if they are authentic, they will never overthrow the fundamental framework that is given in the gospel message and that is intended to be passed on to the next generation of believers.

From the time of the great medieval syntheses, systematic theology has attempted to proceed scientifically. In the eighteenth and nine-teenth centuries, positivist models of science inspired positivist theo-logical systems. By recognizing the tacit and illative foundations of both science and theology, it may be possible to assert the infallibility of the Church through a fallibilist epistemology as part of a larger proj-ect of doing dogmatic theology nondogmatically. The severe, quasi-scientific character of both the neoscholastic tradition and the posi-tivist theological schools tends to cut reflection off from the roots of the tacit, informal reasoning that gives life to faith. The new model of sci-ence as personal knowledge offers theology a chance to operate with renewed confidence in the hidden wellsprings of both faith and reason.

I do not believe that my understanding of the Church flows from my understanding of the epistemologies of Newman and Polanyi in the same way that conclusions flow from the axioms of geometry. Rather, I see the epistemologies as sources of tools for constructing understand-ing. A house is not deduced from a hammer, nor is an automobile a conclusion from its parts. My vision of the Church is not formally de-rived from post-critical epistemology, but is, I hope, developed, sup-ported, and strengthened by thinking about the personal and tacit di-mension of knowledge.

The same tools used to construct the house of faith can be used to deconstruct it. By taking everything apart, it can be shown that a house is nothing but a collection of raw materials. Such analyses render the house uninhabitable. To enter into the intellectual dwelling provided by the faith, we must let the pieces fall into place and remain in place through the tacit integration of subsidiaries. In the years since I began this study, I have had the opportunity to learn more about Eastern reli-gions. The first line of the *Tao Te Ching* has become more and more im-portant to me as I have wrestled with the mystery of the limits of lan-guage: "The Tao that can be put into words is not the real Tao." I have rung dozens of changes on this theme for myself over the last few years. Within the realm of philosophy, it is a reminder that we know more than we can tell, not only because the thing that can be put into words is not the real thing but also because the thought that can be put into words is not the real thought. Our contact with reality, both external and internal, is always deeper than we can tell.

It is hard enough to speak well of ordinary realities that lie before our senses. I am constantly frustrated by my inability to express the beauty of the hills in the southern tier of upstate New York. I have spent many delightful days at my family's camp, a tumbledown house nestled between two low hills. Before leaving, I have written a paragraph or two to remind myself of the day. My efforts to speak of the trees, wildflowers, clouds, sunsets, and the night sky fall far short of the everyday marvels that disclose themselves to my eyes—the day that can be put into words is not the real day. The task of saying what we see is much more difficult as we explore the physical world at greater depth. The physics that can be put into words is not the real physics. Real knowledge of the physical world consists of a vision of how the elementary particles are caught up into ever more compex and astonishing interactions, attracted by some forces, repelled by others, spinning, orbiting, fusing, decaying, combining, colliding, jumping, twisting, tunneling—frustrating and delighting those who try to chart the choreography of the great dance of energy and matter on the stage of space and time. When scientists draw on their vision of physical reality, they must disintegrate the vision into a linear sequence of abstractions, speaking one careful word at a time that leaves out far more of reality than it captures.

So, too, in the spiritual life. The faith that can be put into words is not the real faith. At the core of the act of faith is a personal encounter between God and the believer. Newman held that there were two luminous beings in our experience, the self and God. But the very fullness of direct apprehension of the self and God mocks all of our efforts to capture self or God in words. Even in the act of speaking as best we can, we know that the self that can be put into words is not the real self and the God that can be put into words is not the real God. No set of propositions can fully disclose who I am. Even as I try to tell a few truths about myself, my mind surveys other aspects of my interior life that run deep into the tacit dimension. When the words run out, I remain—a mystery even to myself, luminous, real, incommunicable, a small image of the inexhaustible mystery of God. In both cases, the material that resists abstraction and that cannot be communicated in words is not a negligible residue, devoid of intellectual meaning, but is instead the heart of the whole matter and the point of every proposition.

In my view, the purpose of the Church is to make it possible for us to be personally united with Jesus and through him, to be united to all other persons. The institutional structures of the Church are secondary to the central personal relationship between the believer and the Savior. Because the Church is a reservoir of wisdom that has accumulated over the ages, and because of the power the Church holds to make decisions affecting the lives of the faithful, it is easy to lose sight of the heart of the Church in the ocean of words that have accumulated within the Church.

In the beginning of the Church was the Word. The Word that can be put into words is not the real Word. This Word was spoken from before all time, is spoken now, and always will be spoken by the One whom he called Father. The Word is a Person brought forth by a Person and intended to be received by other persons (perhaps in the life of the Trinity, the first recipient of the Word is the Spirit).

When the Word came among us, we did not recognize his glory, for he had emptied himself of his divine power in order to become like us. His disciples were drawn to him for reasons that have not been fully disclosed. Heart spoke to heart, love was kindled, and they followed. They told us quite clearly that they did not understand Jesus at first, that their expectations, hopes, and dreams were foolish and self-centered, and that they were heartbroken by the event which, with the eyes of faith, was later recognized as the moment of Jesus' greatest glory. After his resurrection and ascension, after the coming of the Spirit, and after they had allowed themselves to be transformed by the light of faith, the disciples saw the whole of their personal relationship with Jesus in a new light. In their first enthusiasm for following him, he must have seemed to be invulnerable. His death shattered that expectation. His resurrection was equally shocking to minds numb with grief. Only after reorganizing their whole understanding of Jesus and then dwelling within the new interpretative framework could they grasp how he had made himself weak as an act of love, then received power and glory anew in his resurrection and ascension.

When the new interpretative framework was in place, the disciples were called to tell the good news to others. But the Jesus who can be put into words is not the real Jesus. The real Jesus is a divine Person who has always existed as God, the Son, who reigns now in glory, and who will always be the Way to union with the Father. The real Jesus is also a fully human being, just like us in everything except the darkness of sin, and he knows our state from the inside out. He is both near and far, known and unknown, like and unlike, ordinary and extraordinary, all-powerful and wholly vulnerable. In any moment of speaking of him, we will grasp only one meager aspect and lose the rich totality of the God-Man. The full expression of who he is stumbles over the history of what he has been: pre-existent, incarnate, executed, raised from the dead, taken from this earth, and glorified.

Each proposition about Jesus reveals only one aspect of the Word while obscuring others. There is no stable resting place for the mind which seeks to express the whole of the Christian vision. If we speak of God, we obscure the tri-personal circumincession of Father, Son, and Spirit; if we do not speak of God, we neglect the doctrine of divine unity. If we speak of one Person, we cast the other two into a shadow; if we do not speak of each Person individually, we diminish our awareness of their unique characters. If we speak of Jesus, calling on the name that is now above every other name, it brings his historical human nature to the forefront of consciousness at the expense of the eternal pre-existence of the Son and the glorified humanity now reigning in glory as the eternal Christ.

In the presence of such a tangle of truths, it might seem better to be still and be thought a fool than to speak and be proven to be foolish. But the Word himself commanded his followers to speak of what they had seen with their own eyes, heard with their own ears, and embraced with their own hearts. Not to tell the story would be a far greater disservice to the Word than to stammer about this astonishing Person. Because of his self-emptying love, Jesus made himself vulnerable not only to suffering and death but also to misinterpretation. Because he embraced our human condition totally, it is easy to seize on the evidence of his humanity and to neglect the clues that point to his divinity. This seems to be the characteristic temptation of our age. In earlier times, perhaps, the temptation was to stress the divinity of Jesus to the detriment of grasping his full humanity. Holding the dual natures of Jesus in proper balance is a skill that is exercised and transmitted primarily in the tacit dimension.

Jesus did not communicate himself to his disciples by giving them a list of propositions to memorize. He wrote no catechism. Instead, he poured himself into their hearts both verbally and nonverbally. They knew him, and through him, they came to know the Father and the Spirit as Jesus knew them. The deposit of faith is therefore quintessentially personal. Physics is personal knowledge because the knower is a person; Christianity is far more personal than physics, because both the knower and the known are persons.

Protestant spirituality has much to teach Catholics about the personal dimension of Christianity. While Catholics tend to talk about being "born Catholic," Protestants generally insist that the believer must make an independent decision to surrender themselves to the Lord Jesus Christ. Just as the existentialists taught that no one can take a bath for someone else, so the Protestants recognize that no one else can make a personal commitment to Christ for another. David DuPlessis often preached on the theme that "God has no grandchildren." Each believer is called to be born again as a son or daughter of God in an act of real apprehension and real assent. After hearing of the love of God through human testimony, those who are called to faith must make the discovery for themselves, with the help of God's grace, that the same Jesus who died and rose from the dead thousands of years ago is alive now and is eager to love them directly and personally.

The challenge for Catholics is to bear in mind that all of the articulate treasures accumulated from centuries of development of doctrine must be recognized as subsidiary to the personal relationship between Jesus and his beloved disciples. Seeing Jesus makes sense of all of the structures of the Church. The infallibility of the Church is a function of Jesus' authority and power as true God and true man. The sacramental life of the Church is the risen and glorified Jesus at work in the hearts of his people. The power of the Church to choose disciplines of prayer and fasting reflects the power of the Good Shepherd to lead the flock as a whole.

The dogmatic propositions in the treasury of the Church are precious because they preserve the definitive revelation given once for all time by the incarnate Word. But the dogma that can be put into words is not the real dogma. Many Catholic theologians, especially in the manualist tradition of the nineteenth and early twentieth century, give the impression that knowing all of the facts about Jesus is all that is required. Knowing facts *about* someone is not the same as knowing the person. I know many facts about the President of the United States, more perhaps than I do about many of my friends, but I do not know him personally. For many Catholics, the transition from knowing about Jesus to knowing Jesus personally seems to be inhibited rather than served by the richness of the articulate tradition.

The articulate dimension of revelation is not the enemy of the tacit dimension; speech springs forth from silence. The institutional dimension of the Church is not the enemy of the personal dimension; the structure springs forth from the Person of Jesus. It is all too easy for both Catholics and non-Catholics to focus on subsidiary elements of the Church (dogma, sacraments, discipline) at the expense of the whole, but that does not mean that we can discard the subsidiaries at will. Memorizing a physics textbook is not enough to produce a good scientist; memorizing the catechism of the Church is not enough to produce a personal relationship with Jesus. In each case, the data is insufficient without a personal reorganization, a flash of insight, the opening of the eyes of the mind and heart to a new vision of reality, a discovery that transforms the person from within.

The fact that physics requires far more than can be captured in a physics text does not mean that physics can burn its textbooks. The fact that Jesus cannot be reduced to a set of propositions does not mean that Christianity can cast aside its catechisms. As Polanyi showed, the way to make fresh, new discoveries that transform the scientific tradition is first to dwell within the tradition, absorbing the tacit vision by assimilating the articulate elements into one's own interpretative framework. The only way to contribute to Christianity's future is to embrace its past and present. Jesus made himself, his Father, and his Spirit *known* to his disciples. They, in turn, under the direction of the risen Lord, made him *known* to all generations. This body of knowledge is partly preserved in speech, partly in ritual, and partly in the tacit dimension of personal and corporate consciousness. The Lord who now reigns in glory, uniting all believers in one body by the will of the Father and the work of the Holy Spirit, is the same Jesus who made friends with people in Galilee and led them on pilgrimage to Jerusalem. To know him as he is now is to learn how he was then. To make him known to others is to speak what can be said and to trust both the power of God and the powers of the human mind to complete the transmission of Jesus in the tacit dimension.

Much of the philosophy of science today is infected with a hunger for revolutionary thinking. Everyone wants to be the next Copernicus. No paradigm is worth its salt unless it has recently shifted its own locus or shattered its predecessors. We have been culturally conditioned to feel passionately that the new is good and the old is bad. Within this culture, the form of Christianity that is most deeply embedded in the past may look like the enemy of freedom, creativity, and progress. Our culture is generally not inclined to believe that the key to the healing of all of the ills of the twentieth century lies in the heart of a first-century peasant. We tend to want our answers from within, from the isolated self, operating on the basis of pure reason and personal experience, and unencumbered by the strictures of tradition. Minds nurtured on the rhetoric of revolutionary discoveries may be ill-suited to repeat and renew the essential Christian discovery that Jesus is Lord. The progress of science may be construed as a process of dwelling in the scientific tradition, then breaking out from it, but the progress of Christianity depends on dwelling in Jesus and never departing from him. Breakthroughs—personal and corporate discoveries—are indeed possible in this abiding relationship, but they lead only to a deeper intimacy and union between faithful lovers rather than to dissolution of the bond established in the original conversion experience.

Dogmatic theology has a real but limited value in this love affair between Jesus and the believer. The rigidity and formalization of theology plays exactly the same role in carrying the message of God's love to his people as does a communications protocol in delivering messages over the tangled web of the internet. Unless there are strict rules of interpretation about how to transmit and receive, there will be no communication from one computer to another. All of the elements of the message will fall into disarray and be lost in the noise and confusion of the environment. From time to time, when the message is deteriorating, someone has to trace the circuits and determine why the transmission is being corrupted. When someone is downloading a new piece of software from the internet, for example, they do not want the intermediary computers to add or subtract a single byte from the original. Personal or random reinterpretations of what is sent would destroy the functionality of the program and prevent it from performing as it was designed to perform. Furthermore, the person seeking the new software generally does not want to receive the communications protocol itself. They want the software, not a set of rules and regulations that describe how software may be sent and received. If the rules did not exist, the transmissions could not take place, but the rules are no substitute for the files transmitted by the rules.

The Church exists to transmit Jesus from one generation to the next. To do this faithfully, without error, without loss of anything given by the Father and the Spirit through the Person of Jesus, the Church has had to develop its own operating system and communications protocols. For the vast majority of believers, as for the majority of end users of the internet, all that matters is the message, not the messenger. The love of God poured forth upon the earth in the Person of Jesus is experienced as a present reality, and the means by which this message was received is simply not an issue. In this case, the Church functions transparently, beneath the level of conscious awareness, in the tacit dimension. At various times, the message has been challenged, and the Church has been forced to double-check both the message and the means of communication. By learning from experience, the Church has deepened its grasp of the message and has refined the rules and regulations that preserve the message from being garbled by sin, ignorance, carelessness, or confusion.

The rigidity of formal theology, like the rigidity of operating systems and communications protocols, serves a very useful purpose. At the same time, the whole point of the system is to put persons in touch with persons and to let them have a free, flexible, dynamic, and unbounded relationship. Like John the Baptist, the messengers must decrease so that Jesus may increase in the hearts of his beloved. Just as computer systems are rewritten or discarded in favor of new systems, so dogmatic theology must be open to revisions and replacements. In any shift from one system to another, the same goal must be achieved: to make the love of God in Christ known to the scattered children of God.

At the heart of personal computers is a very rigid, rule-bound, and deterministic operating system. But that code is what makes the computers fun for the people who use them. It is no fun to have a computer that generates random responses to keystrokes, that develops a mind of its own and thinks its own thoughts. The more perfectly the machine adheres to its design, the more it subserves our free choices to express ourselves through its system. At the heart of personal Catholicism there is a rigid, rule-bound, and definitive operating system that is designed to communicate God's love and to set people free. It is great fun when it works the way it was designed to work. The joy of Christianity lies not in its rules of grammar and syntax but in the loving relationships kindled by the good news of God's love. When we know we are loved, then indeed, all is well and all will be well again.

Appendix: A Partial Glossary of Terms

The purpose of this glossary is to allow the reader to see some of the definitions of Newman and of Polanyi in their own words. It is incomplete both in the selection of terms which happen to have made the list and in the selection of texts to define the terms. Though it lacks breadth and depth, it may provide some seeds for thought.

Some of Newman's Characteristic Terms

apprehension
By our apprehension of propositions I mean our imposition of a sense on the terms of which they are composed (*GA* 29).

Apprehension then is simply an intelligent acceptance of the idea, or of the fact which a proposition enunciates (*GA* 36).

assent
. . . it is in itself the absolute acceptance of a proposition without any condition; . . . it presupposes the condition, not only of some previous inference in favor of the proposition, but especially of some concomitant apprehension of its terms (*GA* 32).

Assent is an act of the mind, congenial to its nature; and it, as other acts, may be made both when it ought to be made, and when it ought not. It is a free act, a personal act for which the doer is responsible, and the actual mistakes in making it, be they ever so numerous or serious, have no force whatever to prohibit the act itself (*GA* 189).

indirect assent. Yet there is a way, in which a child can give an indirect assent even to a proposition, in which he understood neither subject nor predicate. He cannot indeed in that case assent to the proposition itself, but he can assent to its truth. . . . Thus the child's mother might teach him . . . and he, in faith on her word, might give his assent to such a proposition,—not, that is, to the line itself which he had got by heart, and which would be beyond him, but to its being true, beautiful, and good (*GA* 33–34).

real assent. [Real Assent] is in itself an intellectual act, of which the object is presented to it by the imagination; and though the pure intellect does not lead to action, nor the imagination either, yet the imagination has the means, which pure intellect has not, of stimulating those powers of the mind from which action proceeds. Real Assent then, or Belief, as it may be called, viewed in itself, that is, simply as Assent, does not lead to action; but the images in which it lives, representing as they do the concrete, have the power of the concrete upon the affections and passions, and by means of these indirectly become operative (*GA* 86).

certitude

Certitude, as I have said, is the perception of a truth with the perception that it is a truth, or the consciousness of knowing, as expressed in the phrase, "I know that I know," or "I know that I know that I know,"—or simply, "I know;" for one reflex assertion of the mind about self sums up the series of self-consciousness without the need of any actual evolution of them (*GA* 163).

. . . mere assent is not certitude, and must not be confused with it (*GA* 168).

A certitude is directed to this or that particular proposition; it is not a faculty or gift, but a disposition of mind relatively to a definite case which is before me. Infallibility, on the contrary, is just that which certitude is not; it *is* a faculty or gift, and relates, not to some one truth in particular, but to all possible propositions in a given subject-matter. We ought in strict propriety, to speak, not of infallible acts, but of acts of infallibility (*GA* 183).

It must be recollected that certitude is a deliberate assent given expressly after reasoning. If then my certitude is unfounded, it is the reasoning that is in fault, not my assent to it. It is the law of my mind to seal up the conclusions to which ratiocination has brought me, by that formal assent which I have called a certitude (*GA* 186–87).

Certitude is a mental state: certainty is a quality of propositions. Those propositions I call certain, which are such that I am certain of them. Certitude is not a passive impression made upon the mind from without, by argumentative compulsion, but in all concrete questions (nay, even in abstract, for though the reasoning is abstract, the mind which judges of it is concrete) it is an active recognition of propositions as true, such as it is the duty of each individual himself to exercise at the bidding of reason, and, when reason forbids, to withhold (*GA* 271).

Christianity

Christianity is a history supernatural, and almost scenic: it tells us what its Author is, by telling us what He has done (*GA* 92).

But the very idea of Christianity in its profession and history, is something more than this; it is a "Revelatio revelata;" it is a definite message from God to man distinctly conveyed by His chosen instruments, and to be received as such a message; and therefore to be positively acknowledged, embraced, and maintained as true, on the ground of its being divine, not as true on intrinsic grounds, not as probably true, or partially true, but as absolutely certain knowledge, certain in a sense in which nothing else can be certain, because it comes from Him who neither can deceive nor be deceived (GA 302).

Christianity, on the other hand, is in its idea an announcement, a preaching; it is the depository of truths beyond human discovery, momentous, practical, maintained one and the same in substance in every age from its first, and addressed to all mankind (GA 334).

conviction

It is an assent, not only to a given proposition, but to the claim of that proposition on our assent as true; it is an assent to an assent, or what is commonly called a conviction (GA 162).

credence

What I mean by giving credence to propositions is pretty much the same as having "no doubt" about them. It is the sort of assent which we give to those opinions and professed facts which are ever presenting themselves to us without any effort of ours, and which we commonly take for granted, thereby obtaining a broad foundation of thought for ourselves, and a medium of intercourse between ourselves and others (GA 60–62).

. . . a spontaneous acceptance of the various informations, which are by whatever means conveyed to our minds, sometimes goes by the name of Opinion (GA 64). [Newman has his own definition, however: assent to a proposition as probably true.]

economy

Hence in science we sometimes use a definition or a *formula*, not as exact, but as being sufficient for our purpose, for working out certain conclusions, for a practical approximation, the error being small, till a certain point is reached. This is what in theological investigations I should call an economy (GA 56).

first principles

. . . in themselves they [first principles] are abstractions from facts, not elementary truths prior to reasoning (GA 69).

human nature

After all, man is *not* a reasoning animal; he is a seeing, feeling, contemplating, acting animal (GA 90).

illative sense

It is the mind that reasons, and that controls its own reasonings, not any technical apparatus of words and propositions. This power of judging and concluding, when in its perfection, I call the Illative Sense, and I shall best illustrate it by referring to parallel faculties, which we commonly recognize without difficulty (GA 276–7).

Thus the Illative Sense, that is, the reasoning faculty, as exercised by gifted, or by educated or otherwise well-prepared minds, has its function in the beginning, middle, and end of all verbal discussion and inquiry, and in every step of the process. It is a rule to itself, and appeals to no judgment beyond its own; and attends upon the whole course of thought from antecedents to consequents, with a minute diligence and unwearied presence, which is impossible to a cumbrous apparatus of verbal reasoning, though, in communicating with others, words are the only instrument we possess, and a serviceable, though imperfect instrument (GA 283).

. . . still the fact remains, that, in any inquiry about things in the concrete, men differ from each other, not so much in the soundness of their reasoning as in the principles which govern its exercise, that those principles are of a personal character, that where there is no common measure of minds, there is no common measure of arguments, and that the validity of a proof is determined, not by any scientific test, but by the illative sense (GA 321).

infallibility

It is persons and rules that are infallible, not what is brought out into act, or committed to paper. A man is infallible, whose words are always true; a rule is infallible, if it is unerring in all its possible applications. An infallible authority is certain in every particular case that may arise; but a man who is certain in some one definite case, is not on that account infallible (GA 183–84).

inference

Inference is the conditional acceptance of a proposition, Assent is the unconditional; the object of Assent is a truth, the object of Inference is the truth-like or a verisimilitude. The problem which I have undertaken is that of ascertaining how it comes to pass that a conditional act leads to an unconditional (GA 209).

instinct

I have spoken, and I think rightly spoken, of instinct as a force which spontaneously impels us, not only to bodily movements, but to mental acts (GA 67).

It is difficult to avoid calling such clear presentiments by the name of instinct; and I think they may be so called, if by instinct be understood, not a natural sense, one and the same in all, and incapable of cultivation, but a perception of facts without assignable media of perceiving. There are those who can tell at once what is conducive or injurious to their welfare, who are their friends, who their enemies, what is to happen to them, and how they are to meet it. Presence of mind, fathoming of motives, talent for repartee, are instances of this gift (GA 263).

knowledge

I have one step farther to make—let the proposition to which the assent is given be as absolutely true as the reflex act pronounces it to be, that is, objectively true as well as subjectively:—then the assent may be called a *perception*, the conviction a *certitude*, the proposition or truth a *certainty*, or thing known, or a matter of *knowledge*, and to assent to it is to *know* (GA 162).

logic

Ratiocination, thus restricted and put into grooves, is what I have called Inference, and the science, which is its regulating principle, is Logic. . . . Verbal reasoning, of whatever kind, as opposed to mental, is what I mean by inference, which differs from logic only inasmuch as logic is its scientific form. And it will be more convenient here to use the two words indiscriminately, for I shall say nothing about logic which does not in its substance also apply to inference (GA 211–12).

memory

Memory consists in a present imagination of things that are past; memory retains the impressions and likenesses of what they were when before us; and when we make use of the proposition which refers to them, it supplies us with objects by which to interpret it. They are things still, as being the reflections of things in a mental mirror (GA 39).

mystery

A mystery is a proposition conveying incompatible notions, or is a statement of the inconceivable. Now we can assent to propositions (and a mystery is a proposition), provided we can apprehend them; therefore we can assent to a mystery, for, unless we in some sense apprehended it, we should not recognize it to be a mystery, that is, a statement uniting incompatible notions. The same act, then, which enables us to discern that the words of the proposition express a mystery, capacitates us for assenting to it. Words which make nonsense, do not make a mystery (GA 55).

natural law

By natural law I mean the fact that things happen uniformly according to certain circumstances, and not without them and at random: that is, they happen in an order . . . And thus we advance to the general notion or first principle of the sovereignty of law throughout the universe (GA 72).

notion

Notions are but aspects of things; the free deductions from one of these aspects necessarily contradict the free deductions from another. . . . We apprehend sufficiently to be able to assent to these theological truths as mysteries; did we not apprehend them at all, we should be merely asserting; though even then we might convert that assertion into an assent, if we wished to do so, as I have already shown, by making it the subject of a proposition, and predicating of it that it is true (*GA* 60).

opinion

I shall here use the word [Opinion] to denote an assent, but an assent to a proposition, not as true, but as probably true, that is to the probability of that which the proposition enunciates; and as that probability may vary in strength without limit, so may the cogency and moment of the opinion (*GA* 65).

presumption

By presumption I mean an assent to first principles; and by first principles I mean the propositions with which we start in reasoning on any given subject-matter (*GA* 66).

profession

Such are the assents made upon habit and without reflection . . .

Such again are the assents of men of wavering restless minds, who take up and then abandon beliefs so readily, so suddenly, as to make it appear that they had no view (as it is called) on the matter they professed, and did not know to what they assented or why (*GA* 52).

propositions

Propositions (consisting of a subject and predicate united by the copula) may take a categorical, conditional or interrogative form (*GA* 25).

Without a proposition or thesis there can be no assent, no belief, at all; any more than there can be an inference without a conclusion (*GA* 108).

ratiocination

. . . the exercise of a living faculty in the individual intellect [and not just] the mere skill in argumentative science (*GA* 240).

rational

. . . "rational" is used in contradistinction to argumentative, and means "resting on implicit reasons," such as we feel, indeed, but which for some cause or other, because they are too subtle or too circuitous, we cannot put into words so as to satisfy logic (*GA* 256).

rationality

We are conscious of the objects of external nature, and we reflect and act upon them, and this consciousness, reflection, and action we call our rationality (*GA* 272).

reason

We reason, when we hold this by virtue of that; . . . (*GA* 209).

religion

Now a religion is not a proposition, but a system; it is a rite, a creed, a philosophy, a rule of duty, all at once; and to accept a religion is neither a simple assent to it or a complex, neither a conviction nor a prejudice, neither a notional assent nor a real, not a mere act of profession, nor of credence, nor of opinion, nor of speculation, but it is a collection of all these various kinds of assents, at once and together, some of one description, some of another; but, out of all these different assents, how many are of that kind which I have called certitude? Certitudes indeed do not change, but who shall pretend that assents are indefectible? (*GA* 196–97).

By Religion I mean the knowledge of God, of His Will, and of our duties towards Him; and there are three main channels which Nature furnishes for our acquiring this knowledge, viz. our own minds, the voice of mankind, and the course of the world, that is, of human life and human affairs (*GA* 303).

revelation

As prayer is the voice of man to God, so Revelation is the voice of God to man (*GA* 314).

speculation

. . . those notional assents which are the most directly, explicit, and perfect of their kind, viz. those which are the firm, conscious acceptance of propositions as true. This kind of assent includes the assent to all reasonings and its conclusions, to all general propositions, to all rules of conduct, to all proverbs, aphorisms, sayings, and reflections on men and society (*GA* 75). [Examples: mathematics, legal judgments, constitutional maxims, determinations of science, and "the principles, disputations, and doctrines of theology."]

theology

Theology, as such, always is notional, as being scientific: religion, as being personal, should be real . . . (*GA* 62).

Theology, properly and directly, deals with notional apprehension; religion with imaginative (*GA* 108).

things

In this world of sense we have to do with things, far more than with notions. . . . We reason in order to enlarge our knowledge of matters, which do not depend on us for being what they are. But how is an exercise of mind, which is for the most part occupied with notions, not things, competent to deal with things, except partially and indirectly? (*GA* 222).

view

First comes knowledge, then a view, then reasoning, and then belief. That is why science has so little of a religious tendency; deductions have no power of persuasion. The heart is commonly reached, not through the reason, but through the imagination, by means of direct impressions, by the testimony of facts and events, by history, by description (*GA* 89).

Some of Polanyi's Characteristic Terms

assertions

If language is to denote speech it must reflect the fact that we never say anything that has not a definite impassioned quality. It should be clear from the modality of a sentence whether it is a question, a command, an invective, a complaint, or an allegation of fact. Since an unasserted declaratory sentence could not stand for an allegation of fact, its modality would be unspecified and could therefore denote no spoken sentence. . . . An unasserted sentence is no better than an unsigned check; just paper and ink without power or meaning (*PK* 27–28).

A declaratory sentence can be asserted, because it is an incomplete symbol, of indeterminate modality; while a question, a command, an invective, or any other sentence of fixed intention can no more be asserted than could my act of hewing wood or of drinking tea (*PK* 28).

There are three main kinds of utterances, namely: (1) expressions of feeling, (2) appeals to other persons, (3) statements of fact. To each of these there corresponds a different function of language. The transition from the tacit to the articulate which I am envisaging here is restricted to the indicative forms of speech, as used for statements of fact (*PK* 77).

An articulate assertion is composed of two parts: a sentence conveying the content of what is asserted and a tacit act by which this sentence is asserted (*PK* 254).

commitment

The arts of doing and knowing, the valuation and understanding of meanings, are thus seen to be only different aspects of the act of extending our person into the subsidiary awareness of particulars which compose a whole. The inherent structure of this fundamental act of personal knowing makes us both necessarily participate in its shaping and acknowledge its results with universal intent. This is the prototype of intellectual commitment (*PK* 65).

It is the act of commitment in its full structure that saves personal knowledge from being merely subjective. Intellectual commitment is a responsible decision, in submission to the compelling claims of what in good conscience I conceive to be true. It is an act of hope, striving to fulfill an obligation within a personal situation for which I am not responsible and which therefore determines my calling. This hope and this obligation are expressed in the universal intent of personal knowledge (*PK* 65).

In passing from the visionary contemplation of an object to its observation, we do make an affirmation, therefore, of something which lies beyond what we had seen before. This is an act involving a commitment which can prove misguided. It establishes a conception of reality experienced in terms of a subsidiary awareness of the colored patches which had previously been experienced as such in an act of contemplation (*PK* 99).

I can speak of facts, knowledge, proof, reality, etc., within my commitment situation, for it is constituted by my search for facts, knowledge, proof, reality, etc., as binding on me. These are proper designations for commitment targets which apply so long as I am committed to them; but they cannot be referred to non- committally. You cannot speak without self-contradiction of knowledge you do not believe, or of a reality which does not exist. I may deny validity to some particular knowledge, or some particular facts, but then to me these are only allegations of knowledge or of facts, and should be denoted as 'knowledge' and as 'facts,' to which I am not committed. Commitment is in this sense the only path for approaching the universally valid (*PK* 303).

comprehension

Comprehension is neither an arbitrary act nor a passive experience, but a responsible act claiming universal validity. Such knowing is indeed *objective* in the sense of establishing contact with a hidden reality; a contact that is defined as the condition for anticipating an indeterminate range of yet unknown (and perhaps yet inconceivable) true implications. It seems reasonable to describe this fusion of the personal and the objective as Personal Knowledge (*PK* vii–viii).

consistency

Only when repeatable utterances are used consistently can they have a definite meaning, and utterances without definite meaning are not language. The poverty of language can fulfill its denotative functions only if utterances are both repeatable and consistent.

'Consistency' is a deliberately imprecise term designating an unspecifiable quality. Since the world, like a kaleidoscope, never exactly repeats any previous situation (and indeed, if it did we would not know it, as we would have no means of telling that time had passed in between), we can achieve consistency only by identifying manifestly different situations in respect to some particular feature, and this requires a series of personal judgments (*PK* 79–80).

definition

Understood in these terms, definition is a formalization of meaning which reduces its informal elements and partly replaces them by a formal operation (the reference to the definiens). This formalization will be incomplete also in the sense that the definiens can be understood only by those conversant with the definiendum. Even so, the definition may still throw new light on the definiendum, in the way a guiding maxim illuminates the practice of an art, though its application must rely on the practical knowledge of the art. Such definitions (like 'causation is necessary succession,' 'life is continuous adaptation') are, if true and new, analytic discoveries. Such discoveries are among the most important tasks of philosophy (*PK* 115).

discipleship

Proponents of a new system can convince their audience only by first winning their intellectual sympathy for a doctrine they have not yet grasped. Those who listen sympathetically will discover for themselves what they otherwise never have understood. Such an acceptance is a heuristic process, a self-modifying act, and to this extent a conversion. It produces disciples forming a school, the members of which are separated for the time being by a logical gap from those outside it. They think differently, speak a different language, live in a different world, and at least one of the two schools is excluded to this extent for the time being (whether rightly or wrongly) from the community of science (*PK* 151).

discovery

To say that a discovery of objective truth in science consists in the apprehension of a rationality which commands our respect and arouses our contemplative admiration; that such discovery, while using the experience of our senses as clues, transcends this experience by embracing the vision of a reality beyond the impressions of our senses, a vision which speaks for itself in guiding us to an ever deeper understanding of reality—such an account of scientific procedure would be generally shrugged aside as out-dated Platonism; a piece of mystery-mongering unworthy of an enlightened age. Yet it is precisely on this conception of objectivity that I wish to insist in this introductory chapter (*PK* 5–6).

The change is irrevocable. A problem that I have once solved can no longer puzzle me; I cannot guess what I already know. Having made a discovery, I shall never see the world again as before. My eyes have become different; I have made myself into a person seeing and thinking differently. I have crossed a gap, the heuristic gap which lies between problem and discovery.

Major discoveries change our interpretative framework. Hence it is logically impossible to arrive at these by the continued application of our previous interpretative framework (*PK* 143).

The act of assent proves once more to be logically akin to the act of discovery: they are both essentially unformalizable, intuitive mental decisions (*PK* 261).

error

. . . Kepler remains a great scientist to us, in spite of his erroneous reference to the Platonic bodies. It is only when he talks of such things as the mind residing in the sun which listens to the planets, and puts down in musical notation the several tunes of the planets, that we no longer regard him as a scientist, but as a mystic. We draw here a distinction between two kinds of error, namely, scientific guesses which have turned out to be mistaken, and unscientific guesses which are not false, but incompetent (PK 144).

framework

A valid articulate framework may be a theory, or a mathematical discovery, or a symphony. Whichever it is, it will be used by dwelling in it, and this in-dwelling can be consciously experienced (*PK* 195).

grammar

Correspondingly, disagreements on the nature of things cannot be expressed as disagreements about the existing use of words. . . . These controversial questions can be attended to only if we use language as it exists to direct our attention to its subject matter and not the other way around, selecting instances of relevant cases to direct our attention to our use of language. 'Grammar' is pre-cisely the total of linguistic rules which can be observed by using a language *without* attending to the things referred to. The purpose of the philosophic pre-tence of being merely concerned with grammar is to contemplate and analyze reality, while denying the act of doing so (*PK* 114). [Directed at Wittgenstein.]

knowing

I regard knowing as an active comprehension of the things known, an action that requires skill. Skillful knowing and doing is performed by subordinating a set of particulars, as clues or tools, to the shaping of a skillful achievement, whether practical or theoretical (*PK* vii).

The learner, like the discoverer, must believe before he can know. . . . an act of heuristic conjecture . . . a passionate pouring of oneself into untried forms of existence (*PK* 208).

maxims

. . . partial formalization of a personal act . . . (*PK* 30).

. . . *rules of art*, which I should like to call maxims. Maxims are rules, the correct application of which is part of the art they govern. The true maxims of golfing or of poetry increase our insight into golfing or poetry and may even give valuable guidance to golfers and poets; but these maxims would instantly con-demn themselves to absurdity if they tried to replace the golfer's skill or the poet's art. Maxims cannot be understood, still less applied by anyone not al-ready possessing a good practical knowledge of the art. They derive their interest from our appreciation of the art and cannot themselves either replace or estab-lish that appreciation. Another person may use my scientific maxims for the guidance of his inductive inference and yet come to quite different conclusions. It is owing to this manifest ambiguity that maxims can function only—as I have said—within a framework of personal judgment. Once we have accepted our commitment to personal knowledge, we can also face up to the fact that there exist rules which are useful only within the operation of our personal knowing, and can realize also how useful they can be as part of such acts. The probability schemes of Keynes and his followers, purporting to represent the scientific process, may be granted some value of this kind (*PK* 31).

meaning

When focusing on a whole, we are subsidiarily aware of its parts, while there is no difference in the intensity of the two kinds of awareness. . . . Also when something is seen as subsidiary to a whole, this implies that it participates in sustaining the whole, and we may now regard this function as its *meaning*, within the whole (*PK* 57–58).

[distinctions: (1) denotative, representative: the meaning of word/language as a whole is another object; (2) existential: the meaning of face or physiognomy as a whole is in itself] (*PK* 58)

objectivity

Such is the true sense of objectivity in science, which I illustrated in my first chapter. I called it the discovery of rationality in nature, a name which was meant to say that the kind of order which the discoverer claims to see in nature goes far beyond his understanding; so that his triumph lies precisely in his fore-knowledge of a host of yet hidden implications which his discovery will reveal in later days to other eyes (*PK* 64).

Our personal participation is in general greater in a validation than in a verification. The emotional coefficient of assertion is intensified as we pass from the sciences to the neighboring domains of thought. But both *verification* and *validation* are everywhere an acknowledgment of a commitment: they claim the presence of something real and external to the speaker. As distinct from both of these, *subjective* experiences can only be said to be *authentic*, and authenticity does not involve a commitment in the sense in which both verification and validation do (*PK* 202).

perception

We owe to Gestalt psychology much of the available evidence showing that perception is a comprehension of clues in terms of a whole. But perception usually operates automatically, and Gestalt psychologists have tended to collect preferentially examples of the type in which perception goes on without any deliberate effort on the part of the perceiver and is not even corrigible by his subsequent reconsideration of the result. Optical illusions are then classed with true perceptions, both being described as the equilibration of simultaneous stimuli to a comprehensive whole. Such an interpretation leaves no place for any intentional effort which prompts our perception to explore and assess in the quest of knowledge the clues offered to our senses. I believe this is a mistake, and shall say more in Part Four of the reasons for recognizing persons who use their senses as centers of intelligent judgment. At this stage it is enough to recall some features of this active personal participation (*PK* 97).

presuppositions

I suggest now that the supposed pre-suppositions of science are so futile because the actual foundations of our scientific beliefs cannot be asserted at all.

When we accept a certain set of pre-suppositions and use them as our interpretative framework, we may be said to dwell in them as we do in our own body. Their uncritical acceptance for the time being consists in a process of assimilation by which we identify ourselves with them. They are not asserted and cannot be asserted, for assertion can be made only *within* a framework with which we have identified ourselves for the time being; as they are themselves our ultimate framework, they are essentially inarticulable (*PK* 60).

religion

Religion, considered as an act of worship, is an indwelling rather than an affirmation. God cannot be observed, any more than truth or beauty can be observed. He exists in the sense that He is to be worshipped and obeyed, but not otherwise; not as a fact—any more than truth, beauty or justice exist as facts. All these, like God, are things which can be apprehended only in serving them. The words 'God exists' are not, therefore, a statement of fact, such as 'snow is white,' but an accreditive statement, such as '"snow is white" is true,' and this determines the kind of doubt to which the statement 'God exists' can be subjected (*PK* 279–80).

science

The exact sciences are a set of formulae which have a bearing on experience. We have seen that in accrediting this bearing, we must rely to varying degrees on our power of personal knowing. . . . Science is operated by the skill of the scientist and it is through the exercise of his skill that he shapes his scientific knowledge. We may grasp, therefore, the nature of the scientist's personal participation by examining the structure of skills (*PK* 49).

We have now before us the following sequence of sciences relying decreasingly on the first and increasingly on the second operational principle of language:

1. the descriptive sciences;
2. the exact sciences;
3. the deductive sciences.

[The sentence above has been re-formatted to highlight the threefold division of the sciences.] (*PK* 86)

Thus has our scientific outlook been molded, of which these logical rules give a highly attenuated summary. If we ask why we accept this summary, the answer lies in the body of knowledge of which they are the summary. We must reply by recalling the way each of us has come to accept that knowledge and the reasons for which we continue to do so. Science will appear then as a vast system of beliefs, deeply rooted in our history and cultivated today by a specially organized part of our society (*PK* 171).

Natural science is an expansion of observing; technology, of contriving; mathematics, of understanding (*PK* 184).

sign/symbol

Like the tool, the sign or symbol can be conceived as such only in the eyes of a person who *relies on them* to achieve or to signify something. *This reliance is a personal commitment which is involved in all acts of intelligence by which we integrate some things subsidiarily to the center of our focal attention.* Every act of personal assimilation by which we make a thing form an extension of ourselves through our subsidiary awareness of it, is a commitment of ourselves; a manner of disposing of ourselves (*PK* 61).

A small set of consistently used symbols which, owing to their peculiar manageability, enable us to think about their subject matter more swiftly in terms of its symbolic representation, can be used to carry information to other people if they can use this representation as we do. This can happen only if speakers and listeners have heard the terms used in similar circumstances, and have derived from these experiences the same relation between the symbols and the recurrent features (or functions) which they represent. Both speakers and listeners must also have found the symbols in question manageable, as otherwise they could not have acquired any fluency in their use (*PK* 204–5).

speaking

To speak is to *contrive* signs, to *observe* their fitness, and to *interpret* their alternative relations; though the animal possesses each of these three faculties, he cannot combine them (*PK* 82).

Spoken communication is the successful application by two persons of the linguistic knowledge and skill acquired by such apprenticeship, one person wishing to transmit, the other to receive, information. Relying on what each has learnt, the speaker confidently utters words and the listener confidently interprets them, while they mutually rely on each other's correct use and understanding of these words. A true communication will take place if, and only if, these combined assumptions of authority and trust are in fact justified (*PK* 206).

technology

Technology teaches only actions to be undertaken for *material* advantages by the use of *implements* according to (more or less) *specifiable rules*. Such a rule is an operational principle (*PK* 176).

theology

But theology as a whole is an intricate study of momentous problems. It is a theory of religious knowledge and a corresponding ontology of the things thus known. As such, theology reveals, or tries to reveal, the implications of religious worship, and it can be said to be true or false, but only as regards its adequacy in formulating and purifying a pre-existing religious faith. While theological attempts to prove the existence of God are as absurd as philosophical attempts to prove the premises of mathematics or the principles of empirical inference, theology pursued as an axiomatization of the Christian faith has an important analytic task. Though its results can be understood only by practicing Christians, it can greatly help them to understand what they are practicing (*PK* 281–2).

Theology comprises biblical exegesis and the principles of biblical exegesis, and in this context it deals also with the question which I have set myself here, namely how religious faith depends on observable facts, or—more precisely—on the truth or falsity of statements concerning observable facts (*PK* 282).

theory

[Three important observations on theory: (a) distinct from the person who holds it; (b) not affected by my personal illusions; (c) may be constructed without reference to 'normal' experience.] (*PK* 4)

a. A theory is something other than myself. It may be set out on paper as a system of rules, and it is the more truly a theory the more completely it can be put down in such terms. Mathematical theory reaches the highest perfection in this respect. But even a geographical map fully embodies in itself a set of strict rules for finding one's way through a region of otherwise uncharted experience. Indeed, all theory may be regarded as a kind of map extended over space and time. It seems obvious that a map can be correct or mistaken, so that to the extent to which I have relied on my map I shall attribute to it any mistakes that I made by doing so. A theory on which I rely is therefore objective knowledge in so far as it is not I, but the theory, which is proved right or wrong when I use such language (*PK* 4).

Facts which are not described by the theory create no difficulty for the theory, for it regards them as irrelevant to itself. Such a theory functions as a comprehensive idiom which consolidates that experience to which it is apposite and leaves unheeded whatever is not comprehended by it (*PK* 47).

truth

Actually, both sides agreed on what they meant by 'true'; namely, that truth lies in the achievement of a contact with reality—a contact destined to reveal itself further by an indefinite range of yet unforseen consequences (*PK* 147).

Today we should be grateful for the prolonged attacks made by rationalists on religion for forcing us to renew the grounds of the Christian faith. But this does not remotely justify the acknowledgment of doubt as the universal solvent of error which will leave truth untouched behind. For all truth is but the external pole of belief, and to destroy all belief would be to deny all truth (*PK* 286).

According to the logic of commitment, *truth is something that can be thought of only by believing it* (*PK* 305).

vision

Our vision of reality, to which our sense of scientific beauty responds, must suggest to us the kind of questions that it should be reasonable and interesting to explore. It should recommend the kind of conceptions and empirical relations that are intrinsically plausible and which should therefore be upheld, even when some evidence seems to contradict them, and tell us also, on the one hand, what empirical connections to reject as specious, even though there is evidence for them—evidence that we may as yet be unable to account for on any other assumptions. In fact, without a scale of interest and plausibility based on a vision of reality, nothing can be discovered that is of value to science; and only our grasp of scientific beauty, responding to the evidence of our senses, can evoke this vision (*PK* 135).

In order to be satisfied, our intellectual passions must find response. This universal intent creates a tension: we suffer when a vision of reality to which we have committed ourselves is contemptuously ignored by others. For a general unbelief imperils our own convictions by evoking an echo in us. Our vision must conquer or die (*PK* 150).

We must now recognize belief once more as the source of all knowledge. Tacit assent and intellectual passions, the sharing of an idiom and of a cultural heritage, affiliation to a like-minded community: such are the impulses which shape our vision of the nature of things on which we rely for our mastery of things. No intelligence, however critical or original, can operate outside of such a fiduciary framework (*PK* 266).

Selected Bibliography

Apczynski, John V. *Doers of the Word: Toward a Foundational Theology Based on the Thought of Michael Polanyi.* Doctoral dissertation, McGill, 1972.

———. "Integrative Theology: A Polanyian Proposal for Theological Foundations." *Theological Studies* 40 (1979): 23– 43.

Aveling, F. "Universals and the Illative Sense." *Dublin Review* 137 (1905): 236-71.

Boekraad, A. *The Personal Conquest of Truth according to John Henry Newman.* Louvain: Editions Nauwelaerts, 1955.

Bohm, David. *Wholeness and the Implicate Order.* Boston: Routledge and Kegan Paul, 1984 (1980).

Bouyer, Louis. *Newman's Vision of Faith: A Theology for Times of General Apostasy.* San Francisco: Ignatius, 1986.

Brunton, J. "The Indefectibility of Certitude." *Downside Review* 86 (1967): 2–50.

Culler, A. Dwight. *The Imperial Intellect.* New Haven: Yale, 1955.

D'Arcy, Martin. *The Nature of Belief.* London: Sheed and Ward, 1958.

Davis, Philip J., and Reuben Hersh. *The Mathematical Experience.* Introduction by Gian-Carlo Rota. Boston: Houghton Mifflin, 1981.

Dessain, Charles S. "Cardinal Newman on the Theory and Practice of Knowledge." *Downside Review* 75 (1957): 1–23.

———. *John Henry Newman.* Stanford: Stanford University Press, 1971 (1966).

Dulles, Avery. *A Church to Believe In: Discipleship and the Dynamics of Freedom.* New York: Crossroad, 1982.

———. *The Craft of Theology: From Symbol to System.* New York: Crossroad, 1992.

———. "Faith, Church and God: Insights from Michael Polanyi." *Theological Studies* 45 (1984): 537–50.

———. "From Images to Truth: Newman on Revelation and Faith." *Theological Studies* 51 (1990): 252-67.

———. *Models of Revelation.* Garden City, N.Y.: Doubleday and Company, 1983.

———. "Newman on Infallibility." *Theological Studies* 51 (1990): 434–49.

———. "Possibilities for Theology in a Post-Critical Age." Address at Weston Jesuit School of Theology in Cambridge, Massachusetts, on April 21, 1982.

———. *The Resilient Church: The Necessity and Limits of Adaptation.* Garden City, N.Y.: Doubleday, 1977.

———. *The Survival of Dogma: Faith, Authority and Dogma in a Changing World.* New York: Crossroad, 1982 (1971).

Evans, G. "An Organon More Delicate, Versatile, and Elastic: John Henry Newman and Whately's *Logic*." *Downside Review* 97 (1979): 175–91.

———. "Newman and Aquinas on Assent." *Theological Studies* 30 (1978): 247–66; 31 (1979): 202–11.

Ferré, Frederick. *Language, Logic, and God.* New York: Harper, 1961.

Ferreira, M. Jamie. *Doubt and Religious Commitment: The Role of the Will in Newman's Thought.* Oxford: Clarendon Press, 1980.

Fey, William R. *Faith and Doubt: The Unfolding of Newman's Thought on Certainty.* Preface by Charles S. Dessain. Shepherdstown, W.Va.: Patmos Press, 1976.

Foster, Durwood. "Pannenberg's Polanyianism: A Response to John V. Apczynski." *Zygon* 17 (1982): 75–83.

Gelwick, Richard Lee. "Discovery and Theology." *Scottish Journal of Theology* 28 (1975): 301–21.

———. *Michael Polanyi: 'Credere Aude.' His theory of Knowledge and Its Implications for Christian Theology.* Doctoral dissertation, Pacific School of Religion, 1965.

———. "Michael Polanyi: Modern Reformer." *Religion in Life* 34 (1964–65): 224–34.

———. "Science and Reality, Religion and God: A Reply to Harry Prosch." *Zygon* 17 (1982): 25–40.

———. *The Way of Discovery.* New York: Oxford University Press, 1977.

Gilkey, Langdon. *Religion and the Scientific Future.* New York: Harper and Row, 1970.

Gill, Jerry H. *On Knowing God.* Philadelphia: Westminster Press, 1981.

———. *The Possibility of Religious Knowledge.* Grand Rapids: Eerdmans, 1971.

———. "Reasons of the Heart: A Polanyian Reflection." *Religious Studies* 14 (1978): 143–57.

———. "Tacit Knowing and Religious Belief." *International Journal for Philosophy of Religion* 6 (1975): 73–88.

———. "The Tacit Structure of Religious Knowing." *International Philosophical Quarterly* 9 (1969): 533–59.

Grene, M. *The Anatomy of Knowledge.* London: Routledge and Kegan Paul, 1969.

———. *The Knower and the Known.* New York: Basic Books, 1966.

Griffin, John R. *Newman: A Bibliography of Secondary Studies.* Front Royal, Va.: Christendom Publications, 1980.

Gustafson, Scott W. *Scientific and Religious Knowledge in the Thought of Michael Polanyi.* Master's thesis, The Catholic University of America, 1979.

Haddox, Bruce. "Questioning Polanyi's *Meaning*: A Response to Ronald Hall." *Zygon* 17 (1982): 19–25.

Hall, Ronald L. "Michael Polanyi on Art and Religion: Some Critical Reflections on *Meaning*." *Zygon* 17 (1982): 9–18.

Harper, Gordon H. *Cardinal Newman and William Froude, F.R.S., A Correspondence.* Baltimore: Johns Hopkins University Press, 1933.

Hicks, J. "Faith and the Illative Sense." In *Faith and Knowledge.* London: Colins, 1966.

Hofstadter, Douglas R. *Gödel, Escher, Bach: An Eternal Golden Braid.* New York: Random House, 1979.

Houghton, Walter. *The Art of Newman's Apologia.* New Haven: Yale University Press, 1945.

Hume, David. *An Inquiry Concerning Human Understanding.* With an abstract of "A Treatise of Human Nature." Edited and introduced by Charles W. Hendel. New York: Liberal Arts, 1955.

Hunt, William Coughlin. *Intuition: The Key to John Henry Newman's Theory of Doctrinal Development.* Doctoral dissertation, The Catholic University of America, 1967.

Jaki, Stanley. *The Relevance of Physics.* Chicago: University of Chicago Press, 1966.

Ker, Ian. *The Achievement of John Henry Newman.* Notre Dame: University of Notre Dame Press, 1990.

————. *John Henry Newman: A Biography.* Oxford: Oxford University Press, 1990 (1988).

————. "Recent Critics of Newman's *Grammar of Assent." Religious Studies* 13 (1977): 63–71.

Koestler, Arthur. *The Act of Creation.* New York: Dell, 1967.

Kuhn, Helmut. "Personal Knowledge and the Crisis of the Philosophical Tradition." In *Intellect and Hope: Essays in the Thought of Michael Polanyi,* edited by Thomas A. Langford and William H. Poteat, pp. 111–35. Durham: Duke University Press, 1968.

Kuhn, Thomas. *The Structure of Scientific Revolutions.* Chicago: The University of Chicago Press, 1962.

Küng, Hans, and David Tracy, eds. *Paradigm Change in Theology: A Symposium for the Future.* Translated by Margaret Köhl. New York: Crossroad, 1989.

Langford, Thomas A., and William H. Poteat, eds. *Intellect and Hope: Essays in the Thought of Michael Polanyi.* Durham: Duke University Press, 1968.

Locke, John. *Essay Concerning Human Understanding.* Edited, introduced, with critical apparatus and glossary by Peter H. Niddich. Oxford: Clarendon Press, 1975 (1690).

The Logic of Personal Knowledge: Essays Presented to Michael Polanyi. London: Routledge and Kegan Paul, 1961.

Lyons, James W. *Newman's Dialogues on Certitude.* Rome: Catholic Book Agency, 1978.

McMannus, E. E. *A Select Newman Bibliography.* Rochester, N.Y.: St. Bernard's Seminary, 1958.

Medawar, Peter. *The Limits of Science.* Oxford: Oxford University Press, 1984.

Meybohm, Richard L. "A Michael Polanyi Bibliography: Primary and Secondary Materials Having Relevance for Theology." Unpublished manuscript, Boston College, 1982.

Milavec, A. *To Empower As Jesus Did: Acquiring Spiritual Power through Apprenticeship.* New York: E. Mellen, 1982.

———. "Modern Exegesis, Doctrinal Innovations, and the Dynamics of Discipleship." *Anglican Theological Review* 60 (1978): 55– 74.

Mullins, Phil. "The Spectrum of Meaning—Polanyian Perspectives on Science and Religion." *Zygon* 17 (1982): 3–8.

Newman, John Henry. *Apologia pro Vita Sua: Being a History of His Religious Opinions.* Edited and with introduction by Martin J. Svaglic. Oxford: Clarendon Press, 1967 (1864, 1865, 1886).

———. *An Essay in Aid of a Grammar of Assent.* Edited with an introduction by Nicholas Lash. Notre Dame: University of Notre Dame Press, 1979 (1870).

———. *Essay on the Development of Christian Doctrine.* New York: Sheed and Ward, 1960 (1845, 1846, 1878).

———. *The Idea of a University: Defined and Illustrated in Nine Discourses . . .* Edited, with introduction and notes by Martin J. Svaglic (1960). Notre Dame: University of Notre Dame Press, 1982 (1852, 1859, 1873).

———. *John Henry Newman: Autobiographical Writings.* Edited with introductions by Henry Tristram. New York: Sheed and Ward, 1957.

———. *The Letters and Diaries of John Henry Newman.* Edited by Charles Stephen Dessain, et al. Oxford and London: Oxford University Press, 1961–.

———. *A Letter Addressed to His Grace the Duke of Norfolk on Occasion of Mr. Gladstone's Recent Expostulation.* In *Newman and Gladstone: The Vatican Decrees.* Introduction by Alvin S. Ryan. Notre Dame: University of Notre Dame Press, 1962 (1875).

———. *Newman's University Sermons: Fifteen Sermons Preached before the University of Oxford, 1826–43.* Introductory essays by D. M. MacKinnnon and J. D. Holmes. London: S.P.C.K., 1970 (1826–43; third edition, 1871).

———. *On Consulting the Faithful in Matters of Doctrine.* Edited with an introduction by John Coulson. New York: Sheed and Ward, 1961 (1859, 1871).

———. *On the Inspiration of Scripture.* Edited with an introduction by J. Derek Holmes and Robert Murray. London: Geoffrey Chapman, 1967 (1884).

———. *The Philosophical Notebook of John Henry Newman.* Edited by Edward Sillem. Louvain: Nauwelaerts, 1969 (1859–1888).

———. *The Theological Papers of John Henry Newman on Biblical Inspiration and on Infallibility.* Edited and introduced by J. Derek Holmes. Oxford: Clarendon Press, 1979 (1861–1868).

———. *The Theological Papers of John Henry Newman on Faith and Certainty.* Edited by J. Derek Holmes, assisted by Hugo M. de Achaval; introduction by Charles S. Dessain. Oxford: Clarendon Press, 1976 (1846–1886).

———. *The Via Media of the Anglican Church Illustrated in Lectures, Letters and Tracts Written Between 1830 and 1841.* London: Longmans, Green and Company, 1901 (third edition, 1877).

Polanyi, Michael. *The Contempt of Freedom*. London: Watts and Company, 1940.

———. "Faith and Reason." *Journal of Religion* 41 (1961): 237– 47.

———. *Knowing and Being*. Edited by Marjorie Grene. Chicago: University of Chicago Press, 1969.

———. *The Logic of Liberty: Reflections and Rejoinders*. London: Routledge and Kegan Paul, 1951.

———. *Meaning*. With Harry Prosch. Chicago: University of Chicago Press, 1975.

———. "On Body and Mind." *New Scholasticism* 43 (1969): 195–204.

———. *Personal Knowledge: Towards a Post-Critical Philosophy*. Chicago: University of Chicago Press, 1962 (1958). "Torchbook Edition" (with unique preface), New York: Harper and Row, 1974 (1962).

———. "Science and Conscience." *Religion in Life* 23 (1953): 47– 58.

———. "Science and Religion: Separate Dimension or Common Ground?" *Philosophy Today* 7 (1963): 4–14.

———. *Science, Faith and Society*. Chicago: University of Chicago Press, 1946.

———. "Scientific Beliefs." *Ethics* 61 (1950): 27–37.

———. *Scientific Thought and Social Reality: Essays by Michael Polanyi*. Edited by Fred Schwartz. New York: International Universities Press, 1974.

———. *The Study of Man*. Chicago: University of Chicago Press, 1959.

———. *The Tacit Dimension*. New York: Doubleday and Company, 1966.

Powell, Jouett Lynn. *Three Uses of Christian Discourse in John Henry Newman: An Example of Nonreductive Reflection on the Christian Faith*. Missoula, Mont.: Scholars Press for the American Academy of Religion Dissertation Series, 1975 (Yale, 1972).

Prosch, H. "Polanyi's View of Religion in *Personal Knowledge*: A Response to Richard Gelwick." *Zygon* 17 (1982): 41–48.

Sagan, Carl. *The Dragons of Eden: Speculations on the Evolution of Human Intelligence*. New York: Ballantine Books, 1977.

Schoen, Edward. *Religious Explanations: A Model from the Sciences*. Durham: Duke University Press, 1985.

Scott, William. T. "A Bridge from Science to Religion Based on Polanyi's Theory of Knowledge." *Zygon* 5 (1970): 41–62.

———. "At the Wheel of the World." In *From Polanyi to the 21st Century: Proceedings of a Centennial Conference*, 341–54. Edited by Richard Gelwick. Biddeford, Me: The Polanyi Society, 1997.

———. "The Question of Religious Reality: Commentary on the Polanyi Papers." *Zygon* 17 (1982): 83–89.

Sobosan, J. G. "The Tacit Dimension of Faith: A Reflection on Michael Polanyi." *Philosophy Today* 19 (1975): 269–79.

Torrance, Thomas. F. *The Ground and Grammar of Theology*. Charlottesville: University Press of Virginia, 1980.

———, ed. *Belief in Science and in Christian Life: The Relevance of Michael*

Polanyi's Thought for Christian Faith and Life. Edinburgh: Handsel Press, 1980.

————. *Theological Science.* London: Oxford University Press, 1969.

Trevor, Meriol. *Newman: Light in Winter.* Garden City, N.Y.: Doubleday, 1963.

————. *Newman: The Pillar of the Cloud.* Garden City, N.Y.: Doubleday, 1962.

Walgrave, Jan H. *Newman, the Theologian: The Nature of Belief and Doctrine as Exemplified in His Life and Works.* Translated by A. V. Littledale. New York: Sheed and Ward 1960.

Wallace, William. "Causality, Analogy, and the Growth of Scientific Knowledge." In *Il Cosmo e la Scienza.* Number 9 of the *Atti del congresso iternazionale Tommaso d'Aquino nel suo settimo centenario.* Napoli: Edizioni Domenicane Italiane, 1978.

————. *Causality and Scientific Explanation.* In two volumes: *Medieval and Early Classical Science* and *Classical and Contemporary Science.* Ann Arbor: University of Michigan, 1972–74.

————. *From a Realist Point of View: Essays on the Philosophy of Science.* Second edition. Lanham: University Press of America, 1983 (1979).

————. "The Intelligibility of Nature: A Neo-Aristotelian View." *Review of Metaphysics* 38 (1984): 33–56.

Weightman, Colin. *Theology in a Polanyian Universe: The Theology of Thomas Torrance.* American University Studies: Series VII, Theology and Religion. Volume 174. New York: Peter Lang Publishing, 1994.

Zeno. *John Henry Newman: Our Way to Certitude: An Introduction to Newman's Psychological Discovery: The Illative Sense and His "Grammar of Assent."* Leiden: E. J. Brill, 1957.

Index

a-critical choices (*see also* fiduciary program, post-critical philosophy): determine interpretative frameworks, 92, 121; determine criteria of plausibility, 110; simple assents, 111; support symbolic representation, 151; tacit knowing is a-critical action, 89

affirmation. *See* assent, commitment

Ambrose, 9

Anglican Evangelicals, x

apologetics, 161–64, 169, 180

Apologia pro Vita Sua, 8, 126, 143, 169–70

appraisal. *See* fact, self-accreditation, self-set standards

apprehension, 191; notional vs. real, 20, 24, 102, 150–51, 152, 185

Aquinas, Thomas, 118

Aristotle, 3, 41, 45, 118, 130–32, 134, 137

articulation (*see also* assertions, commitment, formalization, propositions, self-accreditation, self-set standards, tacit knowledge): accompanied by tacit self-appraisal, 73–74, 86, 111–12, 152, 159; based on tacit knowledge, 62, 69, 85, 108; creates a community of understanding, 153; explicit knowledge, 56, 62; extends range of reason, 135, 151; includes all symbolic representation of knowledge, 73; integrates subsidiaries to a focus, 76; leaves many things unsaid, 183–84; limited in scope, 38, 77, 104–5, 151–52, 181; reflects vision of reality, 104; relies on illative sense, 108, 111, 137

assent, 191 (*see also* commitment, faith, knowledge, logic, reason); accompanied by intellectual satisfaction, 111; action of the intellect, 118; assent to what is not fully understood, 16, 107, 140; assent to what is not proven, 16,

33, 90–91, 95, 101, 106–7, 113, 126; assent vs. inference, 22–23, 33; a conscientious choice, 36, 106; focused on propositions, 17, 20, 22, 25; indirect assent, 23, 191; may be mistaken (*see* fallibility); natural act of the mind, 36; notional vs. real assent, 20, 152, 154, 192; resembles act of discovery, 89 (*see also* faith); simple vs. complex assent, 33–35, 97, 193

assent, types of (notional): profession, 24–25, 35, 196; credence, 25–26, 35, 193; opinion, 26, 35, 153, 196; presumption (*see* presumption); speculation, 29

assertions, 198 (*see also* articulation, propositions); composed of a sentence and a tacit act, 88; embody tacit dimension, 76; require personal endorsement, 66–67, 86, 88

Augustine, xi, xxii, 89, 137, 141, 166

authority. *See* Catholicism, master/apprentice relationship, papacy (Specific Authority), polycentricity, Protestantism (General Authority), religion, science, tradition

awareness (*see also* intellectual passions, knowledge, part/whole relationships, tacit knowledge, thought): cannot be fully articulated, 108; focal vs. subsidiary, 56, 75–76, 80, 109, 125, 127; from-to structure, 56, 128, 159; varies over whole field of consciousness, 72

axiomitization. *See* formalization, logic, reason, thought

axioms. *See* presuppositions

beauty: associated with vision of reality, 80, 121; evokes intellectual passions, 80, 109; linked to truth about nature, 83, 111

belief. *See* assent, commitment, doubt,

belief *continued*
faith, knowledge, post-critical philosophy, truth
breaking out. *See* conversion, discovery,
indwelling, interpretative framework
Bukharin, Nikolai, 52

Catholicism (*see also* Christianity, dogma,
faith, infallibility, Protestantism, religion, revelation, theology): based on
personal knowledge, 134, 183–86;
bound by dogma, 155, 173, 184, 186–
88; claims to know and teach truth,
134, 154, 156, 166, 173, 185; institutional dimension, 186–89; learns from
experience, 188; network of personal
relationships, 183; provides an interpretative framework, 159; relies on
illative sense, 155; a system of beliefs
(notional and real), 157; subsidiary to
personal relationships, 188–89; tacit
dimension ground of teaching, 183,
186; transmits Jesus, 188
certainty, 8, 30n, 34
certitude, 192 (*see also* assent, commitment, faith, knowledge, religion, theology); characteristic of religion, 153;
does not imply infallibility, 156; independent of formal proof, 18; moral in
nature, 8, 117, 119, 135; personal
habit of mind, 8, 18, 30n, 31, 48; unconditional assent, 1, 34–35
Christianity, 192–93. *See also* Catholicism, dogma, faith, Protestantism, religion, revelation, theology
commitment, 198–99 (*see also* a-critical
choices, assent, conscience, fiduciary
program, intellectual passions, knowledge, presumption, self-accreditation,
self-set standards); a kind of discovery, 93; a responsible choice, 32, 93,
95, 111–12, 115, 119; asserts truth,
56; change in Polanyi's understanding
of, 57–58; denial of commitment self-
contradictory, 94; disposition of the
self, 67, 81; goes beyond what is
proven or provable, 90–91, 95; fallible, 60, 93–95, 123–24, 141; precedes
understanding, 89; structure of commitment saves personal knowledge
from subjectivity, 68; uses subsidiaries as extensions of self, 71
comprehension, 199. *See also* apprehension, integration, meaning, thought,
view

comprehensive entities (*see also* fact, integration, part/whole relationships, system): hierarchy of comprehensive entities, 176; known by integration,
129–30; recognized by correlative degree of commitment, 177
communications protocol, 187–88. *See
also* Catholicism (institutional dimension), dogma (limits speculation), theology (dogmatic)
concept. *See* idea, view
connoisseurship, 69–70
conscience (*see also* illative sense, intellectual passions, self-accreditation,
self-set standards): demands objectivity, 117, 120–21; fallible, 140; foundation of scientific activity, 116–17,
120–21, 135, 165; governs act of assent, 8, 37; rules over intuitive faculties, 116; skill of self-evaluation,
120–21; voice of God, 114–15,
144–45, 161, 166
consistency, 199
contact with reality. *See* reality (contact
with)
conversion (*see also* assent, commitment,
discovery [Gestalt switch], faith, interpretative framework, reality [vision
of]): a normal function of the intellect,
81–82, 84; motivated by intellectual
passions, 151; personal reorganization of data, 186
conviction, 193. *See also* assent, commitment, faith
conviviality, 83–84
Copernicus, 173, 187
critical philosophy. *See* objectivism
cumulation of probabilities (*see also* integration, proof, verisimilitude): sense
of fitness, 111; integration of subsidiary clues, 98, 111, 125–28; function of the illative sense, 8–9, 39–40,
48, 103, 106; goes beyond formal inference, 104–6, 164; resembles asymptote, 106, 126, 134–35

definition, 199. *See also* articulation, formalization, logic
deposit of faith. *See* dogma, Jesus
Descartes, René, x. *See also* idea (Cartesian model), reason (Cartesian model)
discipleship, 200. *See also* master/appren-
tice relationship, science (authority
in), tradition